1979

Rediscovering
Hawthorne

Rediscovering
HAWTHORNE

Kenneth Dauber

Princeton University Press
Princeton, New Jersey

Copyright © 1977 by Princeton University Press
Published by Princeton University Press, Princeton, New Jersey
In the United Kingdom: Princeton University Press,
Guildford, Surrey

All Rights Reserved

Library of Congress Cataloging in Publication Data will
be found on the last printed page of this book

Publication of this book has been aided by
The Paul Mellon Fund

This book has been composed in Linotype Primer
at Princeton University Press

Printed in the United States of America
by Princeton University Press, Princeton, New Jersey

For Antoinette

Table of Contents

Preface

THIS book, I would like to think, is the poetics that Hawthorne might have written. It is an abstraction of his art. More than systematizing his various prefatory remarks and applying them to the fiction, it elaborates the fiction into a theory of the novel with potentially broad, if as yet untested, significance. In a sense it is an attempt to do what Percy Lubbock did with Henry James or E. M. Forster did with himself: generalize about the novel from an interested perspective, define the art of fiction from a limited, but therefore coherent, experience. The basic conviction underlying such an attempt is that every writer opens a valuable window onto literature. Every theory of the novel, however restricted, is a corrective to every other. Because no strictly objective view is ever possible, because no critic sees all things equally, the very distortions resulting from extending a particular artist are important as offering neglected glimpses of the field as a whole.

Still and all, some further justification seems necessary. Hawthorne's status as a writer is greatly different from that of James or Forster. However important his insights on the human condition, as novelist, as artist offering us lessons about the condition of the novel, he has never been considered central in the manner of those two others. His relation to "the novel" seems anomalous, and indeed, by calling him a romancer, critics have been able to confine his art, to discuss it as part of a divergent American branch of an English tradition. It is for this reason that a poetics from the point of view of an observer of Hawthorne is potentially a corrective greater than most to notions of fiction that we now have. I take for my subject a writer on the periphery and move him to the middle. I would define fiction from the vantage of his writing and, consequently, see the romance not as an outgrowth of the novel, but the novel as a development of the romance. Historically, this is the situation in American writing, but ontologically, we are now beginning to see, it is also the situation in fiction in general.

The implications of such an enterprise seem to me particularly relevant for criticism as it has been practiced in this country. First readers of this manuscript and students on whom I have tried parts of it, for example, have asked me what relation my ideas have to various recent developments in Continental thinking, particularly structuralism, and whether this study is a deliberate attempt at a European reading of American writing. The answer, as the remarks in the preceding paragraphs should make clear, is quite the reverse. This book is an American book because it approaches the field of fiction through an American writer. Moreover, as will be seen in the chapters that follow, my general approach, despite a continuing interest in theory, is still within the American tradition of empiricism and practicality. Its starting point is the text as formal object, and its end is a book-by-book analysis of Nathaniel Hawthorne. I have been at pains to place what I say in the context of earlier American critics of Hawthorne. Indeed, though it is true enough that I take issue with such critics, that, in a sense, this book is a running argument with some of our prominent critical positions, yet it need hardly be said that I am bound most to the very writers with whom I have been forced to contend. In the long run, after all, our most original efforts owe as much to the predecessors we oppose as to ourselves. In this respect, I would not so much disagree with Hawthorne scholars as depart from them, with both the meanings of freedom and dependency that that term implies. I would build away from, by building upon, the prior achievements of several generations of researchers.

This study, then, though ultimately it would revalue our typical formalist and historical practice, therefore relies upon it. It does not attempt to replace American criticism with European, but assumes as a central principle the legitimacy of individual, let alone national, modalities of thought. Accordingly, it borrows no vocabulary from philosophical systems currently popular on the Continent, but redefines a group of ordinary critical terms to suit the special interests under investigation. If there are relations between my work and that of the Europeans, it is because, finally, we all participate in the spirit of the critical age. I share with structuralism a loss of belief in centers; hence my willingness to construct a system around a figure not often seen as central. I share a general sense that we are cut off from origins, that to follow the objects of our investigation back to their beginnings is impossible; hence my decision to make do with six or seven volumes of literature as complete in themselves and build a total system around them. All of this, however, seems to me as much American as anything else. It is the sense, basic to any democratic sensibility, that no one of our perspectives may any longer be regarded as privileged. As Hawthorne knew, the writer lives a marginal life. He exists between worlds, among modes of fiction that never quite express him and readers who never quite hear. Hawthorne's wisdom, that curious ambiguity which has so often been remarked, is his understanding of the incompleteness of vision. Hawthorne knew the distortions of language. But he wrote, nevertheless, and a critic can but follow his example. This view, the way of looking at novels presented here, is as true as I have known how to make it. But it does not pretend to be the last word; it is only an example that a vast variety of ways yet remain to be developed.

Acknowledgments

It is a little remarkable that—though disinclined to talk overmuch of themselves and their affairs at the fireside and to their personal friends—an autobiographical impulse should take possession of writers in addressing the public. It is an antique fashion of authors to acknowledge openly the most private of their debts, and the obscurest men of letters in America will be heard.

Thanks first of all to my wife, Antoinette. She challenged my reasoning, pushed my thinking, and in general allowed me to get away with so little that the merits of this book are substantially mine, the faults hers alone. Thanks, too, to Laurence Holland, in response to whose stimulating questions and advice most of my fundamental notions were worked out. This project began in his seminar in the American Renaissance at Princeton and continued on as a dissertation, which, above and beyond the call of duty, he supervised long after we had migrated, each to his separate university.

Peter Garrett, Marcus Klein, Carl Dennis, and Michael Bell all read versions of this book at various stages of its development and offered helpful suggestions. Miriam Brokaw at Princeton University Press gave me, when I needed it most, hope, faith, and invaluable aid. Joanna Brent, Pamela Blawat, and Hilda Ludwig assisted with the preparation of the manuscript.

An especial note of thanks goes to my colleagues at the State University of New York at Buffalo, particularly Charles Altieri. Innumerable informal conversations on a variety of seemingly unrelated theoretical matters and a general atmosphere of energetic inquiry have helped shape this book in the most important ways.

Buffalo
April 1976

Rediscovering
Hawthorne

ONE

"Where the Meanings Are"

AN IDEAL of exploration informs American letters. The "rediscovery" of our literature in the 1920's established a dynamic model of literary activity; as a result, a sense of ourselves as discoverers, of writing as a pioneering process, has seemed the dominating influence on our literary life.[1] The great American project recounted in the poems and novels of the nineteenth century, to search out a rich virgin territory, is continued in the work of critics of the twentieth, uncovering a native literature neglected and undervalued. From Melville, unwrapping layer after layer of the "mummy" of truth, to Parrington, "exhuming" "buried reputations," we have considered literary inquiry a process of burrowing, exposing. Lawrence finds a new American literature by looking for it "under the American bushes" of the "old American literature." Williams unearths the "true character" of the country that "lies hid" beneath a chaos of false names and appearances.[2] The frontier

[1] The story is well known. For detailed analyses see, especially, Richard Ruland, *The Rediscovery of American Literature: Premises of Critical Taste, 1900–1940* (Cambridge, Mass.: Harvard Univ. Press, 1967) and, from a wider historical perspective, Howard Mumford Jones, *The Theory of American Literature* (1948; rev. ed. Ithaca: Cornell Univ. Press, 1965). For an account by one of the men involved from the Thirties on, see the number of reminiscences by Robert Spiller, most notably in *A Time of Harvest: American Literature, 1910–1960* (New York: Hill and Wang, 1962); *The Third Dimension: Studies in Literary History* (New York: Macmillan, 1965); and *The Oblique Light: Studies in Literary History and Biography* (New York: Macmillan, 1968).

[2] Melville, *Pierre*, XXI, i; Vernon Louis Parrington, *Main Currents in American Thought: An Interpretation of American Literature from the Beginnings to 1920* (New York: Harcourt, Brace, 1927), II, i; D. H. Lawrence, *Studies in Classic American*

3

of American letters has been opened, and, as it once seemed with the territorial frontier, every achievement in mapping it but points to another area that remains to be mapped. "The emotional discovery of America," as Stuart P. Sherman wrote, "will go on after we are all dead and forgotten . . . and with just as much room for discovery as it offered thirty years ago or as it offers today."[3]

There is a certain innocence in such an attitude, a stubborn, as it were an almost militant, naïveté. In characteristically American fashion, we have refused to acknowledge that an end is ever in sight. Our horizon is illimitable, we insist, and though the scholarship of the past years has carried us far along towards its outer boundaries, we continue to maintain that every further step is an adventure begun as if afresh. A certain, perhaps legitimate, defensiveness is at work here. Our modern criticism originates against the background of a closed set of standards defining literary possibility. The classical orientation of the academic establishment into this century affirmed a relatively fixed canon that allowed little place for an upstart American literature. The thinness of America's institutional life, so the argument ran—"no Oxford, nor Eton . . . no Epsom nor Ascot," as Henry James formulated it—made, inevitably, for a thin and traditionless writing.[4]

Accordingly, nativists like Van Wyck Brooks, cleverly avoiding a confrontation with Europe on its own

---

Literature (New York: Thomas Seltzer, 1923), p. viii; William Carlos Williams, *In The American Grain* (1925; rpt. New York: New Directions, 1956), following title page.

[3] "The Emotional Discovery of America," address delivered to the American Academy of Arts and Letters, December 1924, rpt. in *The Emotional Discovery of America and Other Essays* (New York: Farrar and Rinehart, 1932), p. 8.

[4] *Hawthorne*, rpt. in *The Shock of Recognition: The Development of Literature in the United States Recorded by the Men Who Made It*, ed. Edmund Wilson (1943; rpt. New York: Modern Library, 1955), p. 460.

ground, sought not to deny but to convert what on one level they admitted were our deficiencies into the source of unexpected interest on another. If we lacked institutions, it was our business to create them. Though the absence of tradition was, of course, a handicap, yet each writer could discover a tradition of his own. There was a terrible vacancy in American life, as Brooks frequently lamented. Without a properly developed context, individuality was forced into mere eccentricity, culture into a sterile hypocrisy. But it was creativity, not history, that would fill the gap, the free play of the independent mind. The effect of Brooks's argument was to value in our literature the moments of its greatest daring. A wonderful newness, an original perception, was advanced, which, for all its problematical nature, became established as our official genius and which even our historians have never really challenged.[5] Long after American literature has become a familiar subject, indeed, as its position in the very academies that had rejected it was secured, the premise of originality remains. The most conservative of Americanists who succeeded Brooks—those chroniclers of our literature who, in opposition to him, have insisted on the sufficiency of American life and who have applied themselves to tracing American history in detail—have yet never been content simply to draw lines of development or to delineate influences. Inverting typical historical practice, they have not demonstrated a source for the present in the past, but recreated the past as present, made even the seemingly old new. Here is history turned back on itself to cancel itself. The historians would revive our interest in works that time has worn out. Opening the obscure origins of now conventional

[5] Brooks's radical attitude was modified significantly in the course of his career. But the early Brooks is still the most influential. See, especially, the epoch-making *America's Coming-of-Age* (New York: B. W. Huebsch, 1915) and "On Creating a Usable Past," *The Dial*, 64 (1918), 335–41.

arguments, pursuing the long forgotten springs of tired controversies, they would offer the stalest ideas in the freshness of a sort of eternal beginning. There is a sense of wonder in even the wisest of our historians, an amazement persisting long after our literature should have ceased to amaze. And, increasingly, as an almost inevitable consequence, there is an insistence in our more contemporary criticism that even the most commonplace ideas are novel and new.[6]

Interestingly enough, in this light, New Criticism, which has long seemed a rejection of the main current of nativist thinking that we have been outlining here, appears equally implicated in the matter. Despite the extremes of their theoretical premises, after all, the methods of the New Critics and the historians have often been integrated in typical American practice.[7] Indeed, New Criticism, from our point of view, but re-orders the research of the historians on an axis of interpretation. The literary work absorbs into its own uniqueness the religious, political, and social currents discovered through historical analysis in American culture as a whole. As the historian burrows into the past, the New Critic burrows into the work in isolation. He, too, reveals new and exciting meanings. The work is far more complex than anyone might imagine on first glance. A childish, sentimental fiction—too immature for serious reading, as it was long regarded—reveals, when probed, a profound and often unsettling depth. The simple surface is penetrated, and beneath

[6] The essays assembled in Norman Foerster, ed., *The Reinterpretation of American Literature: Some Contributions toward the Understanding of Its Historical Development* (New York: Harcourt, Brace, 1928) are a good sampling of the earlier historians' position. See, especially, Fred Lewis Pattee, "A Call for a Literary Historian," pp. 3–22, and Foerster, Introduction, pp. vii–xv, and "Factors in American Literary History," pp. 23–38.

[7] F. O. Matthiessen, of course, is the most notable example, particularly his *American Renaissance: Art and Expression in the Age of Emerson and Whitman* (New York: Oxford Univ. Press, 1941).

it lies a dense network of symbols representing the work in the most challenging, the most ambiguous, light. Here is a structuralization of the process of exploration, a formalization of the act of discovery in the order of the text itself. New Criticism hypostasizes the Americanists' pioneering impulse. It makes discovery possible on a more intensive and thoroughgoing level. Even more than historicism, however, it has worked to deny any consolidation of its own otherwise impressive achievements. Procedure replaces substance. To describe is automatically and always to uncover. Originality is taken to its limit because everything is by definition original, and a necessary awareness that we must try a different tack, that we have reached, once and for all, the end of the pioneering era, has been endlessly postponed.

We began by quoting a passage to the effect that the frontier of American letters has appeared, for most of this century, to expand continuously before us. But increasingly doubts have been raised. Harry Levin quips that the study of *Moby-Dick* has replaced whaling among the industries of New England. Robert Spiller, a principal organizer of the major work of American scholarship, *The Literary History of the United States*, remarks that there is now general agreement about the contours of our writing, which in the 1940's, when the *LHUS* was being planned, was not yet possible. The "large dark areas of unexplored fact," as Norman Foerster called them, no longer seem large or unexplored.[8] Extending the project of the *LHUS*, we are beginning to realize, has meant not continuing a vital American criticism, but engaging in an activity yielding fewer and fewer results. We have reached the point of diminishing returns. Uncovering what we should already know, revealing what the work of the past decades has

[8] Levin, quoted in Ruland, p. 280n.; Spiller, Preface to *A Time of Harvest*, pp. v–viii; Foerster, Introduction to *The Reinterpretation of American Literature*, p. viii.

already revealed, we destroy, in our very attempt to recapture it, that excitement which the first Americanists made possible. As our own inability to continue it now makes clear, the real achievement of the early criticism was the liberation of a suppressed enthusiasm; unearthing new information was simply the particular historical form the liberation took. The material the Americanists brought to light was the result of their searching out their own situation. It was a product of finding in themselves a point from which to proceed. So we must look to our own changed circumstances. Our age is filled with discoveries, not in need of them. If we would continue to be explorers in earnest, it must be by taking as the point of any fresh departure our present burdened position, rather than a moment in the critical past more open, perhaps, but unrecoverable.

Such work is already under way. A sense of our current saturation, I think, lies directly behind some of the most interesting of recent criticism. For example, in the so-called New Historicism so much in the air, the turn from history to historiography is surely more than a turn to one more area of American experience in need of analysis; it is a response to the very weight of historical material already accumulated. The New Historians have begun to investigate man not as events express him, but, as overwhelmed by events, he struggles to express *them*.[9] Similarly, in criticism proper, a recent deflection in interest from the text to what we might call textuality at one level simply extends formalism's technical concerns to the boundaries of literature as a whole. More importantly, however, it constitutes a shift

[9] See, for example, Harry B. Henderson, III, *Versions of the Past: The Historical Imagination in American Fiction* (New York: Oxford Univ. Press, 1974). Also note, for related work, Roy Harvey Pearce, "Historicism Once More," *KR*, 20 (1958), 554–91, rpt. in *Historicism Once More: Problems and Occasions for the American Scholar* (Princeton, N.J.: Princeton Univ. Press, 1969), pp. 3–45, and Wesley Morris, *Toward a New Historicism* (Princeton, N.J.: Princeton Univ. Press, 1972).

from concern with the words a novelist writes to the demands that existing words make upon him.[10] Of course, the artist whom such lines of analysis reveal, no more than ourselves seems a pioneer. But the pioneering artist, we know, was in large measure the product of a view no longer viable. As the experience of our criticism teaches, to write is to confront a body of what has already been written and that, if we attempt to ignore it, we must only repeat. So, for our poets and novelists: it is not that we must alter our belief in their originality, that we must challenge what defines their accomplishment for us still. But the originality of the American writer that remains for us to discover will lie rather in his ability to cope than to create. My subject is Nathaniel Hawthorne, and I would wish to be as technical in the matter as necessary.

In the Preface to the third edition of *Twice-told Tales* Hawthorne describes "what the sketches truly are. They are not the talk of a secluded man with his own mind and heart . . . but his attempts, and very imperfectly successful ones, to open an intercourse with the world" (IX, 6).[11] The stories are "attempts," a means toward an end. They depend for their vitality on energy directed toward a certain goal. Hawthorne thus defines his art in purposive terms. His work is never an end in itself but a vehicle to effect intimacy. At the same time, however, the work offers resistance. It is "imperfectly successful." It fails to implement the author's desire fully. It never quite reflects him. Hawthorne cautions us from reading the works as though they were expressions of

[10] Most notable in American studies are two recent books, Warwick Wadlington, *The Confidence Game in American Literature* (Princeton: Princeton Univ. Press, 1975), and Richard H. Brodhead, *Hawthorne, Melville and the Novel* (Chicago: Univ. of Chicago Press, 1976).

[11] Volume and page numbers, unless otherwise noted, refer to the *Centenary Edition*, ed. William Charvat et al. (Columbus, Ohio: Ohio State Univ. Press, 1962-).

his psyche. He locates himself at a remove from his own creation, as a member of the community in which the work operates. The stories "are not the talk of a secluded man with his own mind and heart." They are social discourse, bound to society's habits of speaking. The forms of fiction impose themselves. The characteristics of the medium, the conventions of a culture embodied in literature as what we may call generic pressure, define the conditions in which Hawthorne's purpose may be realized. The attempt to open an intercourse, that is, is an attempt at art as well. Hawthorne aims to be a writer, and to achieve intimacy he must align himself with a mode of speech, a literature constituted before he begins to speak it. In a preliminary way, we may say that purpose is the work's final and genre its formal cause.

This study is not, however, a generic study in the traditional sense. It runs crosswise to genre analysis, considering not the messages convention, or Hawthorne's adaptation of it, conveys, but the action he undertakes in employing convention altogether. I use "purpose," that is, deliberately, to distinguish it from the "intention" of hermeneutics.[12] Our concern is not with what the writer meant to say or, in a broader sense, with what the work in the structure of its rhetoric insists it says. Ultimately, indeed, our study is not hermeneutical at all. Its interest is frankly non-thematic. It is an investigation of the use of Hawthorne's art beyond communication of a message. The referential quality of literature, we shall be arguing, in Hawthorne, is but a necessary condition of literature as a tool of

[12] For notable discussions of "intentionality" see Wayne C. Booth, *The Rhetoric of Fiction* (Chicago: Univ. of Chicago Press, 1961); Paul de Man, "Form and Intent in the American New Criticism," in *Blindness and Insight* (New York: Oxford Univ. Press, 1971), pp. 20–35; and W. K. Wimsatt, Jr., "The Intentional Fallacy," in *The Verbal Icon: Studies in the Meaning of Poetry* (1954; rpt. New York: The Noonday Press, 1966), pp. 3–18.

action. Hawthorne never offers information; he acknowledges it as the inevitable language through which his purpose may be worked out. Communication is a condition of communion, a circumstance enabling but limiting, which the author cannot transcend but may employ. The work is no object; it is an action—a "performative," in J. L. Austin's sense.[13] We do not rule out the possibility that the action the work performs may, in fact, be the stating of a message. But we will need to establish this in particular cases. We will not assume the secondary quality of literature, attribute to it the strictly subordinate function of symbolizing what is prior to it, though, obviously, it does that, too. We would investigate Hawthorne's writing, rather, as a primary process, referential, or symbolic, even semiotic but as a matter of course.

Any attempt at what criticism calls "interpretation,"[14] the paraphrase of poetic expression in expository terms, is accordingly offered but as a starting point for further study. Another way of saying this is that allegorization, "an attaching of ideas to the structure of poetic imagery," as one critic defines it,[15] merely elaborates for us a work we wish to see as it functions in the world. The work is regarded as a code signifying the various levels of a complex culture. The interpreter uncovers those levels to which he has particular access. Perhaps under the pressure of his own peculiar circumstances, he may even expose a latency his own age makes manifest.

[13] *How To Do Things with Words* (Cambridge, Mass.: Harvard Univ. Press, 1962). For an extension of Austin into literature, though one more limited than my own, see Richard Ohmann, "Speech, Action, and Style," in *Literary Style: A Symposium*, ed. Seymour Chatman (New York: Oxford Univ. Press, 1971), pp. 241–54.

[14] See, for example, E. D. Hirsch, *Validity in Interpretation* (New Haven: Yale Univ. Press, 1967).

[15] Northrop Frye, *Anatomy of Criticism: Four Essays* (1957; rpt. New York: Atheneum, 1965), p. 89. Also, pp. 71–73. See, too, Morton Bloomfield, "Allegory as Interpretation," *New Literary History*, 3 (1972), 301–17.

Decoding the work, translating it into more modern terms, he makes it continuous with himself. Such interpretation comprises the bulk of criticism of Hawthorne we now have. In fact, the four levels of medieval allegorical theory are an impressively complete index to it. Heirs of the New Criticism, for example—demythologizers like Richard Harter Fogle or Hyatt Waggoner—address themselves to the work's literal aspects.[16] A broad humanism replaces religion. The work, unlike the Bible to medieval commentators, is admittedly fiction, and the only events that remain factual are linguistic. Thus Fogle analyzes a variety of light-dark polarities, or Waggoner traces fire imagery. Usage is substituted for history, the former domain of literal interpretation, but it is the usage of a community even more extensive than Christianity's, as when Fogle draws upon a Western association of light with "clarity of design" and dark with "tragic complexity," or when Waggoner sees fire as related to human warmth and veils as human separateness. At the second, the moral, level of interpretation we have critics such as Yvor Winters and Randall Stewart.[17] As exegetes did with the *Song of Solomon*, as Hawthorne himself did with the Greek myths in *A Wonder Book*, they locate the work in a tradition of moral inquiry that Western literature may be seen as constituting and that, as exponents of the tradition, they elaborate as their own. Similarly, Christian typologists Austin Warren, Roy Male, and Darrel Abel see the Christian concerns of their era as a renaissance of the theological principles of Hawthorne's

[16] Fogle, *Hawthorne's Fiction: The Light and the Dark* (Norman, Okla.: Univ. of Oklahoma Press, 1952); Waggoner, *Hawthorne: A Critical Study*, rev. ed. (Cambridge, Mass.: Belknap Press, 1963).

[17] Winters, "Maule's Curse, or Hawthorne and the Problem of Allegory," *In Defense of Reason* (Denver: Alan Swallow, 1947), pp. 157–75; Stewart, *Nathaniel Hawthorne: A Biography* (New Haven: Yale Univ. Press, 1948).

modified Puritanism.[18] In this group, too, the Marxists and neo-transcendentalists who dominated the periodical literature in the Sixties may be included as the opposite number of the neo-Christians.[19] Psychologists Rudolph Von Abele and Frederick Crews, substituting id, ego, and super-ego for the devil, man, and God, modernize anagogy.[20] With Freud they see psychology as the fulfillment of Romanticism. The psyche, religion's true heaven and hell, is the elemental self Romantics sought to uncover and the new science an eschatology of the inner man.

Whatever disagreements I may have with the particularities of certain of these interpretations, the general interpretive categories seem unexceptionable. Hawthorne himself encourages them. In the introduction to "Rappaccini's Daughter" he frankly speaks of his surrogate's, "Aubépine's" "inveterate love of allegory." As paraphrases of an avowedly allegorical writer, then, the interpretations are all, at least potentially, immanently correct. They are essential aspects of a message that I take, however, as manipulative. They engage the reader, fix him in relation to a work whose purpose is beyond transmission of a message.

Allegory has always had a functional role in society, and a brief consideration of its history will illuminate Hawthorne's particular use of it. In a Neoplatonic uni-

[18] Warren, *Nathaniel Hawthorne: Representative Selections* (New York: American Book Co., 1934); Male, *Hawthorne's Tragic Vision* (1957; rpt. New York: Norton, 1964); Abel, "Hawthorne's Dimmesdale: Fugitive from Wrath," NCF, 11 (1956), 81–105.

[19] E.g., Nina Baym, "*The Blithedale Romance:* A Radical Reading," JEGP, 67 (1968), 545–69, and Edward H. Davidson, "Hawthorne and the Pathetic Fallacy," JEGP, 54 (1955), 486–97.

[20] Von Abele, *The Death of the Artist: A Study of Hawthorne's Disintegration* (The Hague: Martinus Nijhoff, 1955); Crews, *The Sins of the Fathers: Hawthorne's Psychological Themes* (New York: Oxford Univ. Press, 1966).

verse, Michael Murrin tells us, allegory was anam-
nestic.[21] It was a cosmic mnemonic device whose formal
structures and fanciful fictions easily lodged themselves
in the mind. It was an intimation of God's Word in
man's words, designed to reawaken the vision of God's
truth that lies in all men. With the rise of neoclassicism
a mechanistic conception of the universe replaced vision. Allegory properly so called was supplanted by
didactic exempla. The Romantics, particularly Blake
and Shelley, revived a species of allegory that was
psychological rather than cosmological, that relied on
imagination rather than memory. But Hawthorne, while
eschewing didacticism, retained enough of an Augustan
perspective to affect his whole approach. As visionary
transcription, he finds allegory tied to a bygone era.
"The Celestial Railroad," for example, is what we may
distinguish as secondary allegory, depending at every
turn on a primary referent, *The Pilgrim's Progress*,
without which it is incomprehensible.[22] Here Hawthorne reasserts our continuity with the conservative
values of the past precisely by using as a cultural artifact an allegory he thereby admits is bankrupt as
prophecy. Allegorical messages, in Hawthorne, are
commonplaces by definition, present from the start as
the language of his community. The summarizing
morals at the end of his stories, indeed, are like definitions in a medieval dictionary of symbols. Thus Lady
Eleanore announces she has wrapped herself in pride as
a mantle. Often such explication extends even to local
symbols, as when the wanderer in "Night Sketches" is
declared to be carrying "the lamp of Faith." Hawthorne's

[21] *The Veil of Allegory: Some Notes toward a Theory of Allegorical Rhetoric in the English Renaissance* (Chicago: Univ. of
Chicago Press, 1969), p. 91. I follow Murrin throughout. See,
also, pp. 75–97 and 167–98.

[22] Similarly, Buford Jones, "The *Faery Land* of Hawthorne's
Romances," ESQ, 48 (1967), 106–24, explicates a number of
scenes in Hawthorne by tracing references to *The Faerie
Queene*.

inability at the end of his career to attach satisfactory meanings to the symbols of the unfinished romances is not a failure of vision,[23] but is symptomatic of his ultimate alienation, his inability to speak the new language of a changed American community.

Hawthorne, then, in disdaining visionary transcription, socializes allegory. The reader, paraphrasing the work as a message he has always known, discovers no God, no transcendent principle, but a reflection of his own cultural being. It is a being, of course, that the author himself shares. Hawthorne is eminently social, eminently agnostic. There is no true church in his work, only conventional ones. As Lionel Trilling put it, "He has no great tyrant-dream in which we can take refuge. . . ."[24] Hawthorne does not believe, but he can, as he remarks Melville cannot, "be comfortable in his unbelief." He is not "too honest and courageous not to try to do one or the other."[25] Where Renaissance allegory, as Murrin points out, is frankly elitist, locating the reader in a hierarchy of interpreters from those who grasp the plainest level to those able to see the highest,[26] elitism in Hawthorne is redefined as strictly inclusive. It is to the "Indulgent," "Kind," or "Gentle Reader" addressed in the Preface to *The Marble Faun* that Hawthorne speaks. Sympathy, a widely regarded mid-century virtue, rather than the exclusive intelligence of a less sentimental age, is the chief bond of the elite community here. Hawthorne's "alternative possibilities"[27] further assault the Renaissance hierarchy. When prophecy is absent, when there is no visionary center

[23] This is the traditional explanation, as, e.g., in Davidson, *Hawthorne's Last Phase* (New Haven: Yale Univ. Press, 1949).

[24] "Our Hawthorne," in *Hawthorne Centenary Essays*, ed. Roy Harvey Pearce (Columbus, Ohio: Ohio State Univ. Press, 1964), p. 457.

[25] Quoted by Matthiessen, *American Renaissance*, p. 490.

[26] Murrin, p. 22.

[27] The expression is from Winters, "Maule's Curse," pp. 170 ff.

15

toward which interpretations may tend, a democratic allegory becomes possible. A democracy of form is maintained in which interpretations co-exist, side by side, equally as embodiments of a culture Hawthorne and his audience share.[28] Allegory, in Hawthorne, is never an end. It reflects his historical condition. It is the dead or living weight of culture that Hawthorne uses. To uncover allegory is to uncover a history he manipulates, the conditions of community with which he must contend. It is where criticism must begin, not end.

In a larger sense my argument here is not with allegorization alone, but with a distortion of formalism of which such allegorization as is generally applied to Hawthorne is an extreme case. Too often interpreters mistake the work for its action, its signification for its significance. Hawthorne's purpose, it is held, is to enforce a particular interpretation, when he merely presents it as a given. We have already considered, for example, the New Critics, whose emphasis on analysis over judgment would seem to preclude such distortion. Nevertheless, even such disinterest as theirs has been roundly attacked.[29] The New Critics' deference to the text is rooted in their desire for a reliable external principle. Their ostensible objectivity is a concealed subjectivity that conservative instinct attaches to the work. The result is a confused position. Explication is confounded with the value judgments otherwise opposed,

[28] This is, admittedly, a rather undynamic version of allegory. Indeed, I disagree with the influential formulation of Angus Fletcher, *Allegory: The Theory of a Symbolic Mode* (Ithaca, N.Y.: Cornell Univ. Press, 1964), p. 23, that allegories are "symbolic power struggles." Fletcher's view is a modernist's attempt to redeem an ancient mode. Rather, the end of any "struggle" in an allegory is a foregone conclusion and the struggle itself simply a realistic portrait of a dialectic working toward a resolution determined from the start.

[29] See, e.g., H. Bruce Franklin, "The Teaching of Literature in the Highest Academies of the Empire," in *The Politics of Literature: Dissenting Essays on the Teaching of English*, ed. Louis Kampf and Paul Lauter (New York: Pantheon Books, 1972), pp. 101–29.

as when Fogle speaks approvingly both of Hawthorne's "moral complexity and aesthetic design" or sums up the oeuvre as "a unique and wonderful combination of light and darkness."[30] The New Critics praise wholeness, rather than describe it. Their complex analysis, so far from being analytic, a rationalistic tool to clarify a difficult subject, is a mystification of complexity itself. There is a substitution here that is repeated often in Hawthorne criticism. The message is taken for what we may call its meaning. Interpretation becomes the end of literature, the fulfillment of a text, and a work prized for the easy labor it gives critics in deciphering it. The subtlety with which a work discriminates the elements of the critic's interest is the basis for judging it good or bad.

Of course, it is true that Hawthorne encourages this, too. As a general rule he invites us to be as subjective as we may. But it is precisely for this reason that we should be careful. The alternative possibilities that, as we noted, ask the reader to interpret—at least to choose interpretations from among several given—come to allow him, as they multiply, greater and greater freedom. In "Wakefield," for example, the multiplication can be seen as having already gone so far that Hawthorne asks us to join with him in writing the story. Angus Fletcher notes that allegory often includes its own explication. He defines Frye's "anatomy," in fact, as allegory that explication has totally overcome.[31] Hawthorne's allegory, then, is often as not anatomy in reverse, an allegory so undirected the reader may overcome it with any number of explications of his own. He works his will on the text. He is written into it, and so, in exercising his subjectivity, far from evaluating the text, he paraphrases it, repeats it. Allegorizations are never what the work is about, only what the work is. Hawthorne cuts the ground from under us, incorporates our

[30] Fogle, pp. 7, 4.   [31] Fletcher, p. 319.

response into what he writes, and we are in danger, in praising him, of praising ourselves instead. We perform precisely what Hawthorne asks of us, but in prizing what we perform we overlook the importance of the fact that we have been asked in the first place. I take quite seriously Hawthorne's frequent introductory remarks, his Prefaces inviting the reader into his study. His purpose is to engage us, and we must not mistake his hospitality for anything intellectually more substantial. Hawthorne offers us not conversation, but the opportunity to converse, and in turning the latter into the former we elide his special contribution.

This is, perhaps, an odd attitude to take toward one of America's presumably exemplary Romantics, a naysayer, whose criticism of American life, though admittedly of a rather temperate sort, all the same indicates his insight into what Melville recognized as the "power of blackness." And yet, from our perspective, Hawthorne does not say nay—or, for that matter, aye—to anything. His themes, at almost every level, are too acceptable, too reasonable, to carry imaginative weight. Consider his morality. A devil like Poe is frightening, an angel like Thoreau a model to try to live after. But a man who is neither too good nor too bad, who hates extremes of sanctity as well as of demonism, informs us that we mere human beings are best left unchanged. Or consider his psychology. A man who is all head, as Melville said Emerson was, challenges our intellect. A man who is all heart, a Walt Whitman perhaps, affects our sympathies. But a man who tells us we must be neither all head nor all heart, as Hawthorne does again and again, tells us, simply, that we are what we are. What Melville, therefore, was "shocked" to recognize in Hawthorne, as he put it,[32] was himself, but a self never assumed by Hawthorne, merely accepted. Hawthorne is, as it were, a realist of Romanticism. That is to say, as

[32] "Hawthorne and His Mosses," in *The Shock of Recognition*, p. 199.

we will explain more fully in succeeding chapters, he objectifies his culture's attitudes toward the world, however demonic or angelic those attitudes are, without comment. Charles Feidelson's brilliant thesis about symbolism—the fundamental statement to date on the American Renaissance—is right: the Word, for the American Romantic, retained its prophetic powers, and the project of the writer was to discover the Word, to appropriate the creativity of speech in calling truth into being.[33] But Hawthorne is not, as Feidelson mistakenly supposes, such a writer. We must no longer look to him as a model of visionary activity. To praise Hawthorne by seeing his allegories as symbolic is to devalue him in the very act of appreciation. And, indeed, such praise inevitably leads to criticism, to a comparison with genuine visionaries like Melville and the resulting claim that his allegories are half-hearted symbolism, a refusal, as Yvor Winters, for example, has charged, to "grope his way blindly to significance."[34] We must read Hawthorne according to his own lights. What he teaches is neither, on the one hand, Emersonian piety nor, on the other, a prudent calculation, a fearful drawing back from the dangers of madness. Hawthorne understands from the start, rather, that the truth of words is self-limiting. The action of his speech is never to create; it is to consolidate. Its function is not to synthesize, but to serve as a locus of association, a space into which value may be put. We must read Hawthorne not as a minor Melville, but, full with his own wisdom, as Melville's opposite number.

Melville's case should be inquired into more closely. He insists, in direct opposition to Hawthorne, that the reader give over explicating. "So ignorant are most landsmen of some of the plainest and most palpable wonders of the world," as he says in a famous passage,

[33] *Symbolism and American Literature* (Chicago: Univ. of Chicago Press, 1953). See below, p. 90, for another formulation.
[34] Winters, p. 175.

"that without some hints touching the plain facts, historical and otherwise, of the fishery, they might scout at Moby Dick as a monstrous fable, or still worse and more detestable, a hideous and intolerable allegory." Interpretation is precluded. Moby Dick as Moby Dick presents himself complete, a naked and, as Captain Ahab finds out, unassailable fact of the novel. Even where a novel of Melville's would appear to be incomplete—as Pierre's "Life's last chapter well stitched into the middle" or Isabel's "All's o'er, and ye know him not" suggest of *Pierre*—it is yet an incompleteness that the book establishes as truth.[35] The reader is never asked, as he is in Hawthorne, to finish it himself, because finishing is held to be impossible. Indeed, we might distinguish Hawthorne and Melville, allegory and symbolism, at least of the nineteenth-century variety, by the demands they make of the reader. It is characteristic of symbolism's synecdochic approach to draw the reader into the symbol. Paraphrase, interpretation, are stratagems by which intellect mediates prophecy. But they dissolve in a radical apprehension of the symbolic object as thing in itself. The metaphoric nature of Hawthorne's allegory, on the other hand, requires that the reader turn events of the story into a vehicle for a tenor he is asked to supply.

And yet, it is precisely for these reasons that allegorizations of, say, *Moby-Dick* are a more significant criticism than allegorizations of *The Scarlet Letter*. The symbolism of nineteenth-century America is the prophetic allegory of the Middle Ages in which prophecy, however, has been assimilated from the cosmos into the work itself. Paraphrase of *Moby-Dick* is a first step,

[35] *Moby-Dick*, ch. 45; *Pierre*, xxvi, vi, vii. The passage in *Moby-Dick*, no doubt, is ironic. But the point of the irony is not to protect allegory, but to protect the book from being dismissed, like too many serious books, because it is in part *unavoidably* allegorical. Accordingly, Melville seeks to anchor the allegorical in the real. As I discuss in the next paragraphs, interpretation is only a beginning and must, ultimately, give way.

a beginning in the progress toward the book's untrans-
latable vision. But Hawthorne's works are structures
that contain no vision. From the point of view of his
purpose they are forms without subjects, a notion in
keeping with, although it reverses, the thrust of most of
his critics. It has long been a project of modern criticism to deny the distinction between form and content.
The work in its totality, it is held, expresses a message,
so that even style has thematic consequences. R. S.
Crane, in his influential essay on *Tom Jones*, has thus
demonstrated that plot, so far from an isolatable technique arranging content, is content itself.[36] From our
point of view, however, the point of view of an allegory
whose themes are not its significance, Crane's terms
must be reversed. A work of Hawthorne's translates
what may in life be content into plot. The critic, paraphrasing images as ideas, properly engaged is elaborat-
ing pure form. Improperly engaged, he supplies a content from his own environment, supplies, insofar as his
environment is the work's as well, a content based on
the materials of the work before they become form.[37]

This last, precisely, is what most critics of Hawthorne do. The neutrality of the work is a principle even
avowed formalists in practice neglect. The work, as
structure, asserts a world as yet unaffirmed. It is an
artifact of the society it presents but does not valuate.
In technical terms, we call the work so considered a

[36] "The Concept of Plot and the Plot of *Tom Jones*," in *Critics
and Criticism: Ancient and Modern*, ed. R. S. Crane (Chicago:
Univ. of Chicago Press, 1952), pp. 616–47.

[37] Cf. Roland Barthes, "Style and Its Image," in *Literary Style:
A Symposium*, p. 11. The editor summarizes a discussion that
followed the presentation of Barthes' paper: "How [someone
asked] can one reduce the substantive or contentual choice to
'form'? There must remain some pre-existent material which is
irreducibly content or subject-matter. Barthes replied that for
him 'subject' was an illusory notion. There is no subject expressed by an author; subject is a level in the hierarchy of
interpretation. It is in interpreting the work that the reader
gives it a center, a principle, a content."

genre. Genre is a middle term between society considered as a living organism and the work considered
from the vantage point of the author's purpose. It is a
"neutral territory," in Hawthorne's phrase, culture in its
formal, the work in its archetypal, aspect. I do not,
however, mean that genre is simply normative, a rough
form each writer alters according to his own needs.
Rather, every work exists as genre, and the writer in
transcribing it but articulates a pre-existing structure.
Saussure's linguistics provides an appropriate analogy.
Saussure distinguishes between *"langue"* (language)
and *"parole"* (speech). Language, as he defines it, is
more than the speech that has already been spoken. It
is the possibilities for new speech that rules derived
from the already spoken permit. As each instance of
speech actualizes what was always potential in language, so each work actualizes its genre, which we take
as potential in culture. Of course, the difference between our formulation and Saussure's is crucial. He is
interested in defining an independent linguistic system,
a relation of *langue* and *parole* that can be described
without recourse to anything outside it. He does not
wish to associate culture with speech as we do with the
work, and so, he needs no such middle term as we re-
quire. In effect he denies *langue* any mediating function, specifically warns against it when he notes that it
is rarely co-extensive with culture even in geography.[38]
We may obviate this difficulty, however, by redefining
culture circularly as a community sharing the particular language in question. In fact, narrowly considered,
the culture we are talking about is the culture the work
calls into hypothetical being as determining the conditions of the work's existence. Therefore, at the beginning of this chapter, we used the term "generic," rather
than cultural, say, or social, pressure to describe the

[38] Ferdinand de Saussure, *Course in General Linguistics*,
trans. W. Baskin (New York: Philosophical Library, 1959), pp.
9 ff., 222–28.

limitations on a writer's purpose. What the work communicates, at any rate, is only what the community, however constituted, assumes from the start. The writer makes manifest what is immanent in his world. He writes only to an audience that accepts any message he may relate as implicit in the language they share. The work exists in all its detail before it has ever been written. It is an invention in both the ordinary and root senses of that word, the writer's creation, but, as it were, found. It is speech latent in the literary *langue* of his audience. It is a genre, though *sui generis*, an archetype of which it itself may even be the only instance.

Strictly speaking, it is such an archetypal work that is the proper unit of formal analysis. We recognize this instinctively when we say a work is incomplete or that it goes on too long. In practice, that is, the work as printed may be larger than the unit of analysis—as we shall see when we come to the multiple endings of *The House of the Seven Gables*—or it may be smaller—as in fragments such as "Passages from a Relinquished Work" or "Fragments from the Journal of a Solitary Man." "Ethan Brand," which Hawthorne evidently began as part of a larger work, seems to have asserted its natural size and remained a story. On the other hand, *The Scarlet Letter*, begun as one of several short stories, grew to the size of a novel.[39] The work as printed is to some degree an arbitrary construction. We will throughout attack the ostensible unity of the printed work, to submit ourselves to a unity more pressing, the unity of the integral structures that are the printed work's component parts. These structures may confirm, contradict, or have nothing to do with each other, but each must be granted its own integrity. An attempt to resolve them into a single structure, for example by such terms as "paradox" or "irony," is an application of "interpreta-

[39] "Ethan Brand" is subtitled "A Chapter from an Abortive Romance." For the growth of *The Scarlet Letter* see the Introduction to the *Centenary Edition*, pp. xx–xxii.

tion" beyond its scope. The writer's purpose lies precisely in his employment of a given. His meaning is his
manipulation of forms independent of him, and it is
critically important not to put into the form a writer
who is using it.

At the same time, however, I do not mean to suggest
the necessity of a psychological or biographical approach for evaluating the significance of a work. The
psyche as an area of special investigation is a category
outside the confines of our study. The attempt to open
an intercourse with the world, we have said, is an
attempt at art as well, and the Hawthorne we are investigating, therefore, is properly no psyche, but a
disposition toward works of literature. The former Hawthorne, indeed, impinges on the latter. But like the culture with which *our* Hawthorne would unite, he is
reconstituted in the work as generic pressure. Psychoanalytic interpretation remains viable—indeed, we shall
practice it often—but only *as* interpretation, as we have
defined that term. When Jean Normand speaks of
Ethan Brand as reflecting Hawthorne's diabolism or
Crews of Reuben Bourne as enacting a hostility directed toward Hawthorne's father, what they say may
be accepted. But these are by no means privileged
analyses, pre-eminent among others, offering some
ulterior key.[40] Psychoanalysis can never explain purpose, quite the reverse. Purpose valuates psychoanalysis. It is a disposing subject manipulating whatever interpretations we may make. It discriminates
levels of paraphrase. It valuates by arranging. Only as
it "places" the messages we read will they be of interest.
And, reciprocally, only within the context of the messages as they *are* placed, does purpose come into being.

[40] Normand, *Nathaniel Hawthorne: An Approach to an Analysis of Artistic Creation*, trans. Derek Coltman (Cleveland: Case
Western Reserve Univ. Press, 1970); Crews, *op.cit.* See Crews,
"Reductionism and Its Discontents," *Critical Inquiry*, I (1975),
543–58, for his own recent placing of psychoanalysis in a new,
more limited role than the one he originally claimed for it.

Purpose, no mere mental phenomenon, lies at the center of a series of works that have already incorporated the writer's mind within themselves. It provides for them a progress, ordering meaningfully what else are items describable, paraphrasable, allegorizable, but ultimately, in our context, inexplicable. Purpose may be known neither in the mind outside the work, nor in the work as a representation of the mind, but only in its place in the progress, only "between" works, in the difference of one from the next and the direction of successive differences.

In effect, we are redefining literary history as a self-contained development. We insist that the practice of writing is a primary subject of investigation, a discipline whose value is self-guaranteeing. Our insistence on literature as a progress, however, makes more urgent than ever the need to distinguish its particular units. To leave no place for value, to ignore the point that determines the significance of all else, is to deny the very meaningfulness that gives the critical enterprise its justification. To absorb purpose into a text artificially held to be integral is but to dissolve its existence, to dissipate its force as effectively as making it anterior to the text eliminates it altogether. It is, as it were, to allegorize purpose, to include within interpretation precisely the uninterpretable and, accordingly, quite unconsciously, to take as validated an interpretation whose status has not as yet been determined.

Consider, as an example, "Rappaccini's Daughter." It is usual to look at the story in one of two ways. For Roy Male, "The inner world of human experience is a complex and ambiguous mixture of good and evil. . . ." He sees Beatrice as the shattered but nourishing fountain, "potential spiritual perfection" in a base of "mortal clay," or rather, as the purple shrub, "a brilliant or lurid intermixture of the two, [which] mirrors her paradoxical state since the Fall." Giovanni "would like to possess her physically, or he would be content with her as a pure

25

ideal; but he cannot grasp the fact that she offers both sin and eventual redemption."[41] Male's language, here, is a creative adaptation of New Critical to Christian terms. The "paradox" of Cleanth Brooks[42] is associated with a paradox of Christian mythology. The world, like a text for the New Critics, is "ambiguous," but the ambiguity is one of "good and evil." Male offers an allegorical criticism, a formalist reading paraphrased at the third, or Christian, level of interpretation. But in attempting to resolve the alternatives that he quite properly notes Beatrice presents, he extends formalism beyond its scope. For Male the dialectic of *felix culpa*, the fall from grace into sin leading to an even greater manifestation of God's grace in salvation, resolves two structures that, in the story, are mutually exclusive. Male, assuming the integrity of the work as printed, overlooks the component, and in this case opposing, structures that are the only proper units of interpretation. Giovanni cannot be blamed for failing to unite what from his standpoint is not a unit. Giovanni, indeed, makes no such body-spirit division as Male presupposes. For him the material world contains the spiritual. Either he sees the flower he tosses to Beatrice wither and, therefore, regards her as evil, or he regards Beatrice as good and, therefore, what he sees as an illusion. Male, by labeling "paradoxical" two readings that to Giovanni are an outright contradiction, would explain out of existence the very point between works in which Hawthorne's purpose lies. He makes of what is a series of contradictions at the level of Hawthorne's self-guaranteeing writing, a single term at a level of critical writing which he himself must guarantee.

As E. H. Gombrich notes, ambiguity, at least of a visual sort, is perceived only at a stage of abstraction higher than perception itself. Gombrich discusses a

---

[41] Male, pp. 57, 68.

[42] See, e.g., *The Well-Wrought Urn: Studies in the Structure of Poetry* (New York: Harcourt, Brace and World, 1947).

certain optical illusion, a sketch that looks now like a rabbit, now like a duck: "We can train ourselves to switch more rapidly," he maintains, "indeed to oscillate between readings, but we cannot hold conflicting interpretations." "Ambiguity . . . can never be seen as such. We notice it only by learning to switch from one reading to another and by realizing that both interpretations fit the image equally well."[13] Male's resolution, then, fails to resolve anything. It but ignores the question it addresses, subsumes the problematical in an assertion belonging to a level of statement in which no such problem exists. And yet, there is no reason to assume that the writing of a critic is any more coherent than that of a novelist. At a level higher still, may not Male but replace one question with another? If Male's reading of Beatrice synthesizes a contradictory Hawthorne who is the subject of his criticism, as subject itself it is but a restatement, an archetypal "work," in a series potentially as contradictory as Hawthorne's own. We would need to investigate this in some detail. For example, conceiving, within the parameters Male provides, a single, symmetrical opposition analogous to that in "Rappaccini's Daughter"–hypothesizing but the easiest possible situation, the simplest series of works a higher criticism will need–evil leading to good stands opposed to good leading to evil. At this point we are faced again with our initial problem, but we have exchanged Hawthorne's purpose for Male's own. We may explain out of existence this purpose, too, but the procedure is as endless as it is pointless, a matter of moving farther

[13] *Art and Illusion: A Study in the Psychology of Pictorial Representation*, 2nd ed., rev. (Princeton: Princeton Univ. Press, 1961), pp. 236, 249. We make all too much of so-called paradoxes. There is a television commercial in which the announcer proclaims, "It's not fake anything, it's real Naugahyde." Similarly, Max Beerbohm, "The Mote in the Middle Distance," in *A Christmas Garland* (London: William Heinemann, 1912), p. 7, parodies James: "It was simply a difference of plane. Readjust the 'values,' as painters say, and there you were!" We have a case here, too, of Gombrich's rabbit or duck.

and farther from what we set out to solve. A proper formalism resists such temptation, accepts mutually exclusive alternatives as they are presented and refuses artificially, according to the special aims of the interpreter himself, to resolve the unresolvable.

A second way of looking at "Rappaccini's Daughter" is the psychological approach offered, for example, by Crews. Though somewhat more current, its essential fault is similar to Male's. Crews identifies the contradictory ways Giovanni looks at Beatrice with the Oedipal child's view of his mother, now as virgin, now as whore. Surely Crews is correct here, and his interpretation is in the best tradition of an informed hermeneutics. The story is one of a large number of nineteenth-century American stories in which the hero is caught between a light lady and dark lady identifiable as sister or mother surrogates.[44] The story is a cultural artifact, and it exhibits the neuroses of its culture, the neuroses of Hawthorne himself as a member of the culture. But Crews goes beyond interpretation when he suggests that the admitted "inconsistencies" of Beatrice's nature, the "crude and unbalanced alternatives" she represents, may be explained by Giovanni's—and, ultimately, Hawthorne's—"morbid curiosity," his prurient interest in a sexuality he hates precisely because he loves. To give what Crews calls "unity" to Beatrice by suggesting that her innocence is a defense against her sexuality[45] is an attempt to resolve mutually exclusive terms in an abstraction whose opposite might be, say, sexuality as a degradation of innocence. As with Male, it is an assimilation of purpose into the structures between which purpose exists. It is to regard the forms of one level of statement in light of the forms of another.

[44] See Leslie A. Fiedler, "The Revenge on Woman: From Lucy to Lolita," in *Love and Death in the American Novel*, rev. ed. (New York: Stein and Day, 1966), pp. 291–336, for a survey of the topic.
[45] Crews, pp. 119, 124, 128.

Let us remain, instead, within the boundaries the story itself provides. We do not, at this point, have much to work with. We have not as yet begun to investigate the sweep of Hawthorne's career, have not seen enough of the successive forms to know their direction, to uncover the purpose between them. Nor have we, as yet, described a mechanism of succession. Ultimately, as we have said, our analysis of any particular work derives support from its place in the total history of works, and the subsequent chapters of this study will address just that totality. Let us, for the sake of demonstration, however, limit Hawthorne's career to "Rappaccini's Daughter" alone. Here is the sole extant work of a writer—or perhaps, we should say, with Hawthorne, the sole available work of an otherwise untranslated writer named Aubépine—and we wish to understand what it is all about. There is little biographical help. The brief headnote does not tell us much about Aubépine's life except, presumably, if we assume he has a certain sympathy with his publisher, that he is an "anti-aristocrat" and believes in "liberal principles." About the works we will never see, we know—if we trust the critic who wrote the headnote—that they are allegories and that they tend to be disquieting mixes of opposites like the material and the transcendental or the popular and the esoteric. In particular, they are neither quite real nor yet purely fantastical, and as a result, they are sometimes amusing, but difficult to take very seriously.

From the standpoint of interpretation this little information is sufficient. Formalistically considered, the story is an independent unit constituting in itself the only world we need to know about, or, to take formalism in its more general practice, reconstituting in itself elements of the world outside and advancing them at the level of message. Aubépine is an allegorist, so we are probably justified in reading the characters as representing various general ideas. Aubépine is a democrat, so perhaps the ideas are political. Or, perhaps, if he is

29

not quite a transcendentalist, the ideas belong to an ethical or moral or philosophical system that is not quite transcendentalism. Crews and Male, of course, have suggested other allegories that, in the wider context available to them, are equally plausible. We know, too, that Aubépine tends to think in dichotomies, to mix opposites, and with this hint—after reading the story carefully, of course—we determine that "Rappaccini's Daughter" is a story about a man caught between democracy and autocracy, or good and evil, or salvation and sin, or innocence and sexuality, or fantasy and reality, or any number of such pairs. Aubépine, in keeping with his liberal principles, in each case favors the former, and the moral of the story, if we allow ourselves to moralize, is something like "Be true," or "Be faithful," or "Be good."

But what action does "Rappaccini's Daughter" perform? What is Aubépine's purpose in writing it? We do not have, as we have said, any other story to work with. Purpose must remain obscure unless, forced back on the single printed work, we discover in it, even if only as fragments, adumbrations of those archetypal works which are the proper units of analysis. Indeed, "Rappaccini's Daughter," I would maintain, is two works simultaneously presented, two stories arranged not sequentially, one after the other, as is generally the case, but vertically along an axis of interpretation. I do not mean that purpose may be found "between" Male and Crews, say. The differences in their descriptions of what the story is about are not, from our point of view, important. The very notion of allegory, the principle on which the idea of polysemous interpretation is predicated, is the equivalence of interpretive levels, their unitary force. They are all versions of each other, different ways of saying the same thing appropriate to different circumstances. But within each "sema" itself there are, in "Rappaccini's Daughter," contradictions. "Rappaccini's Daughter" is the story of an innocent (or democratic or good or imaginative or whatever) girl destroyed by a faithless love, *and* it is the story of a dangerous woman enticing an innocent boy. Though the one title serves for the whole, though the two stories are told within a single narrative frame, yet there are discontinuities, odd dislocations that suggest a co-presence of tales that retain their individuality. The tales reside on the same printed spot, as it were, but follow independent logics. As Aubépine narrates, he emphasizes now one, now the other, now both simultaneously. But it is as if each story is complete from the start, and Aubépine, shifting back and forth, is keeping them both going, preventing them from receding from the narrative surface they both inhabit.

Thus the story of the innocent boy enticed: "It mattered not whether she were angel or demon; he was irrevocably within her sphere, and must obey the law that whirled him onward, in ever lessening circles, towards a result which he did not attempt to foreshadow" (x, 109). But at the end, when a now faithless Giovanni would recant, the story of the innocent girl deserted: "Oh, weak, and selfish, and unworthy spirit, that could dream of an earthly union and earthly happiness as possible, after such deep love had been so bitterly wronged as was Beatrice's love by Giovanni's blighting words! No, no; there could be no such hope. She must pass heavily, with that broken heart, across the borders of Time—she must bathe her hurts in some fount of Paradise, and forget her grief in the light of immortality—and *there* be well!" (x, 126).

Here are two incompatible expositions. Yet there is a breathlessness in each of them, an inexorable pressure through an inevitable sequence of events, as if the narrative of "Rappaccini's Daughter" were possessed now by one pre-existing structure, now by another. Aubépine is not being ambiguous. He is quite clear in each case. But one clarity runs counter to the other. Indeed, ambiguity seems totally beyond the intellectual resources

of poor Aubépine, and his celebrated love of dichotomies, after all, seems to consist simply of the ability to
recount, side by side, structures that, if they do not precisely exclude each other, he still makes no attempt to
resolve. Baglioni, for example, is now a true friend of
Giovanni's father, a wise old uncle devoted to the protection of his inexperienced steward, now a meddling,
selfish academic. Conceivably, of course, a man might
be a blend of both. Aubépine, however, does not conceive of him so. Thus, "Giovanni!–my poor Giovanni!"
Baglioni, "with a calm expression of pity," advises the
boy against Rappaccini. "Listen; for, even should you do
violence to my gray hairs, it shall not silence me" (x,
118). But, a page later, without a word from Aubépine
to indicate that Baglioni might have mixed motives or
ambivalent feelings, a differently construed Baglioni
restates the reasons for his opposition: ". . . let us confess the truth of him [Rappaccini], he is a wonderful
man!–a wonderful man indeed! A vile empiric, however, in his practice, and therefore not to be tolerated
by those who respect the good old rules of the medical
profession!" (x, 119–20). Two men seem to occupy the
same body–two conventional men belonging to two conventional but different stories, instead of one ambivalent man in one complex story.

Similarly, Dame Lisabetta, the chambermaid, is hor-
rified when Giovanni assumes that the garden of poisonous plants belongs to her house. She is a simple,
God-fearing peasant, a stock piece of machinery to introduce the stock unholiness of Rappaccini's enterprise.
But when a stock character of an opposite sort is needed, when the progress of events requires a pandering,
gold-grubbing go-between in the service of Rappaccini,
Aubépine, rather than create anyone new, uses what is
available to him and gives the same figure of Lisabetta
different qualities. This is an unusual procedure. But it
happens too frequently to dismiss, and it interferes with
the notion that "Rappaccini's Daughter" is a consisent

unit capable of being consistently interpreted. The rhetoric of the story shifts. Aubépine's intention—the intention of the text—points in different directions at different places. Giovanni, the text insists, is capable of
the highest faith. He is a Giovanni who, in reply to
Beatrice's plea that he "Believe nothing of me save what
you see with your own eyes," responds that "you demand too little of me. Bid me believe nothing, save what
comes from your own lips" (x, 111–12). But Giovanni
alternately interpreted, the text declares quite as clearly, is shallow enough to spend time admiring himself in
front of a mirror at the very moment before he will
challenge Beatrice about the horror he has discovered
(x, 121). Either Aubépine is incompetent, or he has
written a larger number of stories than it might at first
have appeared. I have suggested two. Belonging to the
innocent-boy-enticed story we would include the positive figures of Baglioni and Giovanni, the negative
figure of Beatrice, and Rappaccini. Belonging to the
deserted-girl story would be the negative Baglioni and
Giovanni, the positive Beatrice, and, perhaps, even a
positive Rappaccini—a Rappaccini who, though heart-
less and coldly intellectual on the surface, is a loving if
misguided father inside, attempting to shield his daughter, as he tells her, from all potential earthly dangers
(x, 127). Dame Lisabetta, in both her aspects, belongs
to both stories.

No doubt other divisions, perhaps even other stories,
are possible. There is a suggestion, for example, particularly at the beginning and end of "Rappaccini's
Daughter," of a star-crossed lovers' tale, a *Romeo and
Juliet* as Aubépine's sentimental age might have understood it: a positive Giovanni and a positive Beatrice are
kept apart by the rivalries of their respective negative
elders. But as we have introduced "Rappaccini's Daughter" for the sake of demonstration, it is perhaps best to
keep things simple. Besides, we must always be governed by the text, and I do not think the star-crossed

lovers' tale, or any other such we might find, is of any consequence. One general point, however, should be made. To be governed by the text does not mean to suppose the unity of what is printed, even if, as a practical matter, to delimit the extent of what we will investigate initially, we must make this assumption on a working basis. Rather, it is to define the very body of the text purposively, to constitute it as a result of its place in the larger development of the writer's career. If dislocations, shifts in rhetoric of the sort we have noticed, are the practical basis for the entities so established, this idea of place in the career, ultimately, is the theoretical ground. No doubt this is to go around in a circle. We have uncovered the units of analysis on the basis of what we see as the writer's purpose and the writer's purpose on the basis of the units of analysis. In the case of "Rappaccini's Daughter" the difficulty is compounded because we have nothing else to work with. For all the procedural problems it presents, however, the approach remains sound in its substance. Concerning my study of Hawthorne, I admit quite freely that in working on particulars I was governed from the start by an intuition, a premature projection in advance, of the whole. But this projection, too, has altered as the particulars changed. In any case, it is better to admit the self-containedness of any system of analysis—to hope it is, as measured by simple common sense, useful or interesting—than to pretend to an objectivity, a privileged vision of the truth which no critic may have.

Owning beforehand, then, the perhaps tautological nature of our criticism, admitting, indeed, the even worse situation in the case of "Rappaccini's Daughter," I take Aubépine's purpose to be the most circular project of all, the elimination of purpose. It is the attempt, by authorially affirming opposite interpretations of the same fiction, by linking in a single printed text two contradictory stories, to create a fiction that affirms

34

itself. To return to the headnote, it is to solve the problem of the unreality of his works by making the fantastical itself real. Indeed, the history of Aubépine's career
is the development of what I take to be realism—a term
we must wait to define more fully until a discussion of
The Blithedale Romance. In a preliminary way, however, we may say that the mode of a fiction is based,
properly, on neither its subject matter nor its form, but
on the author's presence in or absence from it, or to
speak strictly, on his disposition towards it, the use to
which he is putting it, read back onto it *as* a presence.
Purpose, that is, is the only real guide to modality,
which accordingly, though dependent upon interpretation, is finally distinct from it. It is a matter not of what
a work says, even if how a thing is said is considered to
be part of what it says, but of the writer's relation to the
work. It is a question of the status—as self-validating,
authorially validated, culturally validated, and so forth
—of the truth the work speaks as opposed to the truth
itself.

It will perhaps be objected that we have not been
talking about anything much. No matter how many
stories we find in "Rappaccini's Daughter" the message
is the same in each. Aubépine, as noted at the very start,
clearly is on the side of innocence, against the side of
evil. One truth that "Rappaccini's Daughter" speaks is
that innocence is good and evil bad. Our point, however, is that purpose refuses, here, to establish the
status of the characters within the framework of good
and evil. Aubépine will not tell us if Beatrice is one or
the other, or rather, he tells us both, which is his means
of disengaging himself, of moving toward a position
that will enable us to interpret "Rappaccini's Daughter"
as self-validating object, without worrying about purpose, to interpret, assuming all the while that the validity of what we describe is assured. Admittedly, this is
to come a long way without having gotten very far. We

are back where we started, as we might have expected, given the circumscription with which we had to define Aubépine's career. But at least we have established from general principles the special areas in which interpretation applies. We have traveled over ground that in the course of a career more extended than Aubépine's we will traverse with considerably more results.

Let us consider, then, a case more significantly related to the special concerns of this study, involving quite directly the opening of an intercourse that is the reason for Hawthorne's career. Here we will have to allow for the possibility not only of separating what most critics have taken to be one, but of taking as one what critics have separated. Hawthorne's Prefaces, it is generally acknowledged, are especially noteworthy. Genre critics have long turned to them for assistance in defining such problematical terms as novel and romance. Students of ideas have found valuable opinions on politics, sociology, and religion. Biographers have discovered clues to Hawthorne's reaction to the Salem patronage affair, his affection for Franklin Pierce, his state of mind in Italy, and so forth. Since the New Criticism, however, analysts of Hawthorne of all sorts—generic, historical, biographical—have attempted to relate each Preface more integrally to the particular novel it introduces. It is no longer held proper to explain "The Custom-House" simply, say, as Hawthorne's attack on the politicians who had cost him his job. For Frank MacShane, for example, Hawthorne's ambivalence over taking a sinecure as Customs Inspector rather than writing is parallel to Dimmesdale's guilt over his hypocritical role as pastor. Larzer Ziff, focusing on the aesthetic formulations of "The Custom-House," compares Hawthorne's discussion of the need to enrich the actual with the imaginary with the characters' understanding of the present as vitally involved with the past. Sam Basket compares Hawthorne's feelings about Salem to the mixture of attachment and antipathy in Dimmesdale and Hester to the Puritans.[46]

As with interpretation of Hawthorne's other work, I have no particular argument with any of these views per se. They are important insights into the thematic connections between the two pieces. But the focus on theme in disregard of purpose is inadequate in two respects. First, it leads to an artificial construction of the subject to be interpreted. The critic presumes from the first the point he ought to demonstrate, the unity of the material at issue. Implicit in all the usual interpretations is an attempt to consider "The Custom-House" as though it were a chapter of *The Scarlet Letter*. As Basket remarks, " 'The Custom-House' clarifies and extends the meaning of the romance and thus should be read as a significant part of the total work." Clarification and extension are the criteria of unity, a definition, as we have discussed, that makes interpretation itself the end of a work. The possibility that clarification is a distinct action is denied, and two pieces that exist in relation to each other are thus resolved into one that is transcendent. Given such a focus, of course, few writers are capable of any genuine progress, of a career in any real sense. The development of a man like Hawthorne, who returns again and again to the same themes, is reduced largely to a matter of refining—perhaps, if *The Scarlet Letter* is his greatest work, of confusing—what he has said earlier. In effect, this is precisely the attitude of too many of Hawthorne's critics, whose interpretations of one work will serve, with minor alterations, for any other. By eliding purpose, by refusing to consider the different uses to which even the same structure may be put, they neglect Hawthorne's real

[46] MacShane, "The House of the Dead: Hawthorne's Custom House and *The Scarlet Letter*," *NEQ*, 35 (1962), 93–101; Ziff, "The Ethical Dimension of 'The Custom House,' " *MLN*, 73 (1958), 338–44; Basket, "*The* (Complete) *Scarlet Letter*," *CE*, 22 (1961), 321–28.

originality. They rob him of what he does best, of re-defining his limits as liberties, revaluing the dead body of the past, as he called it, as the ground of a new future. They focus on a work as if it were timeless, on what it says as though it took no part in the circumstances of its saying.

Second, then, the elision of purpose leads to an over-valuing of the subject of interpretation in isolation. In the absence of any progress, with a work unplaced, the various themes a writer may repeat are given a significance they do not, in fact, have. If all the works are the same, if we concentrate on the oppositions—writing vs. working, past vs. present, attraction vs. repulsion—that *Letter* and "The Custom-House" share, we lose sight of the more important opposition between *Letter* and "The Custom-House" taken as simple units. Thematic oppositions may constitute a purposive whole. *The Scarlet Letter*, for all its complexity taken alone, presents a seamless front from the perspective of "The Custom-House." Discrepancies internal to a work disappear in the context of the larger discrepancy between two works, each of which is now taken as indivisible. Accordingly, it is well and good to analyze the various ideas with which *The Scarlet Letter* and "The Custom-House" deal, but to do so and to discover that the configurations of these ideas have a certain relation is not to answer but to pose a question. In other terms, theme, as we have maintained, is structure. To notice that certain themes are of continued interest is not to verify their significance, but to demonstrate structural duplication. If MacShane, Ziff, and Basket are correct, they have demonstrated, so far from the unity of the two pieces, the reconstruction of *The Scarlet Letter* as a Preface to itself. They do not explain the reason for the reconstruction: why Hawthorne wrote the structure twice rather than once. The presence side by side of two equivalent forms is our central problem.

It is perhaps well to consider the circumstances of the composition of the works. Hawthorne, unhappy with Fields's decision to publish *Letter* alone, would seem to have slipped in at least one of the stories he had wanted to add to the volume by the front door of an introduction. So far from regarding "The Custom-House" as simply a "clarification" or "extension," he seems always to have seen it as a separate piece, an additional bullet, as he put it, to bring down his quarry, the reader.[47] It was the sketch, he was to maintain, that gave the novel its vogue. It was the sketch, he said, that was the more characteristic, if not the better work.

For us this attitude is difficult to understand. We recognize *The Scarlet Letter* proper as America's first masterwork of fiction. It is the great American novel, the work by an American about America that critics from the beginning of the century had been calling for. Hawthorne's contemporaries recognized this as well. Fields thought it "marvellous" after he had seen only its "germ." It fixed firmly Hawthorne's position in American literature, established him, as he always wished he would be established, as equal to the best of the "scribbling sons of John Bull."[48] Surely, in this area, Hawthorne is blind. He wrote better than he knew. We insist in our very attempt to enlarge *The Scarlet Letter*'s sphere, to integrate "The Custom-House" into it, on honoring the man who wrote it as one of our finest, our foremost, men of letters. And yet Hawthorne was not, if we read him right, blind to the merits of *Letter*. His attitude was simply one of admiration rather than affection. As he noted later, in discussing the difficulties of *The House of the Seven Gables*, *The Scarlet Letter*

---

[47] For this and Hawthorne's negotiations with Fields see the introduction to the *Centenary Edition*, especially pp. xx–xxii.

[48] The phrase appears in a letter to his mother, quoted in Hubert H. Hoeltje, *Inward Sky: The Mind and Art of Nathaniel Hawthorne* (Durham, N.C.: Duke Univ. Press, 1962), p. 42.

seemed virtually to write itself. Hawthorne speaks of it resoundingly as a "hell-fired" work, but he speaks coolly, as if he were not in hell himself, as if, as a sensible man, living at least in part in the "cheering light" he wished he could introduce into the book, he found this work he had produced too morbid, too powerful, ever to own. It is "either very good or very bad," he could remark, an indication, I think, not that Hawthorne was too close to tell, but that he recognized it as something special, in a way beyond his proper control.[49] In a sense, if Hawthorne elsewhere reacts to the isolation presumably enforced on a writer in New England, he is reacting here to the opposite pressure of acceptance, the burden of being a foremost anything. "The Custom-House," I would suggest, reclaims *The Scarlet Letter* for Hawthorne himself. If, as the analyses of Basket and the others propose, it is a personalized *Scarlet Letter*, "The Custom-House" would appear to be a quite deliberate repossession of what, perhaps even in the writing, Hawthorne saw as an artifact too much of his culture, not sufficiently of him. It is a response to an archetype he has as much transcribed as created. Hawthorne duplicates the archetype to insert himself in it. "The Custom-House" is Hawthorne's assertion that the form of *The Scarlet Letter* is his own form as well.

There is a wonderful story by Jorge Luis Borges that presents the situation most acutely. Pierre Menard engages to write *Don Quixote* some three hundred years after it has already been written. As Borges puts it, "he did not want to compose another *Quixote*—which is easy—but *the Quixote itself*. Needless to say, he never contemplated a mechanical transcription of the original; he did not propose to copy it. His admirable intention was to produce a few pages that would coincide—word for word and line for line—with those of Miguel de Cervantes." In preparation Menard first considers

[49] Quoted in Mark Van Doren, *Nathaniel Hawthorne* (1949; rpt. New York: Viking Press, 1957), p. 141.

immersing himself in Cervantes' world, coming to "know Spanish well, recover the Catholic faith, fight against the Moors or the Turk, forget the history of Europe between the years 1602 and 1918, *be* Miguel de Cervantes." After beginning this procedure, however, he changes his mind and decides, rather, "to go on being Pierre Menard and reach the *Quixote* through the experiences of Pierre Menard."[50] When he dies he leaves two chapters and fragments of another that, to the superficial observer, appear to be, in effect, Cervantes in Menard's handwriting, but are really a new work.

Here is a discussion of the difficulties of writing in a language fully constituted from the start. For Menard as well as for Hawthorne, to write is to repeat what has already been written. His work exists as a cultural imposition before he begins. It is a tyranny he cannot resist. The author has two choices. He may fully embrace what would restrict him. He may give up to the culture embodied in the work, be socialized at the cost of his individuality, "*be* Miguel de Cervantes" at the expense of Menard. Or he may take Menard's ultimate route, so to speak inform the form that is given with an energy that is his own, "reach the *Quixote* through the experiences of Pierre Menard." Though *Don Quixote* "A" is formally identical with *Don Quixote* "B," there is a fundamental difference between the two in their relation to Menard. For in between their composition, Menard the reader becomes Menard the writer. The writer who can never escape the work may yet reconstruct it. *Langue* becomes *parole*. *Don Quixote*, quite literally, is "reformed." The writer, possessed by a work he cannot resist, in turn possesses it to make it also his own. The work is the expression of a mutuality. It affirms a culture, yet includes the writer as an equal member. It is the ground of the intercourse Hawthorne would open with the

[50] "Pierre Menard, Author of the *Quixote*," in *Labyrinths: Selected Stories and Other Writings*, ed. Donald A. Yates and James E. Irby (1964; rpt. Harmondsworth, Middlesex: Penguin Books, 1970), pp. 65–66.

world, the locus of such intimacy as writing may achieve.[51]

We note several important considerations. Is it not difficult to determine, concerning any given form, if a writer has in fact possessed it? May not the writer simply recapitulate a work he will or cannot inform? Indeed, he is even capable of what we might call bad faith, pretending to a mutuality that, in fact, does not exist, claiming, in Borges' terms, to write *Don Quixote* when he is only copying it. We will discuss bad faith more fully in *The Marble Faun*, where it becomes important. But it might be observed parenthetically that unrecognized pretense of this sort has been the source of a good deal of misdirected debate about the nature of Hawthorne's personality. In *The American Notebooks*, for example, Hawthorne casts himself as a latter-day troubadour, happily wandering through the villages of New England. Stewart makes use of this when he debunks the traditional image of Hawthorne as a brooding poète maudit.[52] On the other hand, material such as

[51] Cf. Barthes' "zero degree" in *Writing Degree Zero and Elements of Semiology*, trans. Annette Lavers and Colin Smith (Boston: Beacon Press, 1970), esp. pp. 11, 13, 76–78. It lies between "language"—defined as "a horizon," "the initial limit of the possible"—and "style"—defined as "the transmutation of a Humour"—and is the point at which writing "confronts the innermost part of man." Barthes' "style" and "horizon," however, are for me formally identical, distinguishable only as the work is possessed now by the writer, now by the reader. Barthes comes closer to this position in "Style and Its Image," p. 9: ". . . what would have to control the stylistic work is the search for models, of patterns: sentence structures, syntagmatic clichés, divisions and *clausulae* of sentences; and what would inspire such work is the conviction that style is essentially a citational process, a body of formulae, a memory (almost in the cybernetic sense of the word), a cultural and not an expressive inheritance."

[52] Stewart, ed., *The American Notebooks by Nathaniel Hawthorne* (New Haven: Yale Univ. Press, 1932). See also, *Biography*, p. 37, Stewart's discussion of the exaggeration in Hawthorne's letter of October 4, 1840 to Sophia, describing his "lonely youth" in his "lonely chamber."

Fanshawe and "Passages from a Relinquished Work" has been used as grounds for the opposite view. Hawthorne is an isolated man, morose, unwanted, a writer who must write for no one but himself.[53] Neither conception, I would maintain, is particularly true. Each is a facile copy of a role society sanctions. Indeed, the ease with which Hawthorne shifts from one to the other, the relation, that is, between the archetypes he sets down, demonstrates how little of him they both engage. Thus the *Notebooks* show a Whitmanesque camerado, a poet of the people at home with tavern-keepers and bar girls. It is Hawthorne's presentation of himself in an image his culture directs. The poète maudit is a somewhat more complicated case, but it, too, more than a psychic expression, a simple representation of Hawthorne's alienation, is a projection of himself as a popular post-romantic myth. As he describes his procedure in the Preface to *Twice-told Tales*: ". . . the Author, who, on the internal evidence of his sketches, came to be regarded as a mild, shy, gentle, melancholic, exceedingly sensitive, and not very forcible man . . . is by no means certain, that some of his subsequent productions have not been influenced and modified by a natural desire to fill up so amiable an outline, and to act in consonance with the character assigned to him . . . " (IX, 7). In the long run, whether a work is recreated or merely copied is a question to be answered only by carefully observing the successive structures a writer employs.

A second, more serious, objection, however, may perhaps be raised concerning the culture. Is not the story of Pierre Menard inadequate to explain Hawthorne's situation? For is not Menard free from the consequences of his reconstruction, free from the reaction of Cervantes to the act of appropriation that Menard performs? The author of Hawthorne's work, on the other

[53] For a classic portrait of this type, see Newton Arvin, *Hawthorne* (Boston: Little, Brown, 1929).

hand, is a culture still very much alive. It is an audience that he may be changing in addressing, that in the very violence of possession he may in fact be alienating. As Hawthorne continues to write, culture as writer becomes culture as reader. Society that imposes its tyranny on him becomes, in turn, tyrannized. The alienation in which Hawthorne's career originates thus remains, but inverted. Author and audience still fail to commune. Even more seriously, perhaps, just as the author on occasion exhibits bad faith, so the reader may exhibit no faith at all. He may simply refuse to be possessed, be from the start disinterested—a critic, for example, or a member of a culture different from the one the work embodies.

Hawthorne illustrates the problem in "Alice Doane's Appeal." There the narrator assumes an audience naively susceptible to the grotesque. He casts himself as a writer seeking to penetrate "the seldom trodden places" of two girls' hearts with a tale of admittedly gothic horror. The girls laugh at the story's extravagance, and the writer must shift his ground to historical tales that more nearly relate to them. Here is a case of possessing a form irrelevant for the purpose of opening an intercourse. The writer, inserting himself in a work, joins with a world that does not exist. Of course, theoretically, as we have indicated earlier, the writer may simply assume the presence of an ideal audience. The community to which Hawthorne directs himself, so we have said, is a community of readers whose universe, if it did exist, the work would embody. Hawthorne's "Kind" or "Gentle" reader is presumed on only partial evidence, is part real, part hypothetical. In practice, however, he is vitally concerned that the forms he uses be broad enough to reflect a significant segment of a real population. Uniting with the work of a hypothetical audience, with a genre ultimately self-generated, is a particular kind of narcissism, as we will discuss in the next chapter, which when Hawthorne does attempt, he quickly renounces. It is half the problem he would solve. The progress of his career is toward stabilizing an oscillation between self and other, between the work as the world's, on the one hand, but the work as his, on the other.

This leads to our final consideration. To whose authority, Hawthorne's or his readers', may we attribute any given work? Have we not, for example, artificially assigned "The Custom-House" to one, *The Scarlet Letter* to the other? Indeed, we have isolated the two works from their proper context, in which each will appear as a ground of struggle. It is from the perspective of "The Custom-House" only that *The Scarlet Letter*—which, as we will discuss in considerable detail, Hawthorne loses only after a great deal of effort—appears so clearly to belong to the audience. And, in turn, "The Custom-House," too, though written to assert its author, asserts itself as a coercion in the very process of being written. Here is a mechanism of succession. Hawthorne would open an intercourse with a resisting world. He would join with a work that, even as he invests himself in it, even as he composes it, is reconstituted as generic pressure. His development is dialectical, a fuller and fuller commitment of purpose returning against him, demanding a still fuller commitment.

For a brief moment, in *The House of the Seven Gables*, purpose and genre are in equilibrium. The work is a form reformed from the start. It neither tyrannizes nor is tyrannized. It is a pure expression of a writer at one with his readers. At such a point writing as we know it ceases. Development ends, and literature as celebration replaces progress, succession, indeed, as we shall discover, plot. We call such literature romance. Romance is the attempt to open an intercourse completed, purpose fulfilled. It is freedom from the constraint of literary rules—its original meaning, as applied to medieval romances[54]—or, more properly, since rules may never be escaped, a mutual possession of rules and ruled. We will discuss this more elaborately in *The Scarlet Letter*, but as noted in relation to "Rappaccini's Daughter" and realism, I take literary modality to be defined in purposive terms. The absence of purpose constitutes one mode, its full presence another. Romance, as we shall see, is not complete until *The House of the Seven Gables*. But we are getting considerably ahead of ourselves. We first need to follow Hawthorne's development to this point in some detail. We need, indeed, to begin at the beginning, to establish the elements that at this early stage, so far from uniting, barely even relate.

[54] See René Wellek, "The Concept of Romanticism in Literary History," in *Concepts of Criticism* (New Haven: Yale Univ. Press, 1963), pp. 131–32.

TWO

The Short Stories

DESCRIBING a development such as the one we have elaborated begins with a difficulty of selection. A reasonable account of Hawthorne's growth must include the four major novels. But any set of choices from among the short stories, occasional pieces, and sketches will surely seem arbitrary to a reader whose favorite pieces are omitted. On the other hand, although Hawthorne's output is not especially large, it is still obviously impossible to describe everything. Indeed, perhaps it is not even desirable to describe everything. As we have challenged the unity of the work, we might wonder as well about a hypothetical unity of everything a writer has written. The short pieces are of obvious diversity in quality and appeal. May not some of them be written from some other side of Hawthorne than his main side, by some other Hawthorne? The risks of analyzing everything are as great as analyzing some things at the expense of others. Each method is a selection, each liable to the same charge of arbitrariness. Once again, common sense as it judges the results of analysis after the fact, so to speak, is the only justification for the procedure undertaken. A number of stories, therefore, will be considered chronologically that, together with the novels, seem to provide a coherent and important progress. I believe it is a progress that might readily be supplemented, whose gaps might be filled by other stories we have overlooked. It is a progress that might be expanded to include a great deal of what is not directly discussed. From a common-sense standpoint, for example, I have chosen short stories that seem to explain shortness itself, the fact that Hawthorne begins with small pieces and stops writing them, by and large, when he moves on to lengthier ones with the novels. But if pressed, I do not claim that other selections, that other progresses, are not equally important. And most especially, I do not claim that these particular stories are in any way "representative." Hawthorne's career, we have maintained, is a development, not one transcendent set of themes. A broader consideration of his oeuvre consistent with our thesis would include other stories, not as "like" the ones we will consider, but as filling a place in a history more tortuous than we have been able to describe.

Preliminary: "The Hollow of the Three Hills"

We begin with "The Hollow of the Three Hills." From the secure position of an early work, a piece as yet unembroiled in the complications of later development, of process, it would seem to offer a simple prospect of Hawthorne's career. Preceding the demand of the subsequent work for intimacy, it juxtaposes certain areas whose significance, as yet potential, remains to be explored.

The keynote of the story is a deliberate indefiniteness sounded in the first sentence by the still largely undifferentiated conceptions of time, place, and character: "In those strange old times, when fantastic dreams and madmen's reveries were realized among the actual circumstances of life, two persons met together at an appointed hour and place" (IX, 199). This is a generalized formulation of story as a type, a statement of the primary elements necessary in any particular story. The listing of similarly undifferentiated elements more redolent of Hawthorne's own fiction characterizes the rest of the tale. The primeval hollow is a sort of ur-space. It is prototypical of the spaces—the Province-House, the Custom-House, the House of the Seven Gables, and so forth—the fictional loci in which, as we shall see, author and audience will later become invested. As a magic ground, the "almost mathematically circular" sphere in which the conjurer-witch traditionally stands, the hollow will become the work that presents the artist.[1] Within it, formed by the lap and hood of the witch, another hollow into which the woman places her head and fantasizes about home adumbrates the ground of reader response.

The spaces do not mix. The structure of the tale is paratactical. Ritual juxtaposes elements, associates items that at this stage must not more closely relate. The formal, repeated incantations of the crone, the triplicate structure, the progressive horror of the visions from sorrow to madness to death, locate the spaces in a rhythm of rising intensity. But rhythmic progression is not narrative continuity. Causality and relation remain potential. Are the visions hallucinations of the lady, spells of the witch, or some combination of the two? The elements remain uncombined: "But those strangers appeared not to stand in the hollow depth between the three hills. Their voices were encompassed and re-echoed by the walls of a chamber . . . and when the lady lifted her eyes, there was she kneeling in the hollow between three hills" (IX, 201–202). The scenery of the hollow and the vision in the lap, the details of the artistic sphere and those of the domestic, never unite. Awareness of one fades as the vision of the other appears and returns only when the vision subsides.

Most important of all, the spaces are never allowed to become informed with the interest of writer or reader. Ritual, here, too, serves to obviate any possible union by rigidly closing us off from any possible participation in the work. The familial ties presented in the vision, for example, and the lady's ambivalence toward them, are a potential subject of universal Western scope.

[1] See Millicent Bell, *Hawthorne's View of the Artist* (New York: University Publishers, 1962), for a discussion of Hawthorne's magicians, scientists, and artists as versions of each other.

Here is matter that would engage a culture, a problem that may indeed unify, a common concern latent in Hawthorne and his audience as parents and children. But the latency is never exposed. The allegorical method that Hawthorne will practice later, the invitation to his audience to interpret itself in the work, is absent. The scene is fixed in a symmetrical and self-contained geometry of scenes. Interpretation, such as it exists, exhibits no writer or reader present in the material, but is relegated to a position by and large outside the geometric order. It is disconnected from the event, an afterthought, a function of an observer apart from the object of his observation, an interpretation, indeed, that rather demonstrates that nothing is understood.

Consider the second vision: "Shrieks pierced through the obscurity of sound, and were succeeded by the singing of sweet female voices, which in their turn gave way to a wild roar of laughter, broken suddenly by groanings and sobs, forming altogether a ghastly confusion of terror and mourning and mirth" (IX, 202). Here, potentially, is a primal scene, the origin of the Western family. But the gothic terms in which the scene is described are not interpretation, a psychologization of the scene in some pre-Freudian jargon.[2] They offer themselves strictly as a literal account. Nothing in the passage indicates that they are words in any way explanatory, that they bring us close to the action by elucidating it for us. We will meet, in *The House of the Seven Gables*, action and response to action presented in the same language. Indeed, were "Hollow" written at a later period in Hawthorne's career, or were the other paratactical stratagems we have been discussing absent, we might read the language of the primal-scene passage as

[2] Thus, e.g., Fiedler, p. 128: "The flight of the gothic heroine is . . . through a world of ancestral and infantile fears projected in dreams." And, again, pp. 160–61: "The European gothic identified blackness with the super-ego . . . the American gothic (at least as it followed the example of Brown) identified evil with the id. . . ."

avows: "There was once a time, when New-England groaned under the actual pressure of heavier wrongs, than those threatened ones which brought on the Revolution" (IX, 9). The tyranny of the period of the story is declared, but only at the expense of something else that tradition conceives, or, more properly, is held to conceive of as the sufferings of the Revolutionists. Similarly, when Hawthorne describes the New Englanders assembled in King Street, a catalogue of virtue gradually fades into a catalogue of vice:

"Indeed, it was not yet time for the old spirit to be extinct; since there were men in the street, that day, who had worshipped there beneath the trees, before a house was reared to the God, for whom they had become exiles. Old soldiers of the Parliament were here too, smiling grimly at the thought, that their aged arms might strike another blow against the house of Stuart. Here also, were the veterans of King Philip's war, who had burnt villages and slaughtered young and old, with pious fierceness, while the godly souls throughout the land were helping them with prayer" (IX, 11).

More is involved, here, than simple irony. Hawthorne does not mean to resolve contradictory notions of America. "The Gray Champion" is no unit recasting versions of New England into a coherent whole. Rather, alternatives are presented, positive and negative, the one denying the other. Hawthorne's purpose, as in "Rappaccini's Daughter," lies "between" them, and to read into "The Gray Champion" some compromise is to allegorize purpose. In effect, Hawthorne is not attempting to arrive at some truth about the American colonies, to set the record straight, correct erroneous historical notions. He is interested not in the past, but in a mythology of the past, in the present, that is, as the present embodies itself in stories about the past which it tells. Indeed, we may go further. Hawthorne takes the mythology as a given, seeks ultimately—although along the way it is inescapable—not to engage even myth, but

expressing precisely the union of writer, reader, and story that we are claiming is absent. At any rate, a manifest interpretation of the scene, "merry tunes in a Mad House," is offered only after the gothic language is ended and rather denies, in the explanation of madness, the potential commonality of the incident. Interpretation, here, explains nothing. It is decoration outside an experience that, however universal, is simply never perceived as such. Memory, potentially unifying, instead is short-circuited. Response is prohibited by the rhythm of the story. Reader and author are forced into looking past elements with which they are not allowed to become involved. The story, as yet embodying no one, is not permitted to perform its usual reformative function.

In every respect, then, "The Hollow of the Three Hills" is a preliminary catalogue of the concerns of Hawthorne's career. Author, story, and reader are held in suspension. The next step is to dissolve the suspension by emphasizing the narrative[3] aspect of the work. The nature of narrative will be a constant concern throughout the stories and romances. Hawthorne begins early to probe its possibilities.

The Histories

As a journeyman writer Hawthorne attempted and failed three times to collect and publish a group of American tales—*Seven Tales of My Native Land* while in college, *Provincial Tales* shortly after, and *The Story-Teller* some years later.[4] He was trying to define for

[3] In a sense, "The Hollow of the Three Hills" is not narrated at all. Robert Scholes and Robert Kellogg, *The Nature of Narrative* (New York: Oxford Univ. Press, 1966), p. 4, define their subject: "By narrative we mean all those literary works which are distinguished by two characteristics: the presence of a story and a story-teller." The "teller" of "Hollow," then, is an ur-teller who has yet to differentiate himself.

[4] See Elizabeth Lathrop Chandler, "A Study of the Sources of the Tales and Romances Written by Nathaniel Hawthorne before 1853," *Smith College Studies in Modern Languages*, 7 (July

himself his role as narrator and his consequent relation to the matter of America and his audience of Americans. Even more significant than the stories as they appeared singly as magazine pieces, is the attitude towards them he expressed in attempting to collect them in the way that he did.

He begins in *Seven Tales of My Native Land* and *Provincial Tales* to break down the barriers between reader and writer enforced in "The Hollow" by asserting a common cultural experience. The titles imply the role for the narrator of oral poet, of performer of traditional materials. They assume a single heritage. As Robert Scholes and Robert Kellogg point out, the audience of the oral poet "shares the narrator's knowledge and values."[5] Author and reader, deliberately held apart in "The Hollow of the Three Hills," are here united by the identity of the very sympathies they were formerly prevented from having.

Hawthorne, through two volumes, earnestly attempted to maintain such a relation, but it required a self-effacement he could not long bear. If the tale belongs to the "Native Land," if the author merely rehearses something or someone else's tale, he is, in effect, "refined out of existence."[6] His separate identity is denied. Hawthorne, however, sought an interchange of awareness with his audience—not the loss of self, but

---

1926), 8–9, 12–13, 15–16, and the chronological table, 55–63. She lists the tales probably or certainly collected: "Alice Doane," "An Old Woman's Tale," and "The Hollow of the Three Hills" in *Seven Tales*; "Roger Malvin's Burial," "The Gentle Boy," "My Uncle Molineaux," "Doctor Bullivant," "The Gray Champion," "Young Goodman Brown," and "The May-Pole of Merry Mount," in *Provincial Tales*; and "Mr. Higginbotham's Catastrophe" and "Passages from a Relinquished Work" in *The Story-Teller*. Dating throughout this study follows Chandler.

[5] Scholes and Kellogg, p. 52. The discussion in the next few paragraphs relies heavily on the second chapter, "The Oral Heritage of Written Narrative."

[6] *Ibid.*, p. 53. The phrase is from James Joyce's *A Portrait of the Artist as a Young Man*.

the acceptance of it. He desired, ultima mediate between story and reader, but th mediate between reader and him. By the *Story-Teller*, even in telling his America declares his individuality by asserting his all he narrates. As the title implies, focus is the tale to the teller. "Passages from a Work," the introduction to the projected fully details the character and personal teller so that the author, with the teller as assert his "authority" once and for all.

Only with this background of attitude tories be read. They are Hawthorne's e the usefulness of American traditions fo must write into and ultimately out of th business of knowing and being known He begins, that is, that process of osc have said is the development of his car tion of self to other whose resolution i writing. The tales of the American Re myth of the American past only to reje put forth a point of view as official, in be denied. Whatever the reality of diss voices, and perhaps in deliberate de thorne assumes an audience mainta from which he may declare his inde

The contradictory attitudes of th man, Major Molineux" and "The M Mount" and the later "Endicott and clear. Robin's equivocal laugh, own patricide, is echoed in the balance be Merrymounters and again in the c of the brash, revolutionary Endico docile, Roger Williams. In "The G process of writing in and writing capsule. "New-England's hereditary so that, simultaneously, it may be story espouses as popular histor

the community that expresses itself in myth. Proclaiming an ostensibly popular version of the American past, he would join the American people behind the version.[7] The Champion is the creation of purpose submitting to genre, Hawthorne's attempt, under the influence of Scott, to fashion a fictive representative embodying a common past. But inevitably, as the needs of the two writers differ, the stridently national, almost exclusively public, concerns of the *Waverley* novels Hawthorne so much admired are insufficient to accomplish the deeper intimacy he seeks. The Champion betrays Hawthorne's resistance. He motions to the mob, but only "when at some distance" from them. He stands "obscurely in an open space where neither friend nor foe had thrust himself." He is, from the start, imaginable only as a figure no longer possible: "That stately form, combining the leader and the saint, so gray, so dimly seen, in such an ancient garb, could only belong to some old champion of the righteous cause, whom the oppressor's drum had summoned from his grave" (IX, 15). Representing New England, the Champion yet stands in opposition to it. Hawthorne's description of him implies that a negativity has usurped his place. His antique

[7] Strictly speaking, the American people to whom Hawthorne addresses himself are a hypothetical people the story invents and whom we may know not by reference to history or sociology, but by examining the story itself (see above, pp. 22–23, 44–45). There is some evidence from psychology on what amounts to a "dynamics of literary response," however, to indicate that an actual reader, if he is at all involved in the work, will really become what he is hypothesized to be. He is "reformed" by the parameters the story sets out for him. Gombrich, p. 371, summarizes Charles E. Osgood, George J. Suci, and Percy H. Tannenbaum, *The Measurement of Meaning* (Urbana: Univ. of Illinois Press, 1957): "They conclude that we always place any concept into a structured matrix, what they call the 'semantic space' of which the basic dimensions are 'good and bad,' 'active and passive,' 'strong and weak.'" Accordingly, they could get, Gombrich continues, "a surprising agreement on apparently senseless questions, such as whether a boulder is happy or sad." Hawthorne's audience, therefore, is not so much created as recreated.

stateliness presumably suggests a contemporary vul-
garity, his saintliness a modern secularity. He is an
ideal transparently out of keeping with current existence. Mythology and mythologizers are separated, the
common bond shattered. No story remains to coordinate
writer and reader.

"The Gray Champion" demonstrates, then, a turning
point in Hawthorne's narrative. The way of Scott and
Cooper would not do. Hawthorne demanded a more
personal art. The tale now becomes an instrument for
personal communication. The audience will hear *him*.

The Writer: "The Devil in Manuscript"

In "The Devil in Manuscript," therefore, he opens a
conversation with himself. The audience, prohibited
from providing the matter of the tale, is invited to over-
hear it: "behold us seated by a great blazing fire," the
narrator says, as the exchange is about to begin. The
two characters, whose conversation is the tale, may be
compared to any of several similar pairs in Hawthorne's
work: the author and friend of "Fragments from the
Journal of a Solitary Man," Fanshawe and Edward
Walcott, and, to some extent, even Owen Warland and
Robert Danforth.[8] Oberon, Hawthorne's nickname in
Bowdoin, which he used, as well, to sign several early,
otherwise anonymous stories,[9] is a projection of his
artistic side. The narrator, a man of society, and, that
much, an imposition of the audience on a story that
else would exclude it, is yet at first presented as arising
but in reference to the asocial Oberon whom he inverts.
The two produce each other. "Oberon" is "a name of a
fancy and friendship between him and me"; it does not
exist prior to their friendship. Similarly, the narrator's

[8] Jac Tharpe, *Nathaniel Hawthorne: Identity and Knowledge*
(Carbondale and Edwardsville: Southern Illinois Univ. Press,
1967), pp. 25–39, analyzes the projected pairs in some detail.

[9] Bell, p. 137; Arvin, p. 47. Consider, too, that Oberon as
fairy is Hawthorne's conjurer of "The Hollow of the Three
Hills" presiding over his own enchanted space.

narrative propensities, "a desire to turn novelist," as he puts it, develop only when he reads Oberon's manuscripts (XI, 171). Hawthorne, before writing "The Devil," has incorporated the audience into his own psyche. As the disapproving Puritan ancestor of "The Custom-House" indicates, society's demand for a worldlier occupation than writing has been assimilated in childhood into his personality.[10] The narrator, an ostensibly social man with society's attitudes, is yet intimately associated with Oberon's art and would prevent its destruction. His response to Oberon's assertions are double-edged: "That does make a difference, indeed [that no one will print the stories]. . . . What a voluminous mass the unpublished literature of America must be! . . . The villain [a publisher]! . . . It might not be amiss to pull that fellow's nose. . . . The paltry rogues!" (XI, 172–73). These remarks neatly blend appreciation of the publishers' pragmatism with sympathy for Oberon's own embarrassing position.

"The Devil in Manuscript," then, is a psychomachia, Hawthorne's ego in motion. It is the translation of a divided self into narrative. Its dialogue is bifurcated monologue. A single comment is given opposite meanings. The integrative faculty of the ego fails, as what it asserts is split into conflicting assertions. "Would they were out of my sight!" says Oberon of the manuscripts, thinking how their reality haunts him. "And of mine too" (XI, 171), thinks the narrator, but because, he tells us later, he judges them very poor things. The

---

[10] *The Scarlet Letter*, p. 10: "Doubtless, however, either of these stern and black-browed Puritans would have thought it quite a sufficient retribution for his sins, that, after so long a lapse of years, the old trunk of the family tree, with so much venerable moss upon it, should have borne, as its topmost bough, an idler like myself. . . . 'What is he?' murmurs one gray shadow of my forefathers to the other. 'A writer of story-books! What kind of a business in life,—what mode of glorifying God, or being serviceable to mankind in his day and generation,—may that be? Why, the degenerate fellow might as well have been a fiddler!' "

structural basis of the story is a pun: "[I was] privately of opinion," says the narrator, "in spite of my partiality for the author, that his tales would make a more brilliant appearance in the fire than anywhere else" (XI, 173); at the climax of the tale, when the cause of the city's fire has been revealed, "Here I stand—a triumphant author!" says Oberon, "Huzza! Huzza! My brain has set the town on fire! Huzza!" (XI, 178). The narrator sets himself on the side of actuality. The metaphoric brilliance of Oberon's stories is denied by the literal brilliance they would produce in burning. But Oberon exalts the metaphor. For him metaphor replaces reality; the artistic creation envelops the city.

There is an opposition, here, that the narrative never moves to resolve, and, in consequence, no real story, in Hawthorne's mature sense, evolves. Hawthorne refuses, that is, to embrace an attitude that more and more, in the course of the tale, he sees as belonging to a culture he would define himself against. He will not undertake to recreate it as his own, but disengages the action of "Devil" from it, instead. From a personal standpoint, unification with the city, with society, is a consummation that Hawthorne devoutly wished. Formally speaking, it is a synthesis whose dialectic would articulate itself in the form of a story, like his best, compounded of self and other. But he has not yet that confidence in his art as an instrument effective for constructing intimacy. As "The Devil" progresses, the narrator moves outward toward an audience whose disapproval remains too far removed from the central action ever to affect it. A man whose "fancy," at the start, is fully equal to Oberon's own, a whimsical personality, who, spreading his cloak "like a mainsail and scud[ding] along the street" capsizes lesser "navigators" (XI, 170), begins to move out of the fictive sphere. The active agent of the first paragraphs becomes, as he deprecates Oberon's words, a commentator on the action in the middle portion of the story. Soon, even his role as deprecator is usurped: "The wind blows a gale [says Oberon], and wherever it whirls the flames, the roofs will flash up like gunpowder. Every pump is frozen up, and boiling water would turn to ice the moment it was flung from the engine. In an hour, this wooden town will be one great bonfire! What a glorious scene for my next— Pshaw!" (XI, 177).

Oberon, interrupting himself with the deprecating "Pshaw," absorbs the narrator's part as antithesis in the would-be dialectic and goes on to assert a synthesis in his punning resolution. The narrator, on the other hand, becomes pure spectator, asserting one meaning of the pun against the other, asserting the reality principle against the claim of art as second reality.[11] He remains apart, watching the artist in what now seems an ecstasy, quite literally a standing outside reality, performing extra-human feats, as "with a wild gesture of exultation, he leaped almost to the ceiling of the chamber." The narrator moves away from the action, becomes one with the uninspired audience, and safely, sanely observes Oberon in the grip of a demonic "frenzy" (XI, 178).

A mechanism of protection can be seen in the strategy of this tale. Hawthorne, though he seeks intimacy, resists exposure. He presents himself divided against himself, mocking one half with another. As "The Devil" progresses, however, the division becomes so great it breaks down. Elements originally interacting, the one opposing the other, become simply unrelated. Hawthorne's art, ventured as an instrument of unification, yet excludes the very culture with which he would

---

[11] He tells a peculiar kind of joke. Simon O. Lesser, *Fiction and the Unconscious* (1957; rpt. New York: Vintage Press, 1962), p. 282, quotes Freud, *Collected Papers*, ed. Joan Riviere, V (London: Hogarth, 1950), p. 217: "[Humor] signifies the triumph not only of the ego, but also of the pleasure principle, which is strong enough to assert itself here in the face of the adverse real circumstances." The narrator's pun, then, is anti-humor, asserting reality in the face of an adverse pleasure.

unite. The story, as a result, never evolves, but remains at the end what it was at the beginning, a simple projection. Not until "Wakefield" is there evidence of poetic faith in abundance. There, manifestly, art as an instrument of unification is at work. There Hawthorne sets in motion a genuine conversation, not with himself, but with a reader he seeks to define, through art, in relation to himself.

Writer and Reader: "Wakefield"

One must begin, in "Wakefield," by distinguishing the sketch from the story proper, which is only a part of the sketch. The story proper dramatizes an alienation that the sketch tries to overcome. The action of the piece as a whole, the work it performs in bringing together—though momentarily, as we shall see—reader and writer, validates the theme of alienation the story proper may therefore be said to represent. Toward the greater end of creating intimacy, the introductory portion of "Wakefield" seeks to define the reader and control his attitude toward the story. Once again, as in the histories, the question of authority must be considered. The "outline" of "Wakefield" is reported as material given, as something akin to what James would call his "donnée." No special knowledge is available to the writer. The given strikes the author and the reader—indeed, the author is himself presented as reader "In some old magazine or newspaper"—with the same force. It may be more or less factual, probably more, as it is "told as truth," but the author makes no attempt to affirm it on the grounds of authorial omniscience. It has meaning for him only as he is a man like other men, and it is on the grounds of an assumed common humanity that he asserts its reality as at least subjective:

"But the incident, though of the purest originality, unexampled, and probably never to be repeated, is one, I think, which appeals to the general sympathies of mankind. We know, each for himself, that none of us would perpetrate such a folly, yet feel as if some other might. To my own contemplations, at least, it has often recurred, always exciting wonder, but with a sense that the story must be true, and a conception of its hero's character" (IX, 130–31).

The reader, that is, like Hawthorne, shares in Wakefield's alienation. Wakefield is "our friend," as Hawthorne calls him.

To such a reader Hawthorne then extends an invitation: "If the reader choose, let him do his own meditation; or if he prefer to ramble with me through the twenty years of Wakefield's vagary, I bid him welcome . . ." (IX, 131). He is asked to participate in writing the story, and he does: "What sort of a man was Wakefield? We are free to shape out our own idea, and call it by his name. . . . Let us now imagine Wakefield bidding adieu to his wife" (IX, 131–32). A successful advance toward intimacy has been made. Writer and reader have joined in the exploration of their separation through art. It is important to consider, however, how much they learn from their joint venture, how much achieved intimacy is conserved. To put it another way, how much of the lesson of the story proper is carried over into the sketch? Only "a portion," Hawthorne himself acknowledges.[12] The story moves toward a moment of crisis, a point of expanded consciousness when the self confronts its situation in society. But Hawthorne is ultimately unwilling to recognize it. He would bypass his alienation rather than reform it. Afraid he will be overcome, he no longer admits there is anything *to* overcome.

Throughout, Hawthorne malingers, refuses to get on with the narrative. He would avoid the very problem he has invited the reader to join him in analyzing: "Would that I had a folio to write, instead of an article of a

[12] "He has left us much food for thought, a portion of which shall lend its wisdom to a moral; and be shaped into a figure" (IX, 140).

dozen pages! Then might I exemplify how an influence, beyond our control, lays its strong hand on every deed which we do, and weaves its consequences into an iron tissue of necessity" (IX, 136–37). And again: "Watch him, long enough to see what we have described, and you will allow, that circumstances—which often produce remarkable men from nature's ordinary handiwork—have produced one such here" (IX, 137).

Time pauses for a moment; the progress of events stops as Hawthorne generalizes about mankind. The subject of his generalizations, however, is inevitability. Holding off the story of the alienated Wakefield, he sees the tale imposed upon him, finds it a form that his refusal to encounter has turned into a coercion. So far from being "free to shape our own idea," as he initially claimed, he is free but to resist for a moment a progress that must sooner or later continue despite him. At one point he sidetracks the story into a discussion of Wakefield's wife. But the story will not be contained: "But, our business is with the husband. We must hurry after him, along the street, ere he lose his individuality, and melt into the great mass of London life. It would be vain searching for him there. Let us follow close at his heels, therefore . . ." (IX, 133).

When, irresistibly, the crisis is precipitated, when Wakefield, after accidentally meeting his wife, rushes home, throws himself on his bed, and "cries out passionately" his awareness of himself, Hawthorne escapes in the only way left. He couches the experience in a language that would isolate Wakefield from the writer and reader, a language designed to short-circuit *our* awareness, whatever Wakefield has come to know. "Wakefield! Wakefield! You are mad!" he has him say. Nor, much as he assumes in "Hollow," are we all mad, Hawthorne tells us. Our "friend" is no longer very close to us, for a great "transformation" has made him a "nincompoop." The "frolic" and "whim-wham" that earlier had been said to appeal to our "generous sympathies" have become a madness "unprecedented." They are excluded from the well-regulated world in which Hawthorne increasingly assures us we live. Wakefield's condition is not our condition.

Moreover, when the moment comes for transferring the lesson of the story into the sketch—that is, when the moment of crisis in the sketch comes—it is blocked by being telescoped into the end of the story. After twenty years Wakefield returns to his wife. We are not told, however, what happens then. "We will not follow our friend across the threshold," Hawthorne says. For the story, it is not necessary to do so. The crisis is over, the moment of awareness come and gone. But it is precisely what the sketch has promised it *would* do, drive home to the reader an awareness of his alienation, describe intimately the relation of a man to his family. Hawthorne reneges. He will not follow Wakefield. In formal terms, the end of the story engrosses the crisis of the sketch. To put it another way, a "closed" story imposes its closed form upon a potentially "open" sketch. I use these words, with some modification, in Alan Friedman's sense. By "open" he means "an ending which does not contain or close off the rising pressures of conscience in a novel," where "conscience" is defined as a matter of the perceived relation of self to society.[13] Though, as he says, this obliges him to focus on one character as the center of any action, we might extend his definition to a case where the center of "conscience" is the writer and the writer-reader. Telescoping the

[13] *The Turn of the Novel* (New York: Oxford Univ. Press, 1966), pp. xv–xvi. See, too, for a related definition, Robert M. Adams, *Strains of Discord: Studies in Literary Openness* (Ithaca: Cornell Univ. Press, 1958), p. 32. Adams compares *Oedipus Rex* and *The Bacchae* as prototypically open and closed works: "The difference is simply that between a work which, by resolving its given problems, leaves the audience in a state of psychological repose, emptied of passion, and one which, by failing or refusing to resolve its given problems, leaves the audience in a state of psychological tension, of unreleased anguish."

crisis of the sketch into the end of the story, then, closes off the rising pressure of the reader's awareness of his own alienation. Identification with Wakefield, already damaged by the opinion of his madness, stops altogether. Reader and writer cease to participate in an analysis of their separation. A makeshift bond designed to reunify author and audience by locating them in a common metaphysical situation is asserted in the platitude of the last sentences: "Amid the seeming confusion of our mysterious world, individuals are so nicely adjusted to a system, and systems to one another, and to a whole, that, by stepping aside for a moment, a man exposes himself to a fearful risk of losing his place forever. Like Wakefield, he may become, as it were, the Outcast of the Universe" (IX, 140). Here is the well, but superficially, regulated world upon which Hawthorne must now insist. There is little here, however, besides resounding rhetoric to enlist our sympathies.

The problem, simply, is too imposing for Hawthorne's as yet slippery method to grasp. The call to a reader to write with him is, finally, unproductive, a call for intimacy that must remain momentary. It is an avoidance of genre that restricts but that may, as we have discussed in the first chapter, enable as well. It is a denial of the very notion of development, of career, since the only intimacy ever accomplished here is the intimacy of beginning, never of achieving. It is an intimacy of starting together on a joint project, never of fixing in a completed project a relation that, if it is imperfect, may yet, in its own turn be reformed. Hawthorne has not yet gone far enough in attempting to resolve his dilemma. Though the other against which the self is asserted in the earlier stories is here joined with self, the united self and other yet stand extracted from genre, which, for a writer, remains inescapable. Hawthorne must either stay in a state of perpetual beginning to write, without, however, actually writing, or, in writing, give himself over to a form he has still not renewed. He needs, that is, despite the distance he has already traveled, to broaden his scope still wider. He must fix his accomplishments in a work, must establish some ground where intimacy invited may also be conserved.

"Legends of the Province-House"

That ground is the image of the house. We have already alluded to it in our discussion of "The Hollow of the Three Hills." It is a form that Hawthorne invests with his own and his readers' concerns. *Legends of the Province-House* establishes a permanent basis for intimacy by inventing, in the sense we have used that word, finding and creating, a space that is the locus of a collective unconscious, an unconscious of Hawthorne and Hawthorne's public at one.

A good deal of work has gone into analyzing houses in literature. Gaston Bachelard, most notably, proceeding from an analysis of childhood experience, finds that, because we have lived in them, they are places of a self-reflexive revery. They are "one of the greatest powers of integration for the thoughts, memories and dreams of mankind." The house is "the topography of our intimate being." "Our soul is an abode. And by remembering 'houses' and 'rooms,' we learn to 'abide' within ourselves." The particulars of Bachelard's poetics need not detain us here at any great length. But his conclusions, concerned as they are with images general, or generalized by the work, to reader as well as writer, are of especial interest. The implications for Hawthorne are clear. It is the function of the poetic house, Bachelard finds, by calling up a "reverberation" in all those selves which dwell in houses to unite author and audience.[14] Accordingly, Hawthorne opens to his readers the "Manse" in which he resides. His "caverns of the heart," "chambers under the eaves," "halls of fancy," the secluded places in which he sees himself

[14] *The Poetics of Space*, trans. Maria Jolas (New York: The Orion Press, 1964), pp. 6, xxxii, xxxiii, xii.

sequestered, are reconstituted in a more capacious structure. He finds a home in the house of New England's provincial governors. An historical landmark becomes the place in which Hawthorne, too, will now live. In the Province-House Hawthorne and New England meet. The personal and the national join in a form that expresses them both.

Legends begins by bringing together two eras. A sign proclaims the "Old Province-House, kept by Thomas Waite." The home of the "old royal governors" arrests Hawthorne's march along Washington Street, reminding him of a partially obscured yet still present purpose to visit the mansion. Accordingly, he removes himself from "modern Boston" to confront the past, not as an influence on the present, but face to face as coexisting with it. The old brick is "overlaid" with a recent coat of paint. The edifice "hides" behind a modern building yet is never supplanted by it. History here is superposition, not imposition. Events, so far from producing one another, exist side by side. If, indeed, past and present are separated, if one must be "transported" through a "passage" to reach one or the other, yet as *Legends* proceeds they come to occupy the same space. The House fixes time spatially in the still bent bow of the wooden Indian keeping the same attitude in which he was carved some seventy years before. The Indian, like the ceiling, ready at any moment "to shake down the dust of ages," like the "beams and rafters" reviving "the echoes of half a century," conserves concretely the events of times long gone. Action is maintained outside time: "The most venerable and ornamental object, is a chimney-piece set round with Dutch tiles of blue-figured China, representing scenes from Scripture; and, for aught I know, the lady of Pownall or Bernard, may have sate beside this fire-place, and told her children the story of each blue tile" (IX, 240). Events, however discrete, are functionally equivalent as decorations of a coherent space. Narrative is collapsed. The tiles render "story" as "scene," reduce to a single picture action with a beginning, middle, and end. Events coexist, here, outside the logic of sequence. History becomes association and, *ipso facto*, psychology.

Significantly, then, Hawthorne terms Bela Tiffany's memories "historical reminiscences." It is a phrase that links public and private experience. The "anecdotes of famous dead people, and traits of ancient manners" that Hawthorne hears are based on "gossip" and "tradition" even older than his "elderly" raconteur. They constitute a folk-memory, much as in *Tales of My Native Land*, in which every American may participate and which, in epic fashion, has been embellished by teller upon teller. Bela Tiffany, for example, is a "legendary friend," participates so thoroughly in the stories he tells that he has himself become a legend. More importantly, however, the self-denial that *My Native Land* threatened is prevented. Reconstructing psychology, the house binds society and self together. As the stories descend deeper and deeper into the past, from 1775 to 1770 to 1716, they move back, as in "My Kinsman, Major Molineux," toward a childhood of American man. A new man, a new consciousness, with a psycho-historical existence, is created. The house becomes a valorization, as Bachelard would say, of our common American self, the locus of childhood being in which each of our Salem psyches abides. It becomes a form doubly informed, the place at which writer and reader, possessing each other's experience, are one.

We should note and answer an objection that is liable to be raised. The following discussion will be a heavily psychoanalytical analysis of what are generally taken to be overtly historical tales. How, from the perspective of a purposive criticism, however, can the languages of either psychology or history be justified as privileged to describe what *Legends* is about? Is *Legends* not, in fact, without a content—that is, pure form, "about" nothing—and psychology and history simply allegorizations, levels of interpretation among many others, included from the start in a culture-embodying text? Do we not, in offering psychological or historical interpretations, repeat the labors of Crews or Stewart, offer but two more paraphrases equally applicable to the words of the tales and translating, in effect, each other? The aim of this study throughout, it should be repeated, however, has not been to discredit allegorization, merely to put it on a sounder footing, to validate it from a new perspective. It is one of the intentions of this section to show that we can analyze far more complexly and undogmatically than conventional psychoanalysis even while using psychoanalytic language, when we first have a reason for using it. Purpose selects its allegories. Seeking, as we maintain, to integrate the psychic and the national, it situates itself between two levels of interpretation it defines not as equal to others, but as of special significance. Nor are the levels simply paraphrases, capable at any point of being substituted one for the other. We have, here, not polysemy, but sema that interact, that are located in a process which places them. The movement toward conjunction, regression toward a psycho-historical man, transforms the levels from tale to tale, maintains them not in a static equality, but in a dynamic relation as elements of a dialectic whose progress is Hawthorne's overriding goal: intimacy, the interanimation of the language of self and the language of other.

On the one hand, from the standpoint of a history free of psychology, the tales' plausibility decreases. The masquerade of "Howe's Masquerade" requires no special belief in the power of imagination. It is only a metaphor, a fictive emblem of the reality of Howe's retreat. It is a dramatization, re-enacting outside Howe's world an action whose authenticity, thoroughly documented, it in no way disturbs and that Howe himself, as a character first in politics and only secondarily in fiction, is powerless either to call into being or dismiss. The portrait of "Edward Randolph's Portrait," however, appears as a projection of Hutchinson's own doubts about his action. It very nearly prevents him from signing the orders bringing English troops to American soil and is said to affect the aspect of his dying hour. The mantle of "Lady Eleanore's Mantle" goes one step further. An emblem of Lady Eleanore's pride, it becomes itself the sole cause of the plague. On the other hand, from the standpoint of imagination, the narrator, of whose "literal and absolute truth" we at first see Hawthorne despairing, begins to speak in "truth-telling accents" of events, some of which "might have been worth the notice of the grave historian," and about which "how scrupulous is Mr. Tiffany to settle the foundation of his facts." As history increasingly gives way to fiction, so fiction is said to be history. Here is a progressive assumption of the historical into the fanciful. The authority of one is included in the other. This is a systematic development in which the elements that develop are not independent, but are related by the operation of a kind of principle of conservation. The action maintains a constant historicity, but history itself is increasingly validated by psychic sources. Fact and fancy, public and private, history and psychology, interanimate each other.

It is difficult to say how far and how quickly such interanimation has gone. Even as early as "Howe's Masquerade," for example, languages that ordinarily, as we have said, constitute different levels of a story, seem to exist on the same level: "The spectacle of this evening, if the oldest members of the provincial court-circle might be believed, was the most gay and gorgeous affair that had occurred in the annals of the government" (IX, 243). The event exists as a fantasy of perhaps unreliable men, yet the fantasy, in turn, is verified by historical document. But beyond combing the tales for such superficial marks of psychic signification as reference to the operation of fancy provide, we are faced with the problem, in a pre-Freudian age, of determining what a language of psychology really is. We mentioned, in relation to "The Hollow of the Three Hills," gothicism as one possible language. But it is, after all, only one. Precise determination, in any particular story, of how close to merging psychology and history have actually come must await further research into the broad question of the relation of nineteenth-century language to culture.

At the very least, in *Legends of the Province-House*, however, an overarching psychic development that we shall follow, a movement from story to story in a sort of deep structure—perhaps genuinely hidden, perhaps, due to our present ignorance, but seemingly obscure—recasts each of the American events presented as an element of a psychic regression thereby established at a national level. What appears, taken in itself, as strictly historical, becomes, in context, recreated as psychological as well. The phylogeny of the nation as a whole emerges, as it is retold at the inn, as the ontogeny of any one of the people in particular, and the ontogeny, so far from strictly personal, is informed with nationality.

"Howe's Masquerade," then, locates us at the threshold of a double crisis. The staircase, appropriated by a rebellious new generation from the governors who once walked it, is lined with columns of the phallic order, "quaintly twisted and intertwined pillars, from top to bottom," as Hawthorne says. It is problematical how overtly Oedipal this language is. But the staircase revolution, at however deep a level, is thus cast in a psychological light. George Washington is both a political figure and a son rebelling against a castrating father. He possesses a "sword of immense longitude," but the British masquers, in defense of their own power, represent it in their pageant as "rusty." His army flourishes in full potency outside the walls of the Province-

House, but is conceived inside as "rent and tattered by sword, ball, or bayonet." In retaliation, and in psycho-military terms, Washington asserts himself. He announces his approach with "the roar of artillery," smites the governor with "the deep boom of the cannon." An historical-genital conflict at the doors of the Province-House ushers us to the Oedipal edge of childhood.

It is a childhood, however, and, for that matter, an Oedipal phase, that the movement of *Legends* re-creates. Once again, our psychological interpretation is bound to its relation to the historical, is defined by its place in the movement of the tales as a whole. The phases of human growth, as ego psychologists like Erik Erikson, for example, have emphasized, are not simply the result of the stages that preceded them, but must be understood as they contribute to the child's end in a mature individual, his integration into the adult world.[15] In *Legends*, however, the end is reconceived. Integration is possible, as we have said, but in a childhood of American man. Maturity for the purpose of opening an intercourse is infancy. The stages of the psyche in the progress of *Legends*, while formally identical with the stages of the psyche in the world outside, are reversed in order and in function. Their contribution is to the development not of the adult world Hawthorne sees as alienating, but of a world of the child in which alone integration is held possible.

The Oedipal conflict of "Howe's Masquerade," indeed, is the opposite of a preparation for manhood. So far from coming to terms with genitality, it rejects the genital in favor of an earlier sexual state. The potent George Washington is heard from but never does appear. Opposing the malevolent father, William Howe, rather, is a virtually sterile Colonel Joliffe, formerly

[15] See, e.g., "Identity and the Life Cycle," *Psychological Issues*, 1, No. 1 (1959). Also, *Childhood and Society*, 2nd ed. (New York: Norton, 1963).

71

threatening as a "famous soldier in his day," but "now too old to take an active part in the contest." Similarly, the dangerous dark mother is displaced as "a fair grand-daughter" he protects. Adult intercourse is rejected. The victorious couple is a genital-less anti-couple. In the closing paragraphs of the tale, rebel and rebelled against are castrated. Howe "let fall his sword upon the floor," and the Colonel remarks about his own gray head, "You must make haste to chop it off." Significantly, the overthrown father, the British Empire in the Colonies, is termed "a dead corpse." But the America that inherits its place is equally dead. The coprological symbolism of corpses and lopped limbs, indeed—the wastes of the body, its rotted cast-offs—is especially important. Genitally organized intercourse is succeeded by the auto-intercourse of the anal stage. *Legends* proceeds backward through the troubled phases of child-hood. Specifically, in psychoanalytic terms, it moves through the conflicts attendant upon narrowed sexual focuses to that sexually more indiscriminate, "poly-morphously perverse" state, as Freud called it, where conflict is resolved. It is a world of unity preceding op-position, before the self and other that are Hawthorne's dilemma have been separated out, a world of Thanatos and Eros, again in Freud's terms, in equilibrium. The historical progress that "Howe's Masquerade" ostensibly presents, then, from the point of view of the deep struc-ture of *Legends of the Province-House*, is psychological regress. Forward movement at a level isolated from its dynamic context is recast. Interanimation, which reaches a conclusion, as we shall see, in "Old Esther Dudley," has begun. "Legends" proceeds farther and farther into the past, and the genitality of "Howe's Masquerade" gives way to the anality of "Edward Ran-dolph's Portrait."

Central here is the dirty picture that hangs on the wall—both dirty and fantastical, an objectification out-side the body of the magical power of excremental manipulation.[16] Thomas Hutchinson attempts the child's project of becoming his own father. He writes chronicles—or "annals," as they are called here—demythologizing the legends surrounding the portrait in order to control what is otherwise beyond control. The historian subsumes history, absorbs into his presence the power of the past:

"'You, sir [says the Selectman], have written, with an able pen, the deeds of our forefathers. The more to be desired is it, therefore, that yourself should deserve honorable mention, as a true patriot and upright ruler, when your own doings shall be written down in history.'

"'I am not insensible, my good sir, to the natural desire to stand well in the annals of my country,' replied Hutchinson, controlling his impatience into courtesy, 'nor know I any better method of attaining that end than by withstanding the merely temporary spirit of mischief, which, with your pardon, seems to have infected elder men than myself. Would you have me wait till the mob shall sack the Province-House, as they did my private mansion?'" (IX, 265).

Hutchinson, the author of the lives of our forefathers, would author his own life. Admitting his forefathers as a model for action, he yet internalizes them in himself, opposing himself, now made even stronger, to the only father, the Selectman, he must directly confront. Introjecting his fathers, incorporating internally a properly external power, he in effect fathers himself.

Strictly speaking, in psychoanalytic terms, self-mothering should be at issue. Opposition to the father awaits an Oedipal stage still in the future. The child's assertion of self-creativity is a reaction, instead, to the pre-Oedipal or primal mother. We have maintained throughout, however, the power of the work precisely

[16] See Norman O. Brown, *Life Against Death: The Psychoanalytic Meaning of History* (1959; rpt. New York: Vintage, n.d.), p. 279. I rely heavily, throughout the following, on Brown's excellent "Studies in Anality," pp. 177–304.

to reconstruct the psyche. Indeed, psychoanalysis itself assumes—though it has only begun to investigate the theoretical implications of its assumption—such a reconstruction in the psychoanalytic situation.[17] The order of the stories in *Legends of the Province-House*, based on, but reversing, the natural order of human development, creates us, out of our own associations, anew. Specifically, here, we have a case of what we might call reading back the Oedipal father of the preceding "Howe's Masquerade" into the anal stage as "Edward Randolph's Portrait" invents it.

Hutchinson's grand action, at any rate, precisely at the point when the Province-House—his Province-House, as he seems to take it, the locus of his being—is about to be sacked, is to sign his name, to promulgate himself symbolically in letters. Attendant upon both this action and his claim of self-authoring is the aggressiveness that Freud notes first emerges in the anal state, an aggressiveness designed specifically to deny the passivity that dependence on anything outside oneself entails. The "impatience" Hutchinson so barely restrains, in the cited passage, the exercise against Alice of "energy" that, as Hawthorne notes, "was not, however, his most characteristic feature," the overtly aggressive act of mobilizing an army against the Colonists shortly afterward, are part of an activity-passivity conflict that runs throughout the story.

Hutchinson's attribution of the "mischief" of a young nation to "elder men than myself" neatly confirms this opposition. The ambiguity concerning the age of the rebels mirrors the ambivalence surrounding the anal child's project. The child, seeking to deny the virtual death that begins with separation from the mother at

[17] Especially notable is the pioneering work of Jacques Lacan, which is becoming increasingly influential in literary analysis. A valuable bibliography may be found in Anthony Wilden, trans., *The Language of the Self: The Function of Language in Psychoanalysis* (Baltimore: Johns Hopkins Univ. Press, 1968).

birth, becomes his own parent. But the repressed returns, infecting its opposite. Thanatos informs Eros.
Hutchinson's denial of the gradual, natural separation
of the Colonies from England that the Selectmen advise
produces a violent break. The past, denied, returns to
become the future. The old men are the young men.
Alice Vane and Francis Lincoln are the Selectmen reborn. Behind the dirt of the picture, according to the
legends Hutchinson works so hard to control, stands a
devil, like all Hawthorne's devils, a suppressed thing of
the unconscious, projected outside. Former Governor
Randolph, Hutchinson's second self, the self that is not
oneself, the dead self excreted, the Devil exorcised,
returns now to declare the dominion of death over
self-generation. The "demons [who] abode behind the
blackness of the picture," excrement, the dependent self
which the independent self controls, or, in Norman O.
Brown's remarkable phrase, the "constipating past"
inflicting itself upon the future, returns to assert Hutchinson's connection with an earlier era of even greater
dependence. "Excrement . . . is also aliment":[18] the
blood on which Hutchinson, in his last hours, gasps he
is choking returns us to dependence at the breast and
the orality of "Lady Eleanore's Mantle."

Hawthorne's return to the Province-House this time,
accordingly, is by invitation to "an oyster supper." He
has come to eat, and what he eats has acquired, by a
typically narcissistic piece of self-projection, the shape
of his own voracious mouth. Interestingly, however, the
dinner is a reward for the added custom he has brought
with him. It is "far less than the ingenious tale-teller,
and I . . . had fairly earned," he says. And, indeed, the
pair are "welcomed as benefactors": "Many a segar had
been smoked within his premises—many a glass of wine,
or more potent aqua vitae, had been quaffed—many a
dinner had been eaten by curious strangers, who, save

[18] Brown, p. 293.

for the fortunate conjunction of Mr. Tiffany and me, would never have ventured through that darksome avenue, which gives access to the historic precincts of the Province-House" (IX, 271). Hawthorne must excuse his pleasure. He must justify his narcissism in economic terms. Pleasure and business, orality as sensual ("the oyster supper") differentiated from orality as self-preserving ("the paying diners") locate the Province-House at the second oral, or "oral-sadistic," phase of child development. In technical terms, object-libido (sexuality) and ego-libido (self-preservation) are already at war.[19] The fusion of primal narcissism—the baby at the breast, subject and object at one—has already broken down: "It may be unadvisable, however, to speak too loudly of the increased custom of the house, lest Mr. Waite should find it difficult to renew the lease on so favorable terms as heretofore" (IX, 271–72). The mouth at war with economics is infected by it. Defending its sexuality, as we have seen, in economic terms, the mouth threatens to deny sexuality. Business makes the terms of pleasure unfavorable, and orality is business' mouthpiece. Ego-libido threatens object-libido; the sucking baby begins to bite.

The oral-aggressive nature of "Lady Eleanore's Mantle," then, is especially significant. Hawthorne describes the plague the Lady Eleanore has brought upon the nation: "On the occasion of which we speak, it was distinguished by a peculiar virulence, insomuch that it has left its traces—its pitmarks, to use an appropriate figure—on the history of the country. . . ." Psychoanalysis holds that sarcasm (Gr. *sarkazein*, to tear flesh) represents an oral attack on an object that withholds narcissistic pleasure,[20] and the focus on perhaps mouth-

[19] See Freud, "On Narcissism: An Introduction," in *Collected Papers*, IV (1953), 30–59, for a more complete definition of both terms.

[20] Jim Swan, "History, Pastoral and Desire: A Psychoanalytic Study of English Literature and Society," Diss. Stanford, 1974,

shaped "pitmarks" further points up the orality of,
Hawthorne's aggression. Similarly, the people, "in bitter
mockery," proclaim "a new triumph for the Lady
Eleanore" as the pox claims another victim, and Jervase
Helwyse extends the "triumph" to Lady Eleanore's own
destruction. Verbal wit, as opposed to the phallic hos-
tilities of "Howe's Masquerade" or the excremental wars
of "Edward Randolph's Portrait," is directed against a
lady, a "queenly maiden," the Virgin Mother, described
as harsh, distant, literally "unyielding." She cannot even
weep. The lady is dry, and the child, denied nurture,
his own brain parched by madness, turns the instrument of oral satisfaction against the breast that will not
feed him.

Of course sarcasm is no solution. The "pitmarks," so
called in an act of aggression, cannot be controlled. It
is a "dismal pit," in turn, into which the dead draw the
living. The oral child projects his own mode of hostility
onto a hostile mother. Seeking to swallow her, he is
afraid of being swallowed. His own desires, his subjectivity, denied, he becomes pure object, ready to be
eaten up.

And, indeed, a subject-object conflict, similar to the
activity-passivity opposition in "Edward Randolph's
Portrait," runs throughout "Lady Eleanore's Mantle."
Wild swings between introjection and projection, becoming all subject and all object, define Jervase's existence. We see him first as the lady's footstool, denying
his own life in service of an all-comprehending ideal.
But again, at the ball, offering her wine, he is himself
the origin of the nourishment he seeks. At the end of
the story, on her dying bed, it is to Jervase the lady
calls for water.

Significantly, it is a parching disease that Eleanore

---

p. 251, cites M. D. Faber, "On Jaques: Psychological Remarks,"
University Review, 36 (1969–70), 89–96, 179–82. My discussion
of orality throughout is heavily indebted to Swan.

ultimately develops. Burned in effigy, literally dried up by her own inability to give and take succor, she makes possible, in her death, a world where subject and object may unite. "King Death" destroys the "living queen." The "diseased mortality" of the self-sufficient lady denies her all-encompassing subjectivity, and Jervase, his madness dissipated, unites with the townsfolk in celebrating the new era. The way is prepared for Eros to inherit the Province-House.

A new narrator who still reveres the queen, then, tells the tale of "Old Esther Dudley." With the "bad mother" deposed, the "good mother" remains to keep and protect the earliest childhood space. The polarities of "Edward Randolph's Portrait" and "Lady Eleanore's Mantle," by and large, are resolved. As "a labor of love," Esther Dudley maintains the premises the community "must otherwise have paid a hireling" to do. Economics and sexuality, ego-libido and object-libido, are joined. The tale, freed of conflict, "is a mere sketch, with no involution of plot." Celebration of a completed development replaces what earlier had been progress toward an end.

In this connection, it is significant, too, that the journey into the past should end in the most modern period of time. A story of primal childhood takes place after the events of "Howe's Masquerade." The end is the beginning. Past and present unite. Old "Esther Dudley's most frequent and favored guests were the children of the town." Moreover, *Legends* thus conjoins historical and psychological chronologies. The point of furthest psychic regress is the point of nearest historic progress. The Province-House becomes the place of a coherent phenomenology, of otherwise separate times as well as spaces fully aligned and, as we noted earlier in connection with the wooden Indian, of time and space themselves at one. *Legends* recreates us out of our own substance, as we have said, as unified psycho-historical men. The community of the frame is solidified, its collective memory reformed. It may now accommodate even an "old loyalist" as "no rival" in its midst.

And yet Hawthorne leaves the house, declaring he will never return. He violently and precipitately escapes. It is difficult to account for this precisely. Perhaps there yet lurks in his mind some doubt as to the soundness of his procedure. Or, perhaps, though he establishes intimacy in *Legends*, he is still faced with alienation in the world outside. As we shall see, this problem will present itself once again in *The House of the Seven Gables*. At any rate, despite his efforts at engaging historical and psychological language, Hawthorne seems to feel he has been talking, after all, about himself alone. History has not been sufficiently embodied. The capaciousness of the Province-House notwithstanding, it would seem, the audience has not as yet been stabilized in a form established firmly enough for an extremely alienated Hawthorne to be able to control. His audience is too free—objectified, but not solidly enough. Hence it lurks beyond the borders of the work to trouble him with the fact that he does not engage it. He loses faith in his very achievement, and the resolution he has so carefully established comes unhinged.

We have spoken earlier of "reading back." In this light, John Hancock's disruption of the house at the end of the tale is a re-emergence of that alienated adulthood disposed of in "Howe's Masquerade." In psychological terms, it constitutes a sort of return of the repressed, where what is repressed, however, is the adulthood first rejected. Indeed, a number of the details of the first story are recapitulated here. Howe smites his brow with a more tangible vigor than the masquers on the staircase. The Indian and the cock, emblems of reunification, are declared dead. The reality of adult alienation declares Old Esther Dudley's resolution a flight from reality. Genital organization returns in Hancock—"the ancient woman sank down beside one of the

79

pillars of the portal. The key of the Province-House fell from her grasp, and clanked against the stone"—and with it the adult aggressiveness that the *Legends of the Province-House* had seemed to expel.

Esther Dudley's activities about the house, then, primally narcissistic though they are, demonstrate a narcissism whose primal situation now, however, would seem to be fallen adult existence. So far from uniting her with the world, from establishing objects outside her as yet part of her, a diseased narcissism denies the presence of all that is not pleasurable, puts out into a repudiated external world anything painful. The Province-House, gratifying Old Esther's every desire, enforces her alienation from a troublesome universe. Her love is narcissistic in Freud's neurotic sense, directed exclusively to projections of herself. She spends the bulk of her pension "adorning herself" with clothes that constitute a company, "her silks sweeping and rustling as she went, so that the sound was as if a train of spectral courtiers were thronging from the dim mirror." The mirror itself, in whose "inner world" the old governors, ladies, and courtiers reappear, but reflects back Old Esther Dudley's "own magnificence," the "shadows of her own fantasies." She is locked in her own psyche, celebrating events others must "exercise their memories" to remember, indeed converting matters commonly understood to private images: "Whenever the town rejoiced for a battle won by Washington, or Gates, or Morgan, or Greene, the news, in passing through the door of the Province-House, as through the ivory gate of dreams, became metamorphosed into a strange tale of the prowess of Howe, Clinton, or Cornwallis" (IX, 298). Oral report, tradition of the sort we have seen in *Tales of My Native Land* and recounted by the "legendary friend" of *Legends of the Province-House*, folk memory that throughout Hawthorne's work creates community, is "metamorphosed" into an instrument of alienation.

Once again, therefore, Hawthorne divides himself to save himself. He projects onto the loyalist the isolation of which he is in danger, opposes to an outdated Toryism the popular point of view of "a thorough-going democrat" from which all will be rewritten:

"His feelings, indeed, appeared to me more excitable than those of a younger man. . . . At the pathetic passages of his narrative, he readily melted into tears. When a breath of indignation swept across his spirit, the blood flushed his withered visage even to the roots of his white hair; and he shook his clenched fist at the trio of peaceful auditors, seeming to fancy enemies in those who felt very kindly towards the desolate old soul. . . . Under these disadvantages, the old loyalist's story required more revision to render it fit for the public eye, than those of the series which have preceded it . . ." (IX, 290–91).

The loyalist, alone in a world that exists now only for him, fills it with emotions unconstrained. But Hawthorne transforms it as unsuitable. Disavowing alienation, disowning the very man whom formerly he had claimed to integrate into the community, he tells a story "fit for the public eye," a story ready-made, as it were, reflecting the factitious community that early in his career he had rejected. The old conflict, public against private, returns. The claims of *Tales of My Native Land* are asserted against *The Story-Teller*. Hawthorne fears his fiction, fears most of all that it is his alone.

"The Artist of the Beautiful"

This, precisely, is the burden of "The Artist of the Beautiful." It carries narcissism, and with it Hawthorne's story-writing career, to its inevitable dead end. It is Hawthorne's fullest demonstration of an aesthetic his art otherwise repudiates. Defending the artist against the world, it thereby enforces the very alienation that his art everywhere else would overcome.

Numerous critics have noted the self-projective nature of the story.[21] Self-projection, as in "The Devil in Manuscript," is a matter, however, quite different from the identification we will more typically encounter. It denies the prior existence of the work to be identified with, art as formal cause, generic necessity in need of being reformed. Projection, instead, begins in the psyche. The work follows, dramatizing its creator, affirming, in all its action, a previously determined stance. Thus, for example, Hawthorne describes Owen's rambles: "He wasted the sunshine, as people said, in wandering through the woods and fields, and along the banks of streams. There, like a child, he found amusement in chasing butterflies, or watching the motions of water-insects" (x, 457). Hawthorne projects his own childhood reminiscences onto Owen.[22] The reportorial completeness of "as people said," moreover, obviating partisanship by establishing an aura of apparent objectivity, protects the artist from the possibility of criticism. "Rhetoric" is at work, but of a particularly reflexive kind, affirming a writer in isolation, independent of a reader whose reaction it forestalls.

Similarly, Hawthorne meditates on Owen's peculiar privateness: "Perhaps he was mad. The lack of sympathy—that contrast between himself and his neighbors, which took away the restraint of example—was enough to make him so. Or, possibly, he had caught just so much of ethereal radiance as served to bewilder him, in an earthly sense, by its intermixture with the common daylight" (x, 462–63). Once again, ostensible disinterest—statement of the case for and against Owen's sanity—is at work in the service of the disinterested observer. What we might call naive description, objective or naturalistic observation proceeding from or embroidering the formal fabric of the story, is here "rhetorically" conceived.

The notions of transcendence that "Artist" espouses

[21] E.g., Crews, Von Abele.
[22] See Hoeltje, pp. 29–34, Hawthorne's life in Raymond.

are an aesthetic formulation of this rhetorical function. The work, as a reflection, enforces a self-protective ideality.[23] Poets and painters have "imperfectly copied [their productions] from the richness of their vision." Owen, in his butterfly, seeks "to give external reality to his ideas." As in Plato's cave, art, itself but a shadow, adumbrates a vision, the conception of which Hawthorne had previously rejected. Narrative literalizes previous notions. Owen, arranging a procession of dancing hours across an ancient clock, has quite literally, as the old phrase goes, "trifled with time." In a dull, depressed mood, a "heavy weight upon his spirits," he regulates the "leaden weight" of the town clock with "obtuse gravity." The same process is involved here as in Hawthorne's Notebook projects, to give life to "If," "But," "And."[24] Story is enactment, rhetoric, as we have said, affirming on a human level vision which need not be reformed.

Significantly, vision is related to narcissism through the concept of anamnesis, which, as we have seen, Hawthorne otherwise eschews. For Owen's inspiration, the spirit that hovers about his head, is his own inner light: ". . . he must keep his faith in himself, while the incredulous world assails him with its utter disbelief; he must stand up against mankind and be his own sole disciple, both as respects his genius, and the objects to which it is directed" (x, 454). Devotion to his muse is self-devotion. Faith in spirituality is faith in his own spirit. The ideality Owen as "his own sole disciple"

[23] Critics have debated Hawthorne's opinion of Owen's transcendent art. Fogle, p. 78, sees the story as Hawthorne's "affirmation of the value of art and of the spiritual pre-eminence of the artist's imagination." R. W. B. Lewis, *The American Adam: Innocence, Tragedy, and Tradition in the Nineteenth Century* (1955; rpt. Univ. of Chicago Press, 1958), p. 119, reads it as "ironic." Hawthorne's purpose, however, is to defend his alienation with available conventions. His acceptance of transcendentalism is not at issue, here. Once again, themes are not so much affirmed as employed.

[24] *The American Notebooks*, p. 242.

reproduces is himself. Reproduction, indeed, is important in this double sense throughout the story. As Von Abele, Crews, and others have noted, Owen's butterfly is his substitute for the child he will not father.[25] It "has absorbed my own being into itself." He has "instilled his own life into it." It is a self-projection, the "delicate" production of "a delicate ingenuity," a "piece of minute machinery" from a "mind [that] was microscopic." The emphasis on size, here, should especially be noted. The butterfly, as Owen's child, asserts its smallness against the "main strength" of Robert Danforth and his own sturdy son. Incapable of the massive Danforth's phallic production, Owen retreats. Abdicating genitality, like Hutchinson rejecting intercourse—in both the sexual and social sense—Owen narcissistically generates himself.

The rhetoric of the story, then, affirming transcendence, enforces isolation. At the end, we are left with the artist in possession of an ideality that, however, he alone may enjoy. Speechless while all around him are loudly exclaiming, he is unable even to relate what he sees. Communication fails when community is denied. In fact, the story works to abolish its own existence as communication. "It is impossible to express by words," Hawthorne says, "the glory, the splendor, the delicate gorgeousness which were softened into the beauty of this object." Vision, of course, traditionally is indescribable. Like Owen, Socrates, standing alone in the snow, is speechless. But language in Plato, the Socratic dialogue, is designed to make every man a visionary. The interlocutor leads his audience up a ladder. The final inspirational jump alone remains undescribed. Rhetoric in Plato convinces a reader whom in "Artist" it puts off. The failure of language here is a hedge thrown between writer and reader: "Pass we over a long space of intense

[25] See, too, William Bysshe Stein, " 'The Artist of the Beautiful': Narcissus and the Thimble," *American Imago*, 18 (1961), 36–44.

thought, yearning effort, minute toil, and wasting anx-
iety, succeeded by an instant of solitary triumph: let
all this be imagined. . . ." "Artist" eludes the steps Plato
elucidates. It will not portray the sharable progress to
vision. Narrative's extensiveness, story embodying a
common culture, linking the teller and the listener, is
denied to enforce the narcissism of the ideal.

Indeed, extensiveness is condensed. Narrative, reduced, becomes a rhetorical counter. Owen's interest in
his butterfly, for example, revives: "How it awoke again,
is not recorded. Perhaps, the torpid slumber was broken
by a convulsive pain. Perhaps, as in a former instance,
the butterfly came and hovered about his head, and
reinspired him—as, indeed, this creature of the sunshine
had always a mysterious mission for the artist—rein-
·spired him with the former purpose of his life" (x,
466). The allusion, of course, is to John the Baptist,
inspired by the Holy Ghost in the shape of a pigeon.
Peculiarly, though, Hawthorne denies what earlier—
notably, in his dissection of the way in which the
populace protects its "narrowness and dullness"—has
been his omniscience: "How it awoke again is not recorded." There is nothing wrong with an author's denying he knows everything about his subject. Hawthorne,
however, claiming and denying knowledge as he
chooses, is not interested in his story, but is using it to
indulge himself. The action itself—its detailed reality
in the story—is unimportant. Carrying, as Bible stories
do, positive valuation, it serves simply to affirm Owen's
vocation. Similarly, Hawthorne defends Owen against
the populace:

"There was, however, a view of the matter, which
Annie, and her husband, and even Peter Hovenden,
might fully have understood, and which would have
satisfied them that the toil of years had here been
worthily bestowed. Owen Warland might have told
them, that this butterfly, this plaything, this bridal-gift
of a poor watchmaker to a blacksmith's wife, was, in

truth, a gem of art that a monarch would have pur-
chased with honors and abundant wealth, and have
treasured it among the jewels of his kingdom, as the
most unique and wondrous of them all! But the artist
smiled, and kept the secret to himself" (x, 473).

Hawthorne invokes a fairy tale of the artist and the
king. Once again, there is nothing especially wrong with
fairy tales. But they do not occur in "The Artist of the
Beautiful" except here, just at the moment when Owen
needs reinforcement and, moreover, as a sign of his
material success ("honors and abundant wealth"). The
story is alien to the manner and nineteenth-century
New England setting of "Artist," alien to the very point
it is used to demonstrate. Bearing a kind of sympathetic
charge, though, it validates the work of art. Plot is a
trope. Story abolishes itself. The butterfly is crushed.

Neither Owen nor Hawthorne seems, at this point, to
mind: "When the artist rose high enough to achieve
the Beautiful, the symbol by which he made it per-
ceptible to mortal senses became of little value in his
eyes, while his spirit possessed itself in the enjoyment
of the Reality" (x, 475).

But there is, after this, no more story left to write.
Hawthorne, abandoning the public house, retreats to
the privacy of the Old Manse, writing infrequently for
four years. Like Hester, embroidering the symbol of her
alienation, he repairs to the domestic sphere and fathers
a child, dealing with society impersonally and uncom-
fortably in the Salem Custom-House. Not until *The
Scarlet Letter* does he again engage his audience and
this time on a larger, more inclusive scale than ever
before.

THREE

A "Typical Illusion"

THUS far in his attempt to establish intimacy, Hawthorne has made only a beginning. The communal powers of art have been only tentatively explored. "The Hollow of the Three Hills" does not so much embody an audience as present a survey of potential audience concerns that may in the future be embodied. The early historical tales, similarly, do not engage history, but expose how much of the private self history never engages. Ironic vignettes like "The Gray Champion" cast off the nationalist methods of Scott and Cooper, but provide no substitute program.

Hawthorne's strategy remains largely expository. He would, for example, write of himself, so "The Devil in Manuscript," its plot little more than the extension into narrative of an ego, baldly asserts him. He would have the reader participate in a common self-scrutiny, so "Wakefield," denying its own existence, presents an invitation to be written. A positive course is opened in *Legends of the Province-House*. There a space is defined with potential for intimacy. Psychology reforms a discarded history. The work would integrate public and private. Reformation, however, proceeds too far. The self asserting itself destroys the very nationality with which it would integrate. "The Artist of the Beautiful" elaborates. It is a skeptical reminder of the dangers of the artist's career, an affirmation of the narcissistic potential of art. Denying integration, it declares all association private. The butterfly's box, quite simply, is too small.

The Scarlet Letter, therefore, pursues the direction of *Legends of the Province-House* in a wider context. It guards against over-psychologization, establishing the psyche itself as a subjectivity bound to history. It reconceives genre, that is to say, not simply as in opposition to selfhood, but as the very medium in which the self may emerge. *Letter* engages the problem of the possibilities for an intimate art in letters especially American. The introduction places the writer in his arthistorical situation. Hawthorne's account of his "discovery" of the scarlet "A," personal though it may be, yet acknowledges generic pressure. From time to time, in the midst of the mundane customs work, his formerly active imagination revives. One of these moments arises when, in the attic, he finds the letter and a story attached to it as part of a cache of documents left by Surveyor Pue. Hawthorne comments on the event: "One of the most remarkable occasions, when the [imaginative] habit of bygone days awoke in me, was that which brings it within the law of literary propriety to offer the public the sketch which I am now writing" (I, 27). The activity of poetry is a well-established "habit." A "remarkable" occasion occurs within the bounds of literary "propriety." Hawthorne attributes the material of the story to an ancient manuscript in a self-conscious imitation of an established practice. It is a deliberate parroting of the procedure Brockden Brown and Poe bring to American gothic letters.[1] Indeed, self-consciousness and deliberation, the decision to choose to parrot, are the only imagination Hawthorne, in fact, exercises. Psychologization itself is historicized, creativity submitted to genre. Where Brockden Brown and Poe but claim their works are found, perhaps to arrogate to themselves a greater authority than mere fiction ordinarily warrants, Hawthorne's work, fiction though

---

[1] See Jane Lundblad, *Nathaniel Hawthorne and the Tradition of Gothic Romance* (Cambridge, Mass.: Harvard Univ. Press, 1946), pp. 59–61, for a compendium of gothic elements in *The Scarlet Letter*.

it is, is found in fact. Its authority overpowers him.[2] The existence of the "A" is more genuine than has generally been imagined. *The Scarlet Letter* is a reconstitution of a convention already existing and fully perceived, the purposeful engaging of a cultural form Hawthorne has learned he may use but must not escape.

The narcissism of "The Artist of the Beautiful," then, is permanently at an end. The artist locates himself in society. He is no visionary Owen Warland, or rather, the idea of vision, the transcendental epistemology espoused in "Artist," is seen itself as a social phenomenon. Hawthorne considers the scarlet "A": "Certainly, there was some deep meaning in it, most worthy of interpretation, and which, as it were, streamed forth from the mystic symbol, subtly communicating itself to my sensibilities, but evading the analysis of my mind" (p. 31).

[2] While Brown and Poe are writing, in their own turn, within a well-established English tradition, yet they seem to maintain a certain naïveté about their methods. They are artists so wholly in a certain mode, so thoroughly conventional in intention as well as form, that they cannot, properly speaking, be said to be parroting at all. The mode is their own as much as their society's. To call Poe a plagiarist, as has often been done, is to miss the point. He is himself the man he is said to steal from. Consider, for example, the Preface to *The Narrative of Arthur Gordon Pym*. The story, "Pym" tells us, too marvellous, as he originally thought, for the public to believe, was first recounted as fiction by a man named "Poe." Since the public, however, realized it was true, "Pym" will now present it in his own words:
"This *exposé* being made, it will be seen at once how much of what follows I claim to be my own writing; and it will also be understood that no fact is misrepresented in the first few pages which were written by Mr. Poe. Even to those readers who have not seen the Messenger [of January and February 1837], it will be unnecessary to point out where his portion ends and my own commences; the difference in point of style will be readily perceived."
Neither "Poe" nor "Pym" is a plagiarist. Regardless of who creates whom, they are both parts of Poe himself, always under his authority. Poe, when he pretends to find a manuscript, then, never doubts for a moment that it is really his. Hawthorne's situation, as we are maintaining, is considerably different.

Here, in capsule, is what Feidelson calls the "symbolistic imagination." To elaborate our earlier explanation: writers of the American Renaissance, Feidelson tells us, held in common a program designed to reunite a body divided, in this super-rational Western world, from its spirit. On the epistemological level this meant a reintegration of intellect into body, a return to sensuous apprehension.[3] Accordingly, Hawthorne opposes his "sensibilities" to his "mind." He would understand the "A" by a kind of sympathetic magnetism, reach it directly, unmediated by the order of analytic thought. Nature, according to Feidelson, thus supplants nurture. Subject meets object, the surveyor the surveyed. Understanding is immediate, uncoerced by the forms of a neo-Augustan rationalism.

Hawthorne, however, insists on nurture. Nature, as Melville puts it in *Moby-Dick*, is ever at the little lower layer. The "A" itself is a cultural artifact, the object apprehended but a by-product of Hawthorne's society. He finds it amid chronicles that subsequently document his "Main Street." Indeed, all the material discovered in the attic is bound by his "veneration for the natal soil." It may be "worked up . . . into a regular history of Salem," and its "final disposition," he knows, must be "with the Essex Historical Society" (pp. 30–31). Most significantly, Hawthorne allies symbolism itself to the gothic gambit of the found manuscript. He admits it only as it is itself conventional, an inescapable part of his

---

[3] See above, p. 19. As Feidelson sees it, Melville is the symbolistic writer par excellence in the mid-nineteenth century, the man who attempted this most difficult course no matter what the personal risks. Hawthorne is praised for generally seeing the body-spirit division, but by and large is denigrated for too often accepting it, or, as Feidelson defines the modes, for writing allegorical instead of symbolistic novels. I am suggesting, simply, that Hawthorne saw the symbolistic program and understood it, that his failure was not a lack of art or moral courage, but, as Feidelson himself seems to indicate in *"The Scarlet Letter," Hawthorne Centenary Essays*, pp. 31–77, a refusal to elide two hundred years of history.

generic situation. As in Swift he derives ostensibly unmediated apprehension from a "pedantry" in which
mediation so dominates that it obscures the nature of
what is to be apprehended.[4] He casts himself as but the
other side of symbolistic man, Poe's ratiocinative intelligence. Phenomena that seem "transparently" perceived, in Emerson's term, rather have been reconceived
from the start. Negative capability is, in reality, the
egotistical sublime. The pedant consults authorities
("as I am assured by ladies conversant with such mysteries"), takes accurate measurements ("each limb
proved to be precisely three inches and a quarter in
length"), does archaeological research ("It has been
intended, there could be no doubt, as an ornamental
article of dress"), even threatens, to further his knowledge, to destroy the object of his investigation ("the
stitch . . . gives evidence of a now forgotten art, not to
be recovered even by the process of picking out the
threads") (p. 31). Apprehension is described by a strict
set of analytic procedures, coerced by the actualities of
convention. Relationships are never free, are, from the
start, fully figured. It is, inevitably, with the formed
that a reforming art must begin.

"Not love, but instinct," an "unjoyous attachment for
his native town," then, draws Hawthorne back to Salem.
"Attachment" defines the man-in-the-place. "Unjoyous,"
that is, describes an individual coerced, a psyche historically determined and which is the only psyche
Hawthorne, as writer of *The Scarlet Letter*, has. Con-
strainment is everywhere, a "wretched numbness" that
is both inside and outside. The "torpor" that is a quality
of "intellectual effort" yet "held possession of me," "ac-
companied me home, and weighed upon me in the
chamber which I most absurdly termed my study." The
artist submits to the place. The Custom-House, con-
densing the sterility of the Salem Hawthorne cannot

[4] See, especially, "A Discourse Concerning the Mechanical
Operation of the Spirit."

91

leave, defines his work as the work of the sterile Haw-
thorne-in-Salem. We have seen in the first chapter that,
in "The Custom-House," Hawthorne would assert himself. He writes a sketch to declare his independence.
And yet, even as he speaks, his words, bound up in his
culture, are turned against him. The Custom-House
generates a typology, quite literally a language, whose
terms constitute a medium reinforcing alienation. Typically, metaphor, not logic or chronology, carries the
piece forward:

"It was pleasant, in the summer forenoons,—when the
fervent heat, that almost liquefied the rest of the human
family, merely communicated a genial warmth to their
half-torpid systems,—it was pleasant to hear them chat-
ting in the back entry, a row of them all tipped against
the wall, as usual; while the frozen witticisms of past
generations were thawed out, and came bubbling with
laughter from their lips. Externally, the jollity of aged
men has much in common with the mirth of children;
the intellect, any more than a deep sense of humor, has
little to do with the matter; it is, with both, a gleam that
plays upon the surface, and imparts a sunny and cheery
aspect alike to the green branch, and gray, mouldering
trunk. In one case, however, it is real sunshine; in the
other, it more resembles the phosphorescent glow of
decaying wood" (pp. 15–16).

The image "bubbling with laughter" suggests "the
mirth of children," thus resulting in the final invidious
comparison. Through development of an image the
passage proceeds. The felt heat becomes a metaphor,
and the metaphor rapidly becomes real, not only defining the action of the men—the witticisms are "frozen"
old jokes—but ultimately defining the nature of the
men's existence—"gray, mouldering trunk[s]" whose
liveliness is a "phosphorescent glow." Metaphor, as it
were, envelops them, becomes their world.

In a similar manner, the metaphor of death envelops
Hawthorne. It begins as an image of isolation and ste-

rility. The Salem wharves are old with disuse. But death soon takes a body, as the Custom-House crystallizes the decay. Now the death image begins to define Hawthorne's activity. He sees himself as a potential "exterminating angel" with power "to bring . . . under the axe of the guillotine" the political lives of all the old men (p. 14). He sees himself dying, his "intellect . . . dwindling away" (p. 38), till, with a change of administration, "my own head was the first that fell!" (p. 41). The image becomes all-powerful; it has assumed a life of its own. Salem, the oppressive house of death, takes possession of its world.

At this late stage of "The Custom-House" Hawthorne can offer little opposition. Resistance is impossible, and he must begin all over again. Once more he acknowledges generic pressure. Much as he "found" the "A," so now he finds even himself. The dead Hawthorne is a convention established by Washington Irving. It is a self delimited, but on which Hawthorne, because he fully accepts it, may start to operate anew:

"Meanwhile, the press had taken up my affair, and kept me, for a week or two, careering through the public prints, in my decapitated state, like Irving's Headless Horseman; ghastly and grim, and longing to be buried, as a politically dead man ought. So much for my figurative self. The real human being, all this time, with his head safely on his shoulders, had brought himself to the comfortable conclusion, that every thing was for the best; and, making an investment in ink, paper, and steel-pens, had opened his long-disused writing-desk, and was again a literary man" (pp. 42–43).

Two selves are presented: one passive and one active, one fictive, the other fiction-making. An abrupt break— "So much for my figurative self"—separates them. The man, fully-figured, takes up his pen to recompose himself. Self-consciousness, once again, is to revalue an otherwise intractable form.

In the closing paragraphs Hawthorne further elucidates his practice. He speaks of *The Scarlet Letter* itself. The novel is not really his. Its "sombre aspect" is "no indication . . . of a lack of cheerfulness in the writer's mind." Its "uncaptivating effect is perhaps due to the period of hardly accomplished revolution, and still seething turmoil, in which the story shaped itself" (p. 43). The novel is the product of an age now past. It is Hawthorne's heritage, not his creation. He is disengaged. He now proceeds, however, to re-engage himself. Though the book is not his, he yet would incorporate it in one that is. *The Scarlet Letter* was, ultimately, published alone, but Hawthorne insists on speaking of it as though it were still one of a projected collection of pieces. "Some of the briefer articles, which contribute to make up the volume, have likewise been written since my involuntary withdrawal from the toils and honors of public life, and the remainder are gleaned from annuals and magazines, of such antique date that they have gone round the circle, and come back to novelty again" (p. 43).

The stories are old; therefore, they are fresh. They have been circulated in journals, but were written in private. Hawthorne re-appropriates *Letter*, recreates it in a new context, perhaps as one more of his youthful *Tales of My Native Land* or tales from *The Story-Teller*. Of course, *The Scarlet Letter* is yet to be considered "the Posthumous Papers of a Decapitated Surveyor." The convention Hawthorne appropriates reasserts itself at a higher level as conventional still. There is a significant circularity, a kind of infinite regress in this procedure. The reformed work imposes itself anew; each recreation becomes a coercion. Such is Hawthorne's perpetual dilemma. It may be followed from novel to novel and, as we shall see in *The Scarlet Letter*, within even a single novel. *The Scarlet Letter*, indeed, stands as Hawthorne's most exemplary work, because it so centrally articulates the method characteristic of his fiction in general. It is, as we noted in the first chapter, "The

Custom-House" written large. To the development of an image in "The Custom-House" corresponds the logic of plot in *The Scarlet Letter*. Metaphor, extended over the longer length of a novel, becomes allegory, and the artist attempts to reconstruct the work allegory would too narrowly circumscribe.[5]

The story of *The Scarlet Letter* is presented as it is "about to issue" from a jail (p. 48), a space connected, through its association with the cemetery (p. 47), with the Custom-House, the house of death. Kenneth Burke speaks of what he calls the principle of the "scene-act ratio."[6] Act and atmosphere are inter-dependent, temporal and spatial equivalents translating each other. The jail-cemetery-Custom-House, then, projects its narrative. It defines the action as a dramatization of death. New England society, as architect of the house, creates a world that would define *The Scarlet Letter* as a "tale of human frailty and sorrow." Here, too, resistance is impossible. Hawthorne is confined by material, as we have seen, which he will not this time deny. Recreation, however, proceeds. The book progresses as a series of redactions of events now taken as given. The assembly at "The Prison-Door," for example, are "bearded men, in sad-colored garments, and gray, steeple-crowned hats" (p. 47). But the same assembly in the same area entitled "The Market Place" is "a pretty large number of the inhabitants of Boston" (p. 49). Similarly, the typical demeanor of the Boston populace is stern and even harsh in the sphere of the scaffold. But it is now humane and generous as reconceived in "the great and warm heart" of humanity (p. 127), now avaricious and

---

[5] For two related treatments, see Richard Poirier, "Visionary to Voyeur: Hawthorne and James," in *A World Elsewhere: The Place of Style in American Literature* (New York: Oxford Univ. Press, 1966), pp. 93–143, and R. W. B. Lewis, "The Tactics of Sanctity: Hawthorne and James," in *Hawthorne Centenary Essays*, pp. 271–95.

[6] *A Grammar of Motives* (1945; rpt. Berkeley: Univ. of California Press, 1969), pp. 3–7.

materialistic as it appears in "the New World" (p. 261).
Action created once is created again, is reformed in
other spheres. The same story is redefined by each different image. Events are accepted as inevitable, but the
image revalues them to reinforce its own existence.

It is for this reason that, as Malcolm Cowley notes,
The Scarlet Letter reads like a succession of semi-
autonomous dramatic tableaux.[7] Each chapter encloses
its action, determines its importance in a context discontinuous from its importance in neighboring chapters. The effect, as of the tiles in the Province-House, is
to render story as scene. Causality is denied, and events,
repeated, from the point of view of an ongoing tale,
recur in apparent ignorance of their repetition.

Hawthorne describes Pearl's usual behavior toward
her peers. She stands within an "inviolable circle," and
whenever the children gather around her, she hurls
violent imprecations at them (pp. 93–94). The circle is
a metaphor for Pearl's alienation, and the incident
dramatizes the metaphor. In the next chapter, however,
in order to demonstrate the influence of "The Governor's Hall," an instance of Pearl's behavior is presented
in language virtually identical to the original exposition.
Where, earlier, the children are "disporting themselves
in such grim fashion as the Puritanic nurture would
permit" (p. 94), now "the children of the Puritans
looked up from their play,—or what passed for play with
those sombre little urchins" (p. 102). There Pearl sends
"shrill, incoherent exclamations" at them. Here she
"screamed and shouted . . . with a terrific volume of
sound." Even certain minor differences are, rather,
transformations of the same action. When Pearl's imp-
ishness is being presented it is she who flings rocks at
the children. Here, where the cruelty of Puritan life is
the point, the children fling mud at Pearl. It is not be-

[7] "Five Acts of *The Scarlet Letter*," CE, 19 (1957), 11–16.
Cowley's analysis, however, deals with narrowly aesthetic problems.

cause he has forgotten what he has just narrated that Hawthorne repeats himself. Nor is his imagination at fault, his ability insufficient to create incidents appropriate for dramatizing his particular point. Rather, as he now knows, all creation begins in duplication. Imagination is confined by the material at hand. Action generated in one scene imposes itself as generic pressure in another, but whenever regenerated it occurs as if for the first time.

Consider a further example, Pearl's catechism. "Tell me, then, what thou art, and who sent thee hither?" Hester asks (p. 98). Pearl refuses to answer, and Hester, therefore, informs her, "Thy Heavenly Father sent thee!" Two chapters later the incident "recurs." "Canst thou tell me, my child, who made thee?" Reverend Wilson asks (p. 111), and once again Pearl demurs. Hawthorne comments: "Now Pearl knew well enough who made her; for Hester Prynne, the daughter of a pious home, very soon after her talk with the child about her Heavenly Father, had begun to inform her of those truths which the human spirit, at whatever stage of immaturity, imbibes with such eager interest" (p. 111).

Hawthorne's double-consciousness, here, is remarkable. He frankly admits his earlier use of the material—"very soon after her talk with the child about her Heavenly Father." But the admission has no effect. It is very nearly parenthetical. For the especial sake of the scene at hand, Hawthorne must tell us, though he acknowledges he has already done so in the earlier context, that Hester had, by and large, taught Pearl the proper answer. What is to be made of such disconnected connection? Material described in one chapter is not to be remembered in a second, nor introduced quite as new, nor yet repeated as a reminder of its first appearance. We have not a continuous tale, nor yet a series of separate tales, but one tale, itself discontinuous. Story is fragmented, thoroughly dislocated. *The Scarlet Letter* is remarkably unhinged.

The effect of all this on the reader is particularly important. He is placed under a double pressure, invited to see the work as a continuous pattern, but with each new chapter forced to consider another continuity. His sense of unity is preserved but abused. We are maintaining, here, a certain almost gestalt dynamic of reading. The reader never sees events independently, but locates them in completed structures called plots which he hypothesizes as he reads. As Burke, responding to Frank Kermode's assertion that a novel is an essentially temporal form, notes, "just as we 'read' time into the static forms (consider painting and sculpture) by observing piecemeal how they develop from one point to another . . . so we gradually piece together a set of *fixed* relationships within a progressive form such as a story or an opera."[8] To a certain extent the argument between Kermode and Burke is over a question of metaphor. Form, as we have contended, exists fully formed. Every work is a genre, and even a "fragment" adumbrates its archetype. Whether we call a novel temporal or spatial, it nevertheless exists complete from the start.[9] The reader, reading of events that take place in time, yet disposes them into patterns he continually projects. Apprehension, as Hawthorne has shown us, is never direct. Perception is always conception. We see events only as we order them into conventional structures, what E. H. Gombrich calls schemata,[10] and, indeed, memory itself might be defined as such an ordering of events. Revaluation, repetition, revision are liberties taken with story, and the freedom they produce is a kind of "alternative possibilities" in potential. As in

[8] Kermode, *The Sense of an Ending: Studies in the Theory of Fiction* (New York: Oxford Univ. Press, 1967); Burke, "Kermode Revisited," *Novel*, 3 (1969), 77–82. See, also, Joseph Frank, "Spatial Form in Modern Literature," in *Criticism: The Foundations of Modern Literary Judgment*, ed. Mark Schorer, Josephine Miles, and Gordon McKenzie (New York: Harcourt, Brace, 1948), pp. 379–92.

[9] See above, pp. 22–23.   [10] *Art and Illusion*, p. 272.

"Wakefield," the reader is engaged, is himself invited to participate in reconsideration of what has happened and projection of what is yet to happen.

His participation, however, is never free, but consists of adjusting and readjusting his expectations to generic possibility. He may subject himself to forms multiplied and made equally available by the discontinuity of the novel. Again and again he is presented with definitions that ask to be redefined. As in "The Gray Champion" he is provided with a kind of anti-schema, which exists to be replaced.

All aspects of the book are affected, and the example of character may serve as typical. Each of the principals appears now as an emblem of morality, now as an anguished psyche. Hester, first seen on the scaffold as a symbol of sin, protests against her role. "Could it be true?" she wondered, that "these were her realities," that "all else had vanished" (p. 59). Chillingworth, described, initially, as the implacable arch-fiend, is demythologized in "The Leech and his Patient." When he first sees Hester, "a writhing horror twisted itself across his features" (p. 61). But Hawthorne now remarks, "he had begun an investigation, as he imagined, with the severe and equal integrity of a judge" (p. 129). Hester observes Pearl, "imp of evil, emblem and product of sin," "born outcast of the infantile World," hurl exclamations at the other children that "had so much the sound of a witch's anathemas in some unknown tongue." But "The truth was" a psychological explanation of Pearl's alienation: the "little Puritans" noted how different the two were from the rest of society and hated them for it, while Pearl "felt the sentiment and requited it" (p. 94).

The reader, faced with such contradiction, may choose to see ambiguity or paradox. More properly, however, if he refuses to impose his own world on the world of *The Scarlet Letter*, he is drawn into a point "between" schemata, the creative heart of the book.

Here schematizations are never avoided, but they remain potential. Or, rather, since the schema is itself potential, in the sense that it has as yet to be articulated, the heart of Hawthorne's *Scarlet Letter* is the deeper point between alternative potentialities. Here is a center of pure possibility. It is the beginning of what, in the first chapter, we called Hawthorne's romance, a definition we should now justify more elaborately.

Let us review some of the definitions more usually given. We may divide them into two categories, descriptions according to so-called form and descriptions according to so-called content. In the popular mind the first category is defined as romance signifying a story of not always coherently related adventures and the second as romance signifying a story about love. Critics of form generally elaborate the notion of incoherence in more sophisticated terms. Thus Kathleen Williams speaks of what she calls the fluidity of *The Faerie Queene* before the allegorical Christian quest begins. Similarly, John Arthos notes, as typical of Redcrosse's adventures, a certain aimlessness, mistake and struggle endlessly repeated, error—in the root as well as conventional sense—before his experience in the House of Holinesse reveals to him the typological pattern of his wandering.[11] Critics interested in content offer a variety of romance subjects. While the idea of romance as a love story is universally discredited, Joel Porte, for example, sees romance, at least in America, as an inquiry into "the inner life." On the other hand, G. Harrison Orians, in a now classic article, and William Charvat speak of romance's broadly national scope. John Caldwell Stubbs cites a combination of "verisimilitude and ideality." And Richard Chase, in what is still the standard work for Americanists, mixes nearly everything

[11] Williams, *Spenser's World of Glass: A Reading of the Faerie Queene* (Berkeley: Univ. of California Press, 1966), pp. 1–7; Arthos, *On the Poetry of Spenser and the Form of Romances* (London: George Allen and Unwin, 1956), pp. 40–64.

together, shifts from romance as form ("where the search for unity is not at the center of the stage") to romance as content ("a tendency to plunge into the underside of consciousness") to romance as an ill-defined combination of the two (an "adaptation of traditional novelistic procedures to new cultural conditions").[12]

These definitions, despite their variety, are compatible with our own. It is evident they share a certain sense of romance as that freedom from constraint which was our starting point. As René Wellek notes, the word "romance" originally referred to writings in the Romance languages, which tended, more often than not, to break the "rules" of Greek and Roman literature.[13] We can, however, actually unify the various characteristics cited by defining romance in terms of the dynamic of its writers and readers. Freedom, as we see it, is never, in literature, freedom *from* anything but freedom in the written. Rules, that is, are never broken;

[12] Porte, *The Romance in America: Studies in Cooper, Poe, Hawthorne, Melville, and James* (Middletown, Conn.: Wesleyan Univ. Press, 1969), p. 215; Orians, "The Romance Ferment After *Waverley*," *AL*, 3 (1932), 408–31; Charvat, *The Origins of American Critical Thought, 1810–1835* (Philadelphia: Univ. of Pennsylvania Press, 1936), pp. 134–63; Stubbs, "The Theory of the Prose Romance: A Study of the Background of Hawthorne's Literary Theories," Diss. Princeton 1964, p. 234; Chase, *The American Novel and Its Tradition* (Garden City, New York: Doubleday, 1957), pp. 7, ix, 14.

Part of the divergence of views, here, results from the particular writers with which the critics are concerned. Thus, for example, William Gilmore Simms' remark in the Preface to *The Yemassee* that romance is a prose "epic" and Hawthorne's own comment in the Preface to *The House of the Seven Gables* that the scope of romance is limited to "the truth of the human heart" are variously cited. The definitions of each of the critics, however, are meant as generalizations covering a wide variety of writers. A nominalist view that the term romance is meaningless flies in the face of the feeling of generations of readers that American prose fictions of the nineteenth century, despite their differences, share something that sets them apart from the novels of nineteenth-century England.

[13] See above, p. 46n.

they are re-formed. Romance is indeed a liberty, but a liberty of interanimation. It is a form generated by the mutual possession of writer and reader, the elaboration of a culture in which author and audience are integrated, in which intimacy is achieved from the start. Accordingly, in romance, the distinction between the deeply personal (Porte) and the broadly national (Orians, Charvat) disappears. Both descriptions are correct. Moreover, as the discrepancy between the work as archetype and the work as personal statement evaporates, what we might call "internal difference," where, with Emily Dickinson, we have claimed the meanings are, the point between works in which purpose may be found, dissolves. The meanings are everywhere. Center is circumference. Here, indeed, form and content are indistinguishable, which is precisely why romance is described now as one, now as the other.

In *The Scarlet Letter*, then, romance has begun, although the process is not everywhere complete. The alternative schemata provide a point of potentiality, if not of potential realized, a place of purpose uncoerced, purpose pure, though not, perhaps, embodied. Form is not yet re-formed, but it is at least *un*formed—and not, as in "The Hollow of the Three Hills," because it precedes an engagement with the demands of culture, but because it finds a place in their midst. Thus Hester and Dimmesdale meet, as lovers:

"Life had never brought them a gloomier hour; it was the point whither their pathway had so long been tending, and darkening ever, as it stole along;—and yet it inclosed a charm that made them linger upon it, and claim another, and another, and, after all, another moment . . . while one solemn old tree groaned dolefully to another, as if telling the sad story of the pair that sat beneath, or constrained to forebode evil to come" (p. 195).

The "hour" "inclosed a charm," suggesting not only the irrelevance of the controversy over whether the novel is temporal or spatial, but, as in *Legends of the Province-House*, the coherent phenomenology—a unity of time and space—that exists at the place of intimacy. Significantly, the place exists not independently, but as the center of fatalities it holds off. It is "the point whither their pathway had so long been tending" and a moment which "forbode evil to come." And yet, before and after—pushing back the past, delaying the future—as the lovers "linger upon it, and claim another, and another, and after all, another moment," the logic of events pauses. The groaning trees, "telling the sad story," are a case of action still unenacted. Story is suspended in scene. Scene is story's center, arresting the action but never evading it. In much the same way, Pearl tells us she was plucked off a bush. The scenery is fraught with history. Landscape is story *in situ*.

There are interesting Ovidian echoes in both incidents—a kind of subliminal metamorphosis in which trees talk and Pearl is a pluckable flower. They are products, it would seem, of a private mythology in Hawthorne, never fully publicized, but fitfully at work in *The Scarlet Letter*, nevertheless. It is a mythology, too, that informs his retelling of the classical myths for children in *A Wonder Book* and *Tanglewood Tales*. Hawthorne confuses childhood and the childhood of the race of men.[14] Paganism is associated with Europe in opposition to a Puritanism confined to America. Hawthorne recalls his own semi-invalidical youth, per-

---

[14] Thus Hawthorne reports the narrator's, Eustace Bright's, opinions that the stories are readily adaptable to the "childish purity of his auditors." They are expressions of "the pure childhood of the world. When the first poet or romancer told these marvellous legends . . . it was still the Golden Age. Evil had never yet existed; and sorrow, misfortune, crime, were mere shadows which the mind fancifully created for itself, as a shelter against too sunny realities. . . . Children are now the only representatives of the men and women of that happy era; and therefore it is that we must raise the intellect and fancy to the level of childhood, in order to re-create the original myth" (VII, 179).

haps, and the European romances he so fondly remembered reading that transformed it to happiness. In *The Scarlet Letter*, at any rate, "the New World" is ancient. Weather stains and rust mark the jail as "antique." Though only fifteen or twenty years old, "it seemed never to have known a youthful era." But "Old England" is the place of Hester's "infancy." Reminiscences of childhood are of "other scenes than . . . the Western wilderness."[15] Hester, it is true, remembers a "decayed house" and a "half-obliterated shield" betokening "antique gentility," as well. The association of Europe with childhood and the primitive, as we have said, is private, and in *The Scaret Letter* it is public history that dominates. Nevertheless, Pearl, as "a nymph-child, or an infant dryad" (p. 205), "one of the fairies, whom we left in our dear old England" (p. 206), suggests a primeval existence in a somehow pre-Christian Europe. Primitivism would replace the Calvinist cosmology, a unifying animism the loss of Eden. When Hester proposes to Dimmesdale her European option, she thus holds out, I would maintain, the possibility of a return to origins. The sea "will bear thee back again" (p. 197), she tells him. He can "Begin all anew" (p. 198). Hester would deny the action that has thus far transpired, would retrieve in Europe an age when life is still potential.

The possibilities of the new Old World, however, are never more fully developed. Hawthorne's earlier work has established the necessity of a fully nationalistic art. Moreover, the nation in question has no existence ex-

[15] Cf. Michael Davitt Bell, *Hawthorne and the Historical Romance of New England* (Princeton, N.J.: Princeton Univ. Press, 1971), p. 116: "Like James, if with less firsthand experience, Hawthorne early came to associate 'life' with Europe, with the Old World. In the New World, as Hawthorne read American history, this 'life' somehow withered away; it perished in the soil of the wilderness. This process of withering was important to Hawthorne because, as he saw it, his own America was its result."

cept in terms of the national identity Hawthorne's art projects. The audience Hawthorne addresses is not autonomous, but an audience his work hypothesizes. Europe in 1850, then, lies just beyond the literary expectations created—Washington Irving's "Legends of the Alhambra," for example, or similar travel sketches by others, notwithstanding—by Hawthorne's own short stories. The increasing expatriation during the 1850's,[16] including Hawthorne's own years in England and Italy, would present a viable subject for romance only because *The Scarlet Letter* and *The House of the Seven Gables* had previously engaged the possibilities of romance at home. At this point in Hawthorne's courtship of his New England audience, Europe is an evasion of the communal terms of his work, an association outside what we have called his art-historical situation. The opportunity for escaping alienation in the Salem Custom-House lies in the reaffirmation of intimacy in Salem terms. The house of death must become a house of life; intimate American space must be recovered with power still to define intimate American stories.

In an unformed portion of America, Hester and Dimmesdale recall, for one brief period, an American dream, the virgin world still rich with possibilities. The "dungeon of his own heart," the space of the Custom-House, is exchanged for "the magic circle of this hour" (p. 282). Hester suggests that Dimmesdale leave Boston to work among the Indians. She proposes an American fiction, romance in the style of the Leatherstocking saga, alternative to the Custom-House's "tale of human frailty and sorrow." The terms of the Custom-House, however, must be dealt with. Hawthorne accepts but

[16] For a thorough account of Americans abroad in the nineteenth century see Norman Holmes Pearson, "The Road to Italy," in *The French and Italian Notebooks by Nathaniel Hawthorne*, Diss. Yale 1941, pp. i–xxx. Also useful is Nathalia Wright, *American Novelists in Italy; The Discoverers: Allston to James* (Philadelphia: Univ. of Pennsylvania Press, 1965).

reconstitutes them. And indeed, here, for a moment, romance more fully embodied is actually achieved. The language of Puritanism is revalued. The "mystery of joy" replaces the Christian mystery. Dimmesdale's "transformation" adapts Christian regeneration, as, flinging aside his role of suffering sinner, he is "risen up all made anew." The language of theology becomes lovers' discourse, for in Hester's words, "What we did has a consecration of its own" (p. 195). We have, in effect, a series of puns or pun-like structures, alternative definitions of language from which the couple must choose. Hester and Dimmesdale are located at the intersection of the pun. Dimmesdale is a "minister," but of an "interior kingdom." In the equivoke, his social and his solitary selves are dissolved. Similarly, the woman the community has branded an adultress is, in her personal relations, an "angel." Man and his world are one. Public and private are as yet unseparated. Dimmesdale and Hester unite in a universe that is their own extension when, "as if the gloom of the earth and sky had been but the effluence of these two mortal hearts, it vanished with their sorrow" (p. 202).

It is the Custom-House, however, that ultimately takes control. Celebration is coerced. Reformation has not sufficiently been undertaken, and the pure potential we encounter more often than reformation yields inevitably to the fully formed. Chillingworth, answering Hester's plea to let Dimmesdale go, states the case precisely:

"It is not granted me to pardon. I have no such power as thou tellest me of. My old faith, long forgotten, comes back to me, and explains all that we do, and all we suffer. By thy first step awry, thou didst plant the germ of evil; but, since that moment, it has all been a dark necessity. Ye that have wronged me are not sinful, save in a kind of typical illusion; neither am I fiend-like, who have snatched a fiend's office from his hands. It is our fate. Let the black flower blossom as it may!" (p. 174).

Allegory, a "typical illusion," is the destiny to which each character is doomed. Chillingworth, at this late stage in the novel, would disclaim any ability to change the plot. He does, however, as a good allegorical critic, interpret it, drawing on his "old faith" as key. The allegory is that of the "first step awry," the Christian story of the Fall, specifically Hawthorne's favorite story of the fortunate Fall. It is the Puritan history of sin and regeneration. Its progress is clear: Dimmesdale falls deeper and deeper into error. His sin of passion becomes, as he notes, willful transgression when he resolves in the forest to leave Boston with Hester. Finally, God's grace, speaking through him in the Election Day sermon, enables him to confess and brings regeneration at the door of death. This is the story that seizes control, and its dominance is firmly established in the middle of the book.[17]

In contrast to the scene in the forest, then, stands the great scene on the scaffold. As are the others in the book, it is presented as occurring independently of the surrounding events. It takes place at but a minimally defined time, "On one of those ugly nights" (p. 146). Like other action, it has no effect on subsequent action, for despite the awareness manifest in Dimmesdale's "Who is that man, Hester . . . I hate him, Hester. . . . I tell thee my soul shivers at him" (p. 156), directed at Chillingworth, he is outraged and astonished when Hester gives him an answer some time later. The scene is self-contained; it defines its own world. It is a world, however, with a special importance.

[17] This pattern, of course, is as much as an orthodox Christian approach to *The Scarlet Letter* can determine. (See Charles Child Walcutt, *"The Scarlet Letter* and Its Modern Critics," *NCF*, 7 [1953], 251–64, for a good summary of such an approach.) It is a common pattern for Puritan literature, as G. A. Starr, *Defoe and Spiritual Autobiography* (Princeton, N.J.: Princeton Univ. Press, 1965), demonstrates. Starr, too, however, makes the mistake of taking it for the whole in Defoe, as the orthodox critics do in Hawthorne.

The incident begins with Dimmesdale "Walking in the shadow of a dream" (p. 147). As Hawthorne tells us, shadows, to the untrue man, are the only substance, and his own substance, in turn, a shadow (pp. 145–46). More significantly, however, the dream is the dream-vision of Dante and Hawthorne's favorite, Bunyan, a "moment's peace" in a life of "unspeakable misery." The hero, wandering as in a "maze," as Hawthorne later calls it—Dante's "dark wood"—affirms his commitment to Truth at last revealed. Like Redcrosse in the House of Holinesse, he discovers the pattern in what had seemed an indeterminate wandering. Indeed, the scaffold scene serves precisely the function of the House of Holinesse. Cut off from the expected causality of the narrative, centrally placed, specially validated, it exists at a level as it were "higher" than the scenes that surround it. It distills from the rest of the story elements it advances as critically important.[18] It fixes as inevitable schemata that earlier were but potential. Character, landscape, events, all are reconceived in the terms the dream-vision provides.

The discontinuous technique of *The Scarlet Letter* thus achieves its supreme formulation. The result is the end of any further discontinuity, a final fixing of all that may transpire. The novel is most authoritatively, indeed almost prophetically, reconstructed: a respected minister, in the middle of the night, ascends the public place of shame to join hands, under the eyes of the devil, with his former conspirators in evil. A sign appears in the sky, the letter "A," to show forth his crime. The next day, setting aside his night's work, the minister returns to his pulpit. Ironically, the sign has been interpreted by the community to mean "Angel." The

[18] In the terms of Mircea Eliade, *The Myth of the Eternal Return* (1954; rpt. as *Cosmos and History*, New York: Harper Torchbooks, 1959) it is a "symbol of the center" (pp. 12–17), a "zone of the sacred, the zone of absolute reality" (p. 18). The phrases are cited in Fletcher, pp. 210n., 211.

minister's glove, however, remains, tangible proof to him that his midnight walk was, indeed, real. Here "The Minister's Vigil," as the chapter is entitled, is a sort of combination "Young Goodman Brown" and "The Minister's Black Veil." It is an allegory of the Calvinist type enunciated by Chillingworth.

Let us consider, first, the characters as the allegory defines them. For most of the novel, as we have seen, they are located between forms, alternative psychic and religious constructions. On the scaffold, however, they exist only as figures in a "typical illusion": the Fallen Adam and Eve, joined together by the child, the emblem of their sin, under the ever-watchful eyes of the devil. The psychological alternative is presented, but, as the scaffold story progresses, it rapidly becomes obsolete. Hawthorne first attributes the "A" in the sky "solely to the disease in his [Dimmesdale's] own eye and heart" (p. 155). But by the end of the chapter, as demanded for an ironic close, it is an "A" that the whole community has seen. On first ascending the scaffold, Dimmesdale shrieks. It is "an outcry," as he thinks, "that went pealing through the night." Hawthorne, at first faithful to the psychology of guilt, notes that it "perhaps sounded with a far greater power, to his own startled ears, than it actually possessed" and that in reality, as a result, "The town did not awake" (pp. 148–49). A moment later, however, as the allegorical machinery continues to grind, the cry startles both Governor Bellingham and Mistress Hibbins, the representatives of the theocratic and demonic orders needed for the requisite allegorical contrast. The demands of the narrative, that is, revise out schemata that elsewhere in the book are of great significance.

The theocratic and the demonic, in fact, are the parameters within which all things are now defined. The universe of the scaffold is a world of the sacred and the profane, its very phenomena measured on a scale of God and the devil. We noted that the scaffold incident takes place on "one of those ugly nights." But soon, we are told, it is Saturday evening. Dimmesdale's communion with sin and the devil is contrasted with the communion he will lead the next morning with God. Time itself is bent, informed with religious portent. In much the same way the night, we are told, is foggy and "obscure," so that one "could see but little farther than he might into a mill-stone." The obscurity enables Dimmesdale to ascend the scaffold without danger of being discovered. Or, perhaps, it is a metaphor for Dimmesdale's own inner confusion. The space of "The Minister's Vigil," however, much like its time, is religiously conceived. The devil is clearly visible whatever the state of the landscape. As Dimmesdale looks about him, he observes even "the expression of her [Mistress Hibbins'] sour and discontented face" (p. 149). As characters are described in their function as allegorical personifications, so phenomena are bent to fit the allegorical action.

By far the most important reconstruction that occurs on the scaffold, however, is a reconstruction of events. After the action here, all subsequent action proceeds as a matter of course. It but enacts the world now firmly established. The forest scene, as we have noted, will attempt to revive the possibility of alternative action. And yet the events that do occur are determined by "The Minister's Vigil." Hester, for example, would escape Chillingworth. She takes passage for Pearl, Dimmesdale, and herself on a ship bound from the Colonies. But the relationship established on the scaffold is inexorable. The devil is ever-watchful. Chillingworth takes passage, too. His is the "countenance of an inevitable doom," and Hester, seeing it, realizes she can never be free. She is drawn to the scaffold by an "inevitable magnetism." She knows "her whole orb of life, both before and after, was connected with this spot" (p. 244). The scaffold is inescapable and the relationships established on it her fatality.

Indeed, the conclusion for all the characters takes place on the scaffold, and their actions, as a final demonstration of inevitability, recapitulate almost exactly the events of "The Minister's Vigil." Once again Dimmesdale ascends the platform and again joins hands with Hester and Pearl. So, too, Chillingworth watches and even, once more, invites Dimmesdale to leave. What transpired under an "unvaried pall of cloud" occurs, at the close, "In the open air." Events established as inevitable are publicized. It may be argued, of course, that rather than the action proper it is such publication that constitutes the event in question. Indeed, it has become traditional to read Dimmesdale's confession as the climax, the center, so to speak, of the book. He renounces his hypocrisy, affirms his sin, admits, perhaps even transcends, his guilt. Such a reading is true enough. But it is applicable only within a highly circumscribed view of the book. The significance of Dimmesdale's renunciation, I would argue, is to elaborate the substructures of a greater structure already revealed in an earlier climax. From the point of view of the opposition of the theocratic and psychological possibilities with which "The Minister's Vigil" is concerned, it makes little difference whether hypocrisy is renounced or continued. The notion that Dimmesdale is a hypocrite at all, the definition of him as a seeming saint hiding a glaring sin, itself proceeds from a world where God and the devil are already established as parameters. Whether Dimmesdale remains a hypocrite or admits his "sin," he has submitted to what was merely an alternative in the action that the earlier scaffold scene terminates. To read Dimmesdale's publication of his crime as the center of *The Scarlet Letter* is to impose subordinate forms on the larger form that contains them.

To an extent this is what Hawthorne himself would seem to want us to do. He pulls the string on us, presents the decision to confess as though it were the critical decision of the book. As in "Wakefield," he telescopes one story into another. As Hawthorne abandons his own struggle, Dimmesdale's struggle takes over. And yet, Hawthorne's abdication, his surrender of the alternative potential of the book to Puritan control, is expressed even in the affirmation of Dimmesdale's choice:

"God knows; and He is merciful! [says Dimmesdale]. He hath proved his mercy, most of all, in my afflictions. By giving me this burning torture to bear upon my breast! By sending yonder dark and terrible old man, to keep the torture always at red-heat! By bringing me hither, to die this death of triumphant ignominy before the people. . . . Praised be his name! His will be done! Farewell!" (pp. 256–57).

Here is a complete redaction of Chillingworth's "typical illusion," the situation of "The Minister's Vigil" asserted as inexorable. In Dimmesdale's sermon on "the relation between the Deity and the communities of mankind," his "prophecy" of a "high and glorious destiny for the newly gathered people of the Lord" and for "the New England which they were planting in the wilderness" (p. 249), the world of the forest is socialized, ordered once and for all. Alternatives are disposed of; romance is at its predictable end.[19] Hawthorne has

[19] Much like Natty Bumppo at the end of *The Prairie*, Dimmesdale foretells his end as potential American Adam. An inevitable teleology is espoused—in Cooper, the historiography of the French Encyclopedists; in *The Scarlet Letter*, the emergence of God's immanence. Evolution to higher and higher degrees of order push aside the rich potentiality of a world unformed.

Cooper's growing concern with order, of course, stems from different roots than Hawthorne's, but it is especially interesting, nonetheless. We may follow it as, in successive novels, he portrays Natty from old age to youth. (See, e.g., Roy Harvey Pearce, "The Leatherstocking Tales Re-examined," *SAQ*, 46 [1947], 524–36.) Cooper, in possession of his romance figure full-blown, searches out his history. Significantly, in Cooper's late work, the Littlepage Trilogy, romance has become simple rhetoric to enforce an historical claim against the rent-strikers, squatters, like the primitive Ishmael Bush, who were pressing their demands for the land Cooper's parents had socialized years before.

not yet given up altogether; we never do hear the sermon, never feel the effect of what we are only told is the "rich endowment" of Dimmesdale's voice. Indeed, his voice is "music." It "breathed passion and pathos" conveyed "entirely apart from its indistinguishable words" (p. 243). Perhaps, since the scaffold scene, Dimmesdale's message is so firmly established that Hawthorne need only mention it, and it may be taken as spoken—a procedure, in fact, that Hawthorne practices often, as we shall see, in *The Marble Faun*. More probably, however, Hawthorne remains to some degree resistant. He refuses to articulate an allegory he would wish still to struggle against. The sermon remains a message, but one Hawthorne does not wish to enforce. To some extent he attempts to start again, to recreate, in a sort of rear-guard action, the potential that existed in the beginning. But the attempt is doomed from the start, and generally, its failure may be read even as he tries it.

For example, Hawthorne duplicates his initial order of events. The sequence of chapters following the scaffold scene repeats the sequence before. First Hester is discussed, then Hester with Chillingworth, Hester with Pearl, Hester and Pearl with Dimmesdale, and so on. Here is what, in terms of our first chapter, I take to be a blatant "copy" of a given form, no genuine "rewriting." There is to be, presumably, a refocusing, a character reassessment, an attempt to reinvigorate the principals as figures other than allegorical. Hawthorne would give Hester new potential by converting her simple secret—the identities of her husband and lover—to an indefinable mystery of character. She is "strong . . . with a woman's strength" (p. 161). She is solitary. Brushing aside people who would accost her, "she laid her finger on the scarlet letter, and passed on" (p. 162). Dimmesdale, fixed firmly as a pawn in the working out of the story of sin, is endowed with a mysterious sympathy: "The very contiguity of his enemy, beneath

whatever mask the latter might conceal himself, was
enough to disturb the magnetic sphere of a being so
sensitive as Arthur Dimmesdale" (pp. 192–93). Like
Henry James, reacting, as I would maintain, to the
pressure of an inevitability, in his case socially determined, Hawthorne works against the very principle of
engaging genre he has otherwise espoused. He gives his
hero an "adventure of the mind," defines his existence
narcissistically as free of the very coercion he should
be attempting to reform.[20] Most blatantly of all, Hawthorne attempts to redefine Chillingworth. He becomes,
for a time, the sublimely blasphemous Satan, as the
nineteenth century saw Milton's Satan. He is a pathetic
version of Captain Ahab, intended, with his exclama-
tion points, to inspire the wonder all poetic theory attributed to the power of sublimity: "Yea, indeed!–he
did not err!–there was a fiend at his elbow! A mortal
man, with once a human heart, has become a fiend for
his especial torment!" (p. 172). Here, however, is
rather what R. P. Blackmur calls "putative statement,"[21]
no genuine portrait of sublimity, no fiendish magnificence clearly described, but an assertion that we are to
respond *as if* Chillingworth were magnificent, and that
Hawthorne may change at will, when it suits him. Indeed, as the allegory ends and the devil, in the face of
godliness, loses his majesty and withers away, Hawthorne, still struggling, converts him into a quasi-
Rumpelstiltskin figure, leaving behind him a pile of gold
and, at least with respect to Pearl, a life to be lived, as
it were, happily ever after. Hawthorne is clearly and

[20] James is often accused of failing to understand the pressures of an emerging industrial era. In going underground into
the mind, however, it is precisely such pressures to which he is
responding. James is as much a determinist as Dreiser concerning adventures of the body and, accordingly, he insists on pre-
serving at least one area of relative freedom.

[21] R. P. Blackmur on *Pierre*, "The Craft of Herman Melville:
A Putative Statement," in *The Lion and the Honeycomb: Essays
in Solicitude and Critique* (New York: Harcourt, Brace, 1955),
p. 140.

from a distance manipulating his story. He is hardly engaging it, as we have been led to expect he would. His struggle is lost.

With an instinct for self-preservation, therefore, Hawthorne separates himself altogether from the book, much as he escapes from metaphor in "The Custom-House." Aware of his inability to remain creative, of the final victory of allegory, he even surrenders his proper authority to the vision of his characters. No longer is he responsible for anything that occurs. The story that he presents to us in the first chapter as an especial gift, is now totally beyond his disposition. "Point of view," as James would use it—as Hawthorne himself would, in a related way, develop it in Kenyon in *The Marble Faun*— emerges as an oft-repeated technique. Chillingworth asserts Dimmesdale's sixth sense: " 'He has been conscious of me. He has felt an influence dwelling always upon him like a curse. He knew, by some spiritual sense,—for the Creator never made another being so sensitive as this . . .' " (p. 171). So, too, it is he—"unable to restrain a thrill of admiration too; for there was a quality almost majestic in the despair which she expressed" (p. 173)—who exhibits the wonder that we are supposed to feel at Hester's new mystery. When Chillingworth leaves we see Hester, not Hawthorne, asserting the devil archetype, "looking with a half-fantastic curiosity to see whether the tender grass of early spring would not be blighted beneath him" (p. 175). Even in the forest, a landscape chosen with such a manifest eye to its emblematic signification, it is "to Hester's mind," not Hawthorne's, that the wilderness "imaged not amiss the moral wilderness in which she had so long been wandering" (p. 183).

The end of the book, the final confession, as we have noted, by the laws of its now governing allegory, is inevitable. But Hawthorne manages to save himself for a further attempt at intimacy soon after. In a letter to Horatio Bridge he asserts that the book had somehow gotten beyond his control. It is too dark, darker than he had intended.[22] He washes his hands of it, in effect, and expresses confidence that his next effort will be brighter. Within *The Scarlet Letter*, one character, Pearl, manages a sketchy alternative to life defined by the scaffold. For her the "spell was broken." As, at once, a product of the New World who yet lives her life on the Continent, she perhaps integrates Hawthorne's attitude toward Europe with the possibility of existence in New England. But Hawthorne, here, is rather asserting his artistic intentions than performing them. By and large Hawthorne's involvement with the art of *The Scarlet Letter* has ceased. The satiric distance of "The Custom-House" returns:

"So Pearl—the elf-child,—the demon offspring, as some people, up to that epoch, persisted in considering her—became the richest heiress of her day, in the New World. Not improbably, this circumstance wrought a very material change in the public estimation; and, had the mother and child remained here, little Pearl, at a marriageable period of life, might have mingled her wild blood with the lineage of the devoutest Puritan among them all" (p. 261).

Again Hawthorne takes on the pedantic tone of the historian, collecting his documents ("a manuscript of old date, drawn up from the verbal testimony of individuals" [pp. 259–60]), weighing the available evidence ("In fine, the gossips of that day believed,—and Mr. Surveyor Pue, who made investigations a century later, believed,—and one of his recent successors in office, moreover, faithfully believes" [p. 262]), tying up all the loose ends. Again, this pedantry is associated with an

[22] Recounted in Hoeltje, p. 288. See, also, the Introduction to the *Centenary Edition*, p. xv. Hawthorne was much happier with his next attempt. Mark Van Doren, p. 172, quotes a subsequent letter to Bridge: *"The House of the Seven Gables*, in my opinion, is better than *The Scarlet Letter*. . . . I think it a work more characteristic of my mind, and more proper and natural for me to write."

overly mystic view of things: the gravestone, "so sombre is it, and relieved only by one ever-glowing point of light gloomier than the shadow"; and the motto, "On a Field, Sable, the Letter A, Gules!" (p. 264). The final series of alternative possibilities, the ambiguities as to the mark on Dimmesdale's breast, is one last attempt to dissolve the allegory, to involve the reader, as in "Wakefield," by forcing him to complete the writing, an attempt to return the now fully developed story to a matrix whose potential could perhaps be altered for intimacy. There is no room for that, of course, left in *The Scarlet Letter*, but *The House of the Seven Gables* is not yet begun.

FOUR

The House of the Seven Gables

THE SCARLET LETTER demonstrated conclusively, to Hawthorne, genre's coercive power. He appears, in that book, more Puritan than anywhere else because a Puritan schema, crowding out any potential for intimacy, enforces itself upon him. An allegory of the Fall directs the author's pen along inevitable allegorical lines. The ending, we have noted, attempts to dissolve a now hardened allegory into a matrix that may then be reshaped, but is unsuccessful. Accordingly, in *The House of the Seven Gables*, Hawthorne rather accepts from the start genre's intractability. No struggle with it is necessary, because the failure of struggling has been fully learned.

The Preface opens as a recapitulation of familiar literary theory:[1] "When a writer calls his work a Ro-

---

[1] Consider parallels throughout the Preface with, for example, such an established romance as Scott's *Waverley*. Thus Hawthorne: "The latter form of composition [the novel] is presumed to aim at a very minute fidelity, not merely to the possible, but to the probable and ordinary course of man's experience." Cf. Scott, *Waverley*, ch. 1: "Or again, if my Waverley had been entitled 'A Tale of the Times,' wouldst thou not, gentle reader, have demanded from me a dashing sketch of the fashionable world, a few anecdotes of private scandal thinly veiled, and if lusciously painted, so much the better?"

Again, Hawthorne: "The former [romance]—while, as a work of art, it must rigidly subject itself to laws, and while it sins unpardonably, so far as it may swerve aside from the truth of the human heart—has fairly a right to present that truth under circumstances, to a great extent, of the writer's own choosing or creation." Cf. Scott: "From this my choice of an era the understanding critic may further presage, that the object of my tale is more a description of men than manners." His subject is "those passions common to men in all stages of society, and which have alike agitated the human heart, whether it throbbed under the steel corslet of the fifteenth century, the brocaded

mance, it need hardly be observed that he wishes to claim a certain latitude, both as to its fashion and material, which he would not have felt himself entitled to assume, had he professed to be writing a Novel" (II, I). "It need hardly be observed" points up the conventionality of the definition. As in "The Custom-House," Hawthorne presents the inevitable language of his art. The presentations, however, serve widely different functions.

The Scarlet Letter is a reaction to the narcissism of "The Artist of the Beautiful." *Letter* sets forth convention to establish convention, advances it as an act of solidarity with the society that convention embodies. But *The House of the Seven Gables* responds to *The Scarlet Letter*. In it Hawthorne neither gives himself over to convention nor yet retreats to narcissism. He knows he is under a constraint he can neither evade nor reconstruct. He accepts it, but so fully that he never need submit to it. Rather he familiarizes it, abolishes its otherness, thereby cutting the ground of coercion out from under itself. Phrases like "is presumed to aim at," "to a great extent," "If he think fit, also," "He will be wise no doubt," and "He can hardly be said, however," all within a few sentences of each other, express the perfunctoriness of *House*'s aesthetics. The disposition of the nation to view all American writers as potential Scotts is admitted. Indeed, his own ambition to match the best of the "scribbling sons of John Bull,"[2] is admitted. It is a motive that begins internally in Haw-

---

coat of the eighteenth, or the blue frock and white dimity waistcoat of the present day."

Again, Hawthorne: "Many writers . . . with a moral" (see passage quoted below). Cf. Scott: "Some favourable opportunity of contrast . . . may serve at once to vary and to illustrate the moral lessons, which I would willingly consider as the most important part of my plan. . . ."

Stubbs traces the development of the conventions of romance theory from the eighteenth century to Hawthorne's time.

[2] See above, p. 39n.

thorne, then is externalized as an imperative therefore as much imposed as are cultural demands. But it is so natural, now—has been re-internalized to such a degree —as to be worth mentioning only in passing. Even the ostensibly repressive demand for morality—New England's demand and, as a New Englander, his own—may be acknowledged, because moralizing, though obligatory, is too easily performed: "Many writers lay very great stress upon some definite moral purpose, at which they profess to aim their works. Not to be deficient, in this particular, the Author has provided himself with a moral . . ." (p. 2). Convention has its way, and Hawthorne gives it its due. But it is very nearly his way, too. It is of little moment, its potency defused. Its power to coerce is obviated, incorporated in advance within the author himself.

Hawthorne now begins to defuse the potency of such coercion as the reader may feel as well. Much as social conventions form him, so, he acknowledges, expectations his own work creates may form the reader. In the closing paragraph of the Preface he seeks to contain the fears generated by the introduction to *The Scarlet Letter*:

"The Reader may perhaps choose to assign an actual locality to the imaginary events of this narrative. If permitted by the historical connection (which, though slight, was essential to his plan), the Author would very willingly have avoided anything of this nature. Not to speak of other objections, it exposes the Romance to an inflexible and exceedingly dangerous species of criticism, by bringing his fancy-pictures almost into positive contact with the realities of the moment. . . . He would be glad, therefore, if—especially in the quarter to which he alludes—the book may be read strictly as a Romance, having a great deal more to do with the clouds overhead, than with any portion of the actual soil of the County of Essex" (p. 3).

Here Hawthorne admits the concerns of the audience satirized in "The Custom-House."[3] He concedes the inevitability of satire. If he is to maintain his "historical connection," if he is not to return to the narcissism of his pre-*Scarlet Letter* days, social criticism may not altogether be eliminated. The work as an embodiment of culture, a disinterested presentation of the forms of society, becomes, necessarily, in interpretation—that is, the moment a reader begins to construe it from his particular, interested perspective—a cultural critique. And yet, as with genre in his own case, Hawthorne admits what is necessary only to forestall its action. If he cannot, perhaps, quite expect the reader to internalize the criticism—to criticize himself as a matter of course—he can, at any rate, discharge it of purpose of his own, deny there is, even in the satire, any hostile intention. The "Author," as he says, "would very willingly have avoided anything of this nature." "It has been no part of his object. . . ." "He would be glad, therefore, if . . . the book may be read strictly as a Romance. . . ."

I do not, of course, mean to deny that there is irony in Hawthorne's tone throughout these remarks. Attempting quite seriously to free *The House of the Seven Gables* for intimacy, he does allow himself the luxury of responding in kind to the reception of "The Custom-House." References to "the quarter to which he alludes" and "the actual soil of the County of Essex" cast doubt on the avowed fictionality of his scene. "Not to speak of

---

[3] Stewart, *Nathaniel Hawthorne*, p. 98, cites an attack in the Salem *Register* of March 21, 1850: "Hawthorne seeks to vent his spite . . . by small sneers at Salem, and by vilifying some of his former associates, to a degree of which we should have supposed any gentleman . . . incapable. . . . We almost began to think that Hawthorne had mistaken his vocation . . . he would have been more at home as a despicable lampooner. . . . This chapter has obliterated whatever sympathy was felt for Hawthorne's removal from office. . . . If we had any doubt before, we have not a single scruple remaining in regard to the full justification of the Administration in relieving him."

other objections, it . . . [brings] his fancy-pictures al-most into positive contact with the realities of the moment" is a playful postponement of the question of the reader's fear and an immersion, instead, in aes-thetic questions. Hawthorne toys with his audience, covertly indulges his hostility. I would argue, however, that even such indulgence serves to minimize the opera-tion of hostility in *The House of the Seven Gables* proper. Insofar as bitterness cannot be eliminated, Hawthorne plays it out in a place and persona he is careful to remove from the novel itself. There is a separation between the Preface and the rest of the book that differs widely from the close relation "The Custom-House," for example, bears to *The Scarlet Letter*. There is no pretense to discover the materials of the story in the Preface. Instead, its brevity—two pages—and abrupt-ness—"When a writer calls his work a Romance"—characterize a businesslike voice in sharp contrast to the leisurely, confidential tone of what follows. The per-sonal opening of "The Custom-House"—"It is a little remarkable, that . . . an autobiographical impulse should twice in my life have taken possession of me, in addressing the public"—is incorporated within the space of the novel itself: "Half-way down a by-street of one of our New England towns," "On my occasional visits," "The aspect of the venerable mansion has always af-fected me," "Familiar as it stands in the writer's recol-lection." Hostility is detached. It implicates an "I" in the Preface distinct from the "I" of the *House*. It is "carried off" before it ever takes hold in the fiction.

Indeed, even where the Preface seems to refer to certain material of the novel, it rather repeats it to de-personalize it. It defuses potential hostility while hos-tility yet remains potential. Consider Hawthorne's sum-mation: "He [the author] trusts not to be considered as unpardonably offending, by laying out a street that infringes upon nobody's private rights, and appropri-ating a lot of land which had no visible owner, and

building a house, of materials long in use for constructing castles in the air" (p. 3). "Appropriating" land with
"no visible owner" is a restatement of a significant
theme of the novel. It relates to the story of the Pyncheon inheritance, the deed to vast territories that no
longer has any force. It hardly introduces those themes,
however, separated as the Preface is. Rather, it stands
in their place. Concerns of the sort raised by "The
Custom-House" that threaten to continue in *The House
of the Seven Gables* proper, find their continuation, instead, in the Preface as it replicates *House*.

In the Preface the theme of ownership is closely
allied to the furor over Hawthorne's treatment of the
Salem Custom-House, his "castle" not quite safely
enough "in the air." But its appearance in *The House of
the Seven Gables* thereby is made free, is allowed to be
defined in a context independent of the pressure the
reaction to his last work has attached to it. The un-
owned land, for example, is perhaps an elaboration of
an economic theme in the book, of the question of
capitalism as *The Blithedale Romance* will further
discuss it: man's desire for property as opposed to
another need to live in a kind of commonality. Whatever it is, though, it may be so only because the Preface
has admitted in itself the pressure of existing meanings,
has intruded itself in what is otherwise a coercive continuity. Similarly, Hawthorne remarks that the "personages of the Tale . . . are really of the Author's own
making, or," once again, maintaining his irony, "at all
events, of his own mixing." The threat that Hawthorne's
attitude toward Jaffrey Pyncheon, in so many ways a
modernized version of the New England establishment
opposed in *The Scarlet Letter*, will obtrude on *Gables*,
is similarly deflected. Hostility toward Jaffrey, because
first acknowledged here, becomes, as it appears in
Gables, as we shall see, simple self-expression, directed
at no object at all. Hawthorne will not again be overwhelmed by rage at society, as he was in "The Artist of

the Beautiful," a disavowal made here when he abjures, as a general method, "sticking a pin through a butterfly." Hostility, instead, is admitted but bound to the preliminary matter. The Preface fixes, contains within itself, attitudes that threaten intimacy. It circumscribes them in an area outside the main body of the work. The space under the Seven Gables is preserved for romance.

The house, as Hawthorne describes it, begins in psychological and historical memories. It is associated with early days, both of the race and its individual members, a house "familiar to every town-born child" and rooted in "the annals of all New England." It unites, as we have discussed, therefore, both a private and a public image. Adversity is not excluded. The preservation of pleasure by denial of pain would constitute a narcissism, the creation of an insulated world, Hawthorne has abandoned long ago.[4] The house, rather, bears the traces as well of the "outward" life as the life "within." It is a house of "vicissitudes," of "storm and sunshine," that first world where self and other are as yet undifferentiated, a world of Thanatos and Eros in equilibrium. In the history of the house now one, now the other, takes control. Murder and love threaten to define the book now as a gothic, now as a sentimental, novel. Murder would abolish intimacy, sentimentality reduce it to the level of a cliché. But *The House of the Seven Gables* is neither gothic nor sentimental. It is a house in which conventional form, discharged of hostile intention, as we have seen, may be reconstructed. Hawthorne's *Love Letters* offer something of an analogue. By recasting forces in themselves dangerous, they create a balanced pastoral world. There the sterility of working in the Boston Custom-House constitutes but the threat of urban danger necessary to set up a pastoral world.[5] The avowals of an overwhelming affection but

[4] Cf. above, p. 80, the discussion of "Old Esther Dudley."
[5] *Love Letters of Nathaniel Hawthorne, 1839–1841 and 1841–1863*, 2 vols. (Chicago: The Society of the Dofobs, 1907). For a

respond to the urban threat. So, in the *House*, gothicism and sentimentality exist only in relation to each other, define a space together that neither murder nor love can define alone. Holgrave, would-be destroyer of houses, lives contained in a wing of the Gables. Phoebe, appalled by the very thought of destruction, is yet attracted to Holgrave.

Towards the end of the book the balance is broken down. The marriage of Holgrave and Phoebe, we shall be arguing, is an attempt to resolve in plot an equilibrium that is seen as stagnating. But for the bulk of the novel Hawthorne's narrative is carefully controlled. Struggle, dialectic, progress, indeed, of any sort, is subordinated to the realized balance of the Gables. As in the tiles of the Province House, story is spatialized. The "aspect of the venerable mansion" is an architectural equivalent of story, is "expressive . . . of the long lapse of mortal life, and accompanying vicissitudes that have passed within. Were these to be worthily recounted, they would form a narrative of no small interest and instruction, and possessing, moreover, a certain remarkable unity, which might almost seem the result of artistic arrangement" (p. 5). The shape of the house precedes all action as the novel's structural principle. Plot, as it will arise, is but elaboration of the house, enacting its "aspect."

Hawthorne has learned the lesson of *The Scarlet Letter*. No action issues here from the space to take control of the novel. All action begins, rather, when characters enter into it. On Hepzibah's first day in the store a woman "worn to death by a brute—probably a drunken brute—of a husband, and at least nine children" enters to buy some flour (p. 53). A story in a new mode, Thanatos in the instance, as Howells might call

---

discussion of the point concerning pastoral, see Frank Kermode, ed., *English Pastoral Poetry: From the Beginnings to Marvell* (London: George G. Harrap and Co., 1952), p. 14.

it, of a modern tragedy, enters the house and threatens to upset the balance of the romance. Soon after the woman leaves, however, a drunk whom Hepzibah conceives to be her husband arrives to buy some tobacco. The new mode is turned back on itself before it has the chance to develop; Thanatos is redefined in the house as fantastical. Coincidence disperses tragedy. Necessity, the inevitable, tragic wearing down of the woman to death, is cancelled. Romance is preserved.

It is noticeable how careful Hawthorne is, except at the close, to avoid allegorization. *The Scarlet Letter* is metaphor extended to allegory, but *The House of the Seven Gables*, to forestall limiting definitions of characters, rather delimits metaphor whenever it is used: ". . . her unwonted joy shrank back, appalled, as it were, and clothed itself in mourning; or it ran and hid itself, so to speak, in the dungeon of her heart . . ." (pp. 101–102). Qualified as it is by "as it were," "so to speak," and the choice presented by "or," the danger that the metaphor will enlarge itself is met from the start, and the "dungeon" fails permanently to surround. Soon "laughter" as well as "tears" come gushing from Hepzibah. Similarly, Holgrave tells Phoebe, "in this long drama of wrong and retribution, I represent the old wizard, and am probably as much of a wizard as ever he was" (p. 316). A metaphor is used to add mystical resonance to the character. Its job done, however, the metaphor is quickly removed from further action by presentation of what in contrast appears a reality: old Maule himself was no more a wizard than is a mesmeric dabbler of today.

An opposite case is metaphor functioning as ironic counterpoint to the reality. The consolations of mythic identification are exposed. When Hepzibah sighs, "indeed, her breast was a very cave of Aeolus" (p. 36), Hawthorne says. The comparison is blatantly excessive, the vehicle ridiculously incommensurate to the tenor. Again, when the shop-bell rings, "The maiden lady arose upon her feet, as pale as a ghost at cock-crow; for she was an enslaved spirit, and this the talisman to which she owed obedience. . . . The crisis was upon her! Her first customer was at the door!" (p. 42). Hyperbole keeps us conscious of the metaphoric nature of the metaphor, assures that it never becomes real.

Sometimes the metaphor is simply reduced to absurdity. Phoebe, a beautiful, health-giving flower, impregnates the air "with the perfume of garden-roses, pinks, and other blossoms of much sweetness." But "her petals sometimes drooped a little, in consequence of the heavy atmosphere about her" (p. 143). The image, in close compass, plays itself out. While, in the course of *The Scarlet Letter*, as we have seen, the allegorical existence of the characters deepens, Phoebe, as *The House of the Seven Gables* continues, ceases to be a stereotypical rose. Indeed, unlike the situation in *The Scarlet Letter*, allegorical identification is deliberately localized. Thus Jaffrey, in a single scene, may be associated with Comus, a New England witch, and King Log, and a new mythological tale may be invented around him: "It was he, you know, of whom it used to be said, in reference to his ogre-like appetite, that his Creator made him a great animal, but that the dinner-hour made him a great beast" (p. 275). As Barbara Hardy notes in another context, no single "trail of thematic imagery emerges." Rather a variety of images "crosses and overlaps and confuses classification."[6]

Hawthorne, then, delimits the potency of what was his ultimate limitation in *The Scarlet Letter*, metaphor extended and in control. In *The House of the Seven Gables* any number of metaphors may be employed, but no one ever takes over. The house itself is now a heart, now a head, a part of nature, and an artifact of culture. Metaphors are generated extemporaneously, as it were,

[6] "The Structure of Imagery: George Meredith's *Harry Richmond*," in *The Appropriate Form: An Essay on the Novel* (London: The Athlone Press, 1964), p. 92.

exist side by side in the house that, so far from con-
straining the nature and order of metaphor, is rather an
ur-metaphor in which metaphors of all sorts meet. It is
the place of Hawthorne's romance, as we have defined
that term, the point of purpose in celebration, embodying itself freely in any variety of forms, purpose at one
with, not subordinate to, its material.

We thus are far more closely in touch with Hawthorne uncoerced than we are in *The Scarlet Letter*. It
is for this reason that the personal tone, reserved in that
book, as we have noted, for "The Custom-House," can
be seen everywhere in *The House of the Seven Gables*.
The distance between teller and tale is abridged. Story,
which is found and which Hawthorne must struggle to
appropriate in *The Scarlet Letter*, here is from the start
informed by Hawthorne's presence. He is a "disembodied listener," hovering about the house, a self-
created Hawthorne observing his own existence, which
already is written into his subject.

Consider, for example, the abusive portrait of Hepzibah. A sixty-year-old lady is "Miss Hepzibah" rather
than "Miss Pyncheon." Though aged she must be treated, as she prepares to receive Clifford, as a young girl:
"Far from us be the indecorum of assisting, even in
imagination, at a maiden lady's toilet!" (p. 30). By the
logic of the story, formalistically interpreted, by the
disposition of events considered as self-sustaining, such
ridicule, if not completely gratuitous, is yet belabored.
As aristocrat, as New England lady, as representation
of any number of allegorical themes the book embodies,
Hepzibah might appropriately be criticized. But neither
her age nor her love for Clifford warrants abuse such as
this. At best, even if we choose to see her age as decayed
nobility and her love as misplaced emotion, love deliberately restricted to the aristocratic family, the abuse
is surely disproportionate to the offense. As Hawthorne
says: "Heaven help our poor old Hepzibah, and forgive
us for taking a ludicrous view of her position! . . . For

here—and if we fail to impress it suitably upon the reader, it is our own fault, not that of the theme—here is one of the truest points of melancholy interest that occur in ordinary life. It was the final term of what called itself old gentility" (p. 37).

Hawthorne's "ludicrous view" is supererogatory. In a manner of speaking it is no "view" at all but an imposition of himself on the object ostensibly viewed. It is no reaction but verges on what we might call psychological "expression." Responding to elements of the work conceived as embodying objects Hawthorne hates—say New England aristocracy—is, in accordance with our previous discussion, precluded by the Preface. But Hawthorne yet presents *in* the work, a hostility undirected *toward* the work: "She now issued forth, as would appear, to defend the entrance, looking, we must needs say, amazingly like the dragon which, in fairy tales, is wont to be the guardian over an enchanted beauty. . . . But we must betray Hepzibah's secret, and confess, that the native timorousness of her character even now developed itself, in a quick tremor, which, to her own perception, set each of her joints at variance with its fellow" (pp. 126–27).

The ridicule here is inexplicable in terms generated by the novel itself, and we may be tempted to turn to Hawthorne's psyche for a more ready key. As in "Old Esther Dudley," confrontation at the threshold is associated with sexual resistance. The house is a womb, and the protectress of the intimate childhood, indeed pre-natal, space cannot be forgiven for allowing penetration. Mother would defend her virginity. Hepzibah would bar Jaffrey's admission to the inner sanctum of the house. But her defense is mock defense and her ultimate failure weakness. Alternatively, as Hawthorne elsewhere conceives it, a mother's intercourse with a rival father yields, by a wish-fulfilling reversal, an ironic portrait of a maiden lady who never knew, "by her own experience, what love technically means" (p. 32).

And yet, a strictly psychological explanation is inadequate as well. If the hostility cannot be explained as proceeding from an independent work, neither may the work be seen as a projection of Hawthorne's hostility. More is involved than the simple narcissism of "Old Esther Dudley." Recall that Hawthorne by and large ended his short-story writing career precisely to engage, in *The Scarlet Letter*, the broader forms of his society. We continue to insist with him, that is, on the priority of the work. Hepzibah as New England, then—Hepzibah considered from the allegorical viewpoint embodied in the work as self-sustaining unit—confronts Hepzibah as Hawthorne's psyche, Hepzibah from the point of view of disproportionate abuse, across a single, unifying structure. The audience embodied in the work and the author who, in earlier works such as *The Scarlet Letter*, does indeed react, are brought sufficiently close to each other so as virtually to elide reaction. The work, very nearly, becomes a joint embodiment of a joint writer-reader.

The point is perhaps clearer in relation to the macabre presentation of Jaffrey's death. Jaffrey, as we mentioned earlier, though an authority figure of the sort opposed in *The Scarlet Letter*, cannot, except in a formal way, be associated with the figures of that novel. *The House of the Seven Gables*, however much of the form of *The Scarlet Letter* it employs, never brings along with it Hawthorne's hostility to the form, which is contained, instead, in the Preface. By and large, *The House of the Seven Gables* does not embody some "other," a society against which Hawthorne would define himself. On the other hand, neither are the terms that *The House of the Seven Gables* itself generates sufficient to explain Hawthorne's peculiar acerbity. Once again, Jaffrey, as in the case of Hepzibah, represents New England aristocracy and, like her, is to be abused. Moreover, he is a cheat and usurper, the chief obstacle to the happiness of every one of the other characters. All these, however, I would maintain, are rather attributes of a Jaffrey who never quite symbolizes any one of them. What in particular about Jaffrey Hawthorne is angry at, in what sense his many evil aspects come together, is difficult to determine. For example, aristocracy, in *The House of the Seven Gables*, is everywhere in decay. Jaffrey's potency, I would claim, is more than simply the last gasp of an impotent class. Nor is his psyche ever sufficiently delineated for us to read his meanness as psychological. There is never an approach to the inwardness, the struggle with guilt and anger that, even in Chillingworth, exists until his role takes over. It is as if Jaffrey from the start were cast in a role, the nature of which, however, is unclear. If we seek to allegorize Jaffrey, to interpret his character thematically, we have a case not of the rich "ambiguities" typical of, say Melville, but of what Yvor Winters might call "obscurantism." We need to approach Jaffrey in a wholly different way, not to resolve the evils attributed to him, but to accept as our point of departure Hawthorne's willingness to attribute any evil available.

Significantly, therefore, Hawthorne's hostility is notably personal. Compare Jaffrey's death with his ancestor's, recounted very early in the novel. In both cases the dead owner of the Gables sits in a chair in the house, failing to keep appointments he has previously made. Hawthorne describes the first event:

"One inauspicious circumstance there was, which awakened a hardly concealed displeasure in the breasts of a few of the more punctilious visitors. The founder of this stately mansion—a gentleman noted for the square and ponderous courtesy of his demeanor—ought surely to have stood in his own hall, and to have offered the first welcome to so many eminent personages as here presented themselves. . . . 'It is time that the good Colonel came forth to greet his friends [remarked the

Lieutenant Governor] . . . since he is so much behind-hand, I will give him a remembrancer myself!' " (pp. 12–14).

There is continuity here between the voice of the narrator and the voices of the characters in the scene. It is the "visitors" who are displeased, the Lieutenant Governor who is angry. Hawthorne, remarking that the circumstance is inauspicious, asserting the dictum that the builder of a house should be prompt to the house-warming, speaks but as the consciousness of the wait-ing community. His voice is the voice of the people, or, more properly, the voice of the scene considered inde-pendent of Hawthorne's psyche, the voice generated by the scene as requiring a narrator whose tone is there-fore congruous with it.

In contrast, the communities attending Jaffrey's ap-pearance are removed from the house. The narrator, beyond expressing their impatience, uses the impa-tience to vaunt a hatred that expresses him. The com-munities themselves and Jaffrey's business with them, are as much created on the spot as vehicles of Haw-thorne's hostility as they are a milieu legitimized by the larger demands of the book. Jaffrey's memoranda, it is true, include a number of events that function largely as representative of the sort of action he would seem to perform on a typical day: meeting his stock broker, ordering trees for his country seat, making a political contribution. Another event, the gathering of the party to choose a candidate for governor, while not typical, is perhaps a logical culmination of Jaffrey's career. But his intention to replace the cracked tombstone of his dead wife proceeds from two sources. In particular, his casual attitude toward his wife and his happiness with her death are feelings so closely associated with the theme of familial connections important to *The House of the Seven Gables* as a whole that reference to the tombstone for the first time this late in the book is a manifest compromise between generic considerations and demands external to genre. The whole event is generated both by aesthetic requirements of the novel as self-sustaining and by psychic requirements of the novel as asserting its author.

Even more extraordinary is Jaffrey's intention to buy a piece of real estate adjoining the Pyncheon property that originally belonged to Maule's garden. The connection with the plot's dominating concern—Jaffrey's attempt to recover the lost Pyncheon fortune and the relation of the Pyncheon fortune to the Maules from whom a part of it was stolen—is blatant. As with the tombstone incident, however, the action serves a double purpose. It furthers a theme and is a lash used to beat the dead Jaffrey. It is continuous with the rest of the novel, but a counter for hostility beyond such continuity. It is brought in at will, uncoerced, and rapidly dismissed when the hostility has run its course. Plot, here, for Hawthorne, embodies allegorical themes and provides the occasion for self-expression, the opportunity to generate incidents that at once relate to the incidents of the book and are informed by a meaning beyond them.

Hawthorne, then, is at his best, using his art most effectively. He neither coerces nor is coerced by it. It is his own and other both, which is to say the distinction between self and other is breaking down. Hawthorne speaks to Jaffrey directly: it is a sign of a new, closer relation between author and his material. The characteristic speech of the chapter, in opposition to the neutral stance of the earlier death scene, is apostrophe. The "ancient patrimony," even, is "our" patrimony, the world "our universe." Hawthorne and Jaffrey are closely related. As with Hawthorne and Hepzibah, the Oedipal allegorization perhaps latent in any narrative of a man or woman described as older is validated on a personal level. Hawthorne brings it manifestly into play at the very beginning of the scene. Back to the Gables "does our story now betake itself, like an owl, bewildered in the daylight, and hastening back to his hollow tree" (p. 268). The story of the dead Jaffrey is an "owl," to be associated, accordingly, with that other "owl," Hepzibah, as Hawthorne calls her in the previous chapter, at the moment when she abandons her protection of the "hollow" for her flight with Clifford. The sexual implications are continued in Jaffrey's first projected engagement: "Yes; in a score of drawing-rooms, he would be more than welcome. Mamma would advance to meet him, with outstretched hand; the virgin daughter, elderly as he has now got to be—an old widower, as he smilingly describes himself—would shake up the cushion for the Judge, and do her pretty little utmost to make him comfortable" (p. 269). Presumably, "elderly as he has now got to be" modifies "the Judge." But the odd inversion of the sentence allows it, ambiguously, to mean that the virgin daughter is as old as he. Once again, here is Jaffrey, welcomed by a "Mamma" related to an ancient virgin who has failed to protect her space. He penetrates and dies, and Hawthorne, in both joy and anguish, vaunts over his dead body.

And yet, the point is not that *The House of the Seven Gables* is a private mythology, the projection of Hawthorne's mind. Jaffrey and Hepzibah, indeed their action and all the actions of the book, exist independently of Hawthorne—as elaborations of his psyche, surely, but as elaborations objectified outside the psyche, *parole* as an instance of *langue*. In *The Scarlet Letter* we presented a model of Hawthorne interacting with a form either social from the start or, in the process of the narrative, socialized. In *The House of the Seven Gables* the model still applies, but the circle of interaction is drawn tight, the circumference reduced to center. There is no beginning to the creation of *The House of the Seven Gables*. Arbitrarily we may start with the mind or the work—the mind, for example, projecting a form to which it responds, which response it projects, to which projection it responds again, which continued response it continues to project, and so on. Such ostensibly descriptive passages as "its quaint exterior . . . grew black in the prevalent east-wind," "the very timbers were oozy, as with the moisture of a heart," "The deep projection of the second story gave the house such a meditative look," are, more properly, a description of Hawthorne's reaction to the object "described."

We have an example of the sort of "expressionism" known in painting as "Die Neue Sachlichkeit," "the New Objectivity," expressionism that is objective as well. The subject portrayed, the event stylized, is the event as style has already constructed it. To return to literary terms, we have a conception of art as a kind of interior Aristotelianism. A drama, as modern psychology elaborates on Aristotle, provides a rhythm with which the reader associates his own concerns.[7] A tragic rhythm purges unpleasant associations. A comic rhythm resolves them. In *The House of the Seven Gables*, however, the writer himself has reacted to what he has written. The book incorporates Hawthorne's own response to it. In fact, no purgation is possible. No scapegoat is sent to Azazel, because the goat and the self are indistinguishable. Our continuing interest in the problem of "Who Killed Judge Pyncheon?" as one critic has put it,[8] is a measure of our uneasiness over precisely this point. Jaffrey never is killed, but arbitrarily is said to die. Hawthorne may not destroy Jaffrey, because Hawthorne *is* Jaffrey, or invested in him. Murder is impossible, suicide the only option. Action integrated with the self never carries off hostility, but only exposes it. Narrative turns in on itself, uncovering the self at

[7] Norman N. Holland, *The Dynamics of Literary Response* (New York: Oxford Univ. Press, 1968), p. 52. See, too, Lesser, p. 250.

[8] Alfred H. Marks, "Who Killed Judge Pyncheon? The Role of the Imagination in *The House of the Seven Gables*," PMLA, 71 (1956), 355–69.

the heart of narrative. Writer and written are one. The tyranny of genre fades. The work approaches pure self-expression, expression of the self.

A certain intimacy with his material, then, replaces the distance of interpretation for Hawthorne. Symbols, in *The House of the Seven Gables*, contain their own explanations. Phoebe, Clifford finds, is an "interpretation . . . brought warmly home to his conception." The chicken, as Holgrave says, is "a symbol of the life of the old house; embodying its interpretation, likewise, although an unintelligible one, as such clues generally are" (p. 152). Identity is its own meaning, subsuming within itself the terms of human explanation. Action and interpretation of action are one. The event as object unites with its perceiver. Interpretation interprets drama, which itself but dramatizes the interpretation, which interprets the dramatization, and so on.

Consider a discussion between Hepzibah and Uncle Venner: " 'Yes!—Phoebe is a nice girl,' said Hepzibah, with a scowl of austere approbation. 'But, Uncle Venner, you have known the family a great many years. Can you tell me whether there ever was a Pyncheon whom she takes after?' " (p. 82). Here is a particular action in the novel, a dialogue on the relative merits of aristocrats and plebeians. It but enacts, however, a previous assessment: "As to Phoebe's not being a lady, or whether she were a lady or no, it was a point perhaps difficult to decide, but which could hardly have come up for judgement at all, in any fair and healthy mind" (p. 80). In turn the assessment is but an explanation of a previous monologue: " 'What a nice little body she is! If she could only be a lady, too!—but that's impossible! Phoebe is no Pyncheon. She takes everything from her mother!' " (p. 79). The progress continues. The monologue dramatizes a previous explanation—"by assuming that these active and forcible qualities are incompatible with others, which they choose to deem higher and more important . . . [an awkward person like Hepzibah] was well content to acknowledge Phoebe's vastly superior gifts as a shopkeeper." This explains yet an earlier drama— " 'Was not that well done?' asked Phoebe laughing, when the customer was gone. 'Nicely done, indeed, child!' answered Hepzibah. 'I could not have gone through with it nearly so well. As you say, it must be a knack that belongs to you on the mother's side' " (p. 79). And so it goes on.[9] The passages quoted are contained within a few pages. They are too close together to dismiss as a simple extension of a theme across the novel. The rapid alternation of drama and explanation tends, rather, to superimpose one on the other, to contract rather than extend the message. Practically speaking, of course, the book must start somewhere. But we have, again, that circle of mind and work whose only beginning is arbitrary.

On the whole, the reflexive nature of the book is particularly notable. Characters react to one another and to the objects around them as to themselves. We find Hepzibah "murmuring, in an undertone, as if speaking rather to her own heart than to Phoebe" (p. 103) and Clifford reflecting to himself but loudly enough to be overhead (p. 106). Hepzibah finds Phoebe in her heart, and Clifford does not distinguish between himself and the world. Clifford's delight in the garden's tiny hummingbirds is termed "miniature enthusiasm," and his reaction to Phoebe "seemed rather a perception, or a sympathy, than a sentiment belonging to himself as an individual" (p. 142). There is no relation of this thing to that. Subject and object are one.

Communication, not surprisingly, is, therefore, by silence or sound, almost never signification. Properly speaking, communication, the generic necessity of language, which, as we discussed in the first chapter,

---

[9] The chain actually continues even further: " 'Do not trouble yourself . . . ' " (p. 78) dramatizes "It is very queer . . . to confront a customer" (pp. 77–78), which explains " 'What a nice little housewife . . . ' " (p. 77).

Hawthorne willy-nilly must employ, is bypassed for a more direct communion. Phoebe is necessary to Clifford: "Not that he could ever be said to converse with her, or often manifest, in any other very definite mode, his sense of a charm in her society. But, if she were a long while absent, he became pettish. . . . Phoebe's presence, and the contiguity of her fresh life to his blighted one, was usually all that he required" (p. 138). Or he listens to Hepzibah's "emphasis, which he seemed to detect without any reference to the meaning." Her voice sounds as if it "had been dyed black; or—if we must use a more moderate simile—this miserable croak, running through all the variations of the voice, is like a black silken thread, on which the crystal beads of speech are strung, and whence they take their hue. Such voices have put on mourning for dead hopes; and they ought to die and be buried along with them!" (p. 135).

Words at their best, in *The House of the Seven Gables*, express; they do not denote. The gap between what words say and the people who say them is dissolved. Language as means to effect an interchange among people otherwise apart becomes language as celebration of a union already achieved. Where language does function denotatively, sufficient gloss is generally provided so that any interpretation of what it denotes is included within the denotation itself. The "rank weeds" in Maule's garden are "*symbolic of* the transmitted vices of society" [my italics]. The interpreting reader sees his interpretation in the object he would interpret. His reading is anticipated, his approach to the object included within the object. Similarly, in Phoebe's circle, "it was regarded as by no means improper for kinsfolk to visit one another, without invitation." Yet, "in consideration of Miss Hepzibah's recluse way of life" and, more importantly, the New England reader's own sense of propriety, "a letter had actually been written" (p. 69). The reader's response—his own shock at what Phoebe almost does—much as the writer's elsewhere, is written in.

The intimacy advanced in *The Scarlet Letter*, then, approaches its destination. The writer is at one with materials in which the reader is fully constituted. Reader and writer are exposed—uncovered, uncoerced, in the house. The bulk of the book is celebration of purpose fulfilled. There is little real movement. Language accumulates rather than develops:

". . . a rusty, crazy, creaky, dry-rotted, damp-rotted, dingy, dark, and miserable old dungeon . . ." (p. 261).

". . . this desolate, decaying, gusty, rusty, old house of the Pyncheon family . . ." (p. 28).

"Inaudible, consequently, were poor Miss Hepzibah's gusty sighs. Inaudible, the creaking joints of her stiffened knees. . . . And inaudible, too . . . that almost agony of prayer . . ." (p. 30).

Detail duplicates itself. The decayed hens recapitulate the decaying race of Pyncheons, Jaffrey reproduces his Puritan ancestor, the Holgrave-Phoebe plot matches the Matthew Maule-Alice Pyncheon tale. The town pump of "A Rill from the Town-Pump" is split into a man and a metaphor: "And Uncle Venner, who had studied the world at street-corners, and at other posts equally well adapted for just observation, was as ready to give out his wisdom as a town-pump to give water" (p. 155). Imagination is fertile and reflexive. Incident multiplies in its own image, leading back into itself. *The House of the Seven Gables* goes nowhere, which is at once its virtue and the reason why, ultimately, it fails.

The time comes when a book must end. At such a time our description of reflexiveness and intimacy may be seen, negatively, as a description of stagnation. There is some evidence, even, to suggest that Hawthorne himself saw it so. *The Scarlet Letter*, as we have discussed, virtually wrote itself: ". . . being all in one tone," Hawthorne remarks, "I had only to get my pitch, and could then go on interminably." But *The House of the Seven Gables* "requires more care and thought than the 'Scarlet Letter.' " As Hawthorne neared the time for ending it, he seemed especially to find difficulty: "There are points where a writer gets bewildered, and cannot form any judgment of what he has done, nor tell what to do next."[10] There is a delicate reciprocity in *The House of the Seven Gables*. Work and artist are in equilibrium. Eros and Thanatos, self and other, are one. But Hawthorne's bewilderment, I would suggest, is the beginning of the breakdown of union. The pressure of an end upsets the equilibrium. Self and other declare themselves. Their resolution, written, otherwise, everywhere in the middle, is thrust to the end. They are separated now, composing a dialectic whose progress to resolution is the plot. Hawthorne, caught, I believe, at the moment of the quotation, in one turn of the progress, for a while is lost in himself. The self, unchecked by form external to self, expanded to include every "other" as part of itself, disperses in an accumulation of assimilated and assimilating detail. Eros casts out Thanatos. Clifford nearly jumps from his window into the stream of humanity. The multi-identitied Holgrave threatens to continue in an endless succession of roles.

To counteract dispersion, strategies of miniaturization are employed. Hepzibah is caricatured as a scowl and Jaffrey as a smile (p. 223). The most diffuse Clifford is first presented, quite literally, as a "miniature, done in Malbone's most perfect style" (p. 31). The treatment of most of the characters as quaint or eccentric is a means of sharply defining their individuality in a house through which they are otherwise dissolved.[11]

[10] Quoted in the introduction to the *Centenary Edition*, pp. xvii–xviii.

[11] Cf. Northrop Frye, "Dickens and the Comedy of Humors," in Roy Harvey Pearce, ed., *Experience in the Novel*, English Institute Essays (New York: Columbia Univ. Press, 1968), pp. 49–81. The attempt to control the subversive energy of the hid-

More significantly, miniaturization controls, by narrowing its sphere of power, the hostility by which the self inevitably asserts itself against dissolution. Hawthorne, revolting from the pressure of Eros, but containing the response of Thanatos, fixes the "sultry, dog-day heat" that Jaffrey "diffused" (p. 119) in Holgrave's "sunshine" art. Similarly, he elsewhere reduces the man to his "gold-headed cane" which "had it chosen to take a walk by itself, would have been recognized anywhere as a tolerably adequate representative of its master" (p. 56).

Ultimately, however, the book cannot maintain itself. For a long while the action does manage not to progress.[12] Indeed, only with great reluctance does Hawthorne even tell a story: "Our story must therefore await Miss Hepzibah at the threshold of her chamber. . . . Will she now issue forth over the threshold of our story? Not yet, by many moments. . . . Now, she is almost ready. Let us pardon her one other pause. . . . All this time, however, we are loitering faint-heartedly on the threshold of our story. In very truth, we have an invincible reluctance to disclose what Miss Hepzibah Pyncheon was about to do" (pp. 30–34). Hawthorne would linger in intimacy, would remain at the "threshold," in equilibrium. To begin is, inevitably, to end, and he would delay the end as long as possible.

---

den world of Thanatos and Eros fixates character, produces "humors," people obsessed by a single trait or phrase.

[12] Most critics find this lack of progress a fault. They precisely reverse what I take to be the strengths and weaknesses of the book. Arvin, pp. 212–13, is representative: "The scene is set elaborately . . . the lines are drawn and the colors disposed with the last subtlety; all the properties are in exquisite keeping, and the lights are adjusted and readjusted with marvellous atmospheric skill; but the action, in the midst of this impeccable 'atmosphere,' is halting, torpid, and badly emphasized . . . what happens momentously is painfully out of proportion to what is so copiously told. . . . There are plenty of 'scenes,' to be sure: but the curtain rises and falls upon them too abruptly, and the principle of coherence among them is less dramatic than pictorial."

Holgrave, stabilized at a threshold of his own, exhibits the dilemma most clearly. It is a moment of love on the brink of death. Proposing to Phoebe in a room adjoining the one in which Jaffrey lies dead, he is reluctant to take her outside the house: "Neither was he in haste, like her, to betake himself within the precincts of common life. On the contrary, he gathered a wild enjoyment—as it were, a flower of strange beauty, growing in a desolate spot, and blossoming in the wind—such a flower of momentary happiness he gathered from his present position" (p. 305). Life and death, self and other, join in a "momentary happiness" that may at any point break down. And, indeed, sooner or later Holgrave must bring the situation to a head. Sooner or later Hawthorne must stop writing. He must define his work as self against other so that he may resolve it and put it to a stop. Having gotten us into the house, that is, having united us with it, Hawthorne must now get us out. Three incidents in the second half of the book constitute a sort of progress away from *House*. They are an argument about the possibility of writing in a different way, indeed, at certain points, an argument about not writing at all.

The telling of the Alice Pyncheon story is an idealization of art as Hawthorne had thought to use it. Holgrave narrates to Phoebe. Here is courtship through story of the kind that won Hawthorne the heart of Sophia Peabody and that he would use to win his readers as well. The portrait of Holgrave is a fine parody of typical American authorship or even of Hawthorne's own as the young writer of *Fanshawe*. His work is loaded with dialect—"'Don't know what Massa wants!' answered Scipio"—and wherever possible, packed with excitement, containing "a good deal of action to the parts capable of being developed and exemplified in that manner." But essentially Holgrave's method is much the atmospherical one of the mature Hawthorne, communicating in an interanimated space: "A veil was beginning to be muffled about her [Phoebe], in which she could behold only him, and live only in his thoughts and emotions" (p. 211). Its effect is not to present a message, but to elicit a certain generalized sympathy: ". . . though I don't remember the incidents quite distinctly [Phoebe says], yet I have an impression of a vast deal of trouble and calamity . . ." (p. 212). Holgrave's success, however, is an exercise in wish-fulfillment, the accomplishment of Hawthorne's career-long effort: "He now observed that a certain remarkable drowsiness (wholly unlike that with which the reader possibly feels himself affected) had been flung over the senses of his auditress" (p. 211). The author's intrusion admits of a failure that the surrogate avoids.

But Holgrave abandons his achievement. His courtship is Hawthorne's demonized—literally insofar as he has demon blood, figuratively because it would master a "free and virgin spirit"—and therefore undesirable. Hawthorne, through Holgrave, may thus reject a success only briefly his and be rewarded for the non-sacrifice: "Let us, therefore . . . concede to the Daguerreotypist the rare and high quality of reverence for another's individuality. Let us allow him integrity, also, forever after to be confided in; since he forbade himself to twine that one link more, which might have rendered his spell over Phoebe indissoluble" (p. 212). The self claims "integrity," places itself, that is, against the dispersion of self in atmosphere out of equilibrium. Holgrave respects Phoebe's individuality, her otherness, and is, paradoxically, rewarded with intimacy—"forever to be confided in."

The second incident, Clifford's flight, goes a step beyond abandonment of atmosphere to assume a posture, later exploded, of intimacy outside atmosphere actually achieved. Clifford adopts a transcendentalism that is a positive program for life without houses. Interestingly, Clifford's flight poses the problem of individuality from an opposite perspective. The argument progresses, but the metaphors shift. The assault on atmosphere is maintained, but atmosphere represents, in this action, character assimilated rather than assimilating. The house, for Clifford, is the reverse of Holgrave's space, that is of space made all self: it is a space in which the self is made all other.

Clifford leaves: "The soul needs air; a wide sweep and frequent change of it. Morbid influences, in a thousand-fold variety, gather about hearths, and pollute the life of households. There is no such unwholesome atmosphere as that of an old home, rendered poisonous by one's defunct forefathers and relatives! I speak of what I know!" (p. 261).

Here is a conception of the house much as in *Legends of the Province-House*, but negatively drawn. It is a spatialization of historical being seen, now, as restrictive. Clifford, however, will not be restricted. He presents a vision, instead, of unencumbered humanity, of life outside houses. He would live in the air, open and free. He speaks of the telegraph as a medium for instantaneous communication of love messages. It makes technologically possible unlimited intimacy, life in the Oversoul, of the sort Hawthorne had renounced in "The Custom-House": " 'Is it a fact—or have I dreamt it—that, by means of electricity, the world of matter has become a great nerve, vibrating thousands of miles in a breathless point of time? Rather, the round globe is a vast head, a brain, instinct with intelligence! Or, shall we say, it is itself a thought, nothing but thought, and no longer the substance which we deemed it?' " (p. 264). "Substance" is "thought," existence "a breathless point of time." With forefathers rejected, with houses denied, time and space vanish. Clifford would live "everywhere and nowhere," as Hawthorne puts it elsewhere (p. 261).

Such an existence, however, such boundlessness, is to be resisted as strongly as existence limited by forefathers. In any case, it is untenable. Limitation cannot be overleaped. Clifford denies his past, yet his future, by a sort of return of the repressed, becomes his past in reverse. His reveries are but memories projected onto the future: "'You are aware, my dear Sir—you must have observed it, in your own experience—that all human progress is in a circle; or, to use a more accurate and beautiful figure, in an ascending spiral curve. While we fancy ourselves going straight forward, and attaining, at every step, an entirely new position of affairs, we do actually return to something long ago tried and abandoned . . .'" (p. 259). History can never be abolished. It must be fairly owned and dealt with or it will take over. The House, which is "everywhere" to Hepzibah, set "phlegmatically down on whatever spot she glanced at," is there, when the couple alights, in the broken church and "venerably black" farm-house "with a roof sloping downward from the three-story peak" that first greet them.

The third incident, Jaffrey's death, therefore, returns us to Hawthorne's failure in the house. It acknowledges the defeat of space, the end of intimacy in art, thus pointing toward a new conception of writing. The scene attempts to sum up the book in order that Hawthorne may leave it. The struggle, so long balanced, of life and death—the house as self and the house as other—comes to an apocalyptic end. Each force is intensified, and each, in the process, turns into its opposite. But there is no longer any middle possibility that would stabilize the reversal. Everything is in extremity. Hawthorne is found "Indulging our fancy." Indeed, the "quiver of the moonbeams" provides what he tells us in "The Custom-House" is the ideal condition for his imagination to function in.[13] Significantly, the moonbeams "are re-

---

[13] *The Scarlet Letter*, p. 35: "If the imaginative faculty refused to act at such an hour, it might well be deemed a hopeless case. Moonlight, in a familiar room, falling so white upon the carpet, and showing all its figures so distinctly,—making every object so minutely visible, yet so unlike a morning or noontide visibility,—is a medium the most suitable for a romance-writer to get acquainted with his illusive guests."

flected in the looking-glass." His imagination, that is, has only itself to delimit it. No "other" coerces it. He has "lost the power of restraint and guidance." Unbounded, refusing to restrict himself as Holgrave did, he fills his house. And yet, what his imagination produces is one more of Hawthorne's historical tableaux, a danse macabre of vexed Puritan ancestors. It is the generic other of his career, an embodiment of a disapproving New England culture. In much the same way, at the level of character, Jaffrey occupies the house himself. He has displaced the other residents, turned the Gables into the locus of his being. And yet, Jaffrey is dead, and the signs of his mortality are the forefathers in whose footsteps he now follows. The ghost of Jaffrey joins them in peering at the picture frame. Jaffrey's life, his attempt to recover the lost Pyncheon property, has been but an imitation of the lives of his fathers.

There is no question, I think, of a union of opposites here. Self and other are at war, and between the two of them the universe disintegrates:

"Meanwhile the twilight is glooming upward out of the corners of the room. The shadows of the tall furniture grow deeper, and at first become more definite; then, spreading wider, they lose their distinctness of outline in the dark, gray tide of oblivion. . . . Fainter and fainter grows the light. . . . An infinite inscrutable blackness has annihilated sight! . . . and we, adrift in chaos, may hearken to the gusts of homeless wind, that go sighing and murmuring about, in quest of what was once a world!" (pp. 276–77).

Home is lost. Space is abandoned and with it all attempts to achieve intimacy in space:

"And, hark! the shop-bell rings. After hours like these latter ones, through which we have borne our heavy tale, it is good to be made sensible that there is a living world, and that even this old, lonely mansion retains some manner of connection with it. We breathe more

freely, emerging from Judge Pyncheon's presence into
the street before the seven gables" (p. 283).

Hawthorne, though he would claim the house yet
has some relation to the world outside, is easier now
that he has left it. He would leave the work for the
world. As Holgrave's art eventuates in marriage outside
art, so Hawthorne would turn his work from an end,
complete in itself, to an instrument of a world beyond.
Hawthorne's life in the work is subordinated to his life
outside. What we have called interior Aristotelianism is
externalized: through the agency of plot, by identification with a fiction for purposes not of union, not of
inserting the self in it, but of catharsis, of purgation of
a self with which the fiction may never, finally, be
united, Hawthorne would turn Holgrave's success into
his own.

The ending redefines the book according to plot:
" 'His [Jaffrey's] own death [says Holgrave], so like that
former one, yet attended with none of those suspicious
circumstances, seems the stroke of God upon him, at
once a punishment for his wickedness, and making
plain the innocence of Clifford. But this flight—it dis-
torts everything! He may be in concealment, near at
hand. Could we but bring him back, before the discovery of the Judge's death, the evil might be rectified' "
(p. 304).

Three separate endings are offered: the end as
Jaffrey's death, the end as Clifford's flight after Jaffrey's
death, the end as Clifford's return after his flight. Each
ending would reshape the book in a different way.[14]
Hawthorne, no longer invested in what he writes, will
write anything to accomplish a goal that is beyond
writing. The middle in which he has luxuriated, from
which, for so long, he would not get out, the middle,

[14] Kermode, *The Sense of an Ending*, discusses controlling
"end-fictions," e.g., p. 46: ". . . plotting presupposes and
requires that an end will bestow upon the whole duration and
meaning."

indeed, that so successfully for a while resisted the pressures of development toward anything beyond it-self, is reconceived as a stage in the progress of a form which develops toward an end. Of course, the develop-ment Hawthorne chooses is the love story. In the inti-macy Holgrave and Phoebe achieve in marriage, he provides us with a comic catharsis, a rhythm that re-solves our personal discomforts and integrates us into society. The plot is the typical Aristotelian structure Frye defines, in fact, as comedy.[15] The obstructing father-figure (Jaffrey and the original Pyncheon) pre-cipitates the protagonist's (young Maule's) descent into death (the house) and loss of identity (Holgrave), eventuating in a rediscovery of identity (Maule) and the formation of a new society out of the ruins of the old (marriage of Maule and Pyncheon). The ending, of course, as most critics agree, is forced.[16] It springs not from the discovery of intimacy but from the desire, in the face of alienation, to assert intimacy's existence nevertheless. It is so severely external to Hawthorne that no catharsis is ever really achieved. It is more a reaction to failure than a claim of success, a spurious substitution of wish for fact. But it points to a new direction in Hawthorne's art. *The Blithedale Romance* will carry him further in that direction.

[15] Frye, *A Natural Perspective: The Development of Shake-spearean Comedy and Romance* (New York: Columbia Univ. Press, 1965), pp. 73–79.

[16] Marcus Cunliffe, "*The House of the Seven Gables*," in *Haw-thorne Centenary Essays*, p. 85, summarizes the argument, though disagreeing somewhat with it: "Some critics think that last chapter of *The Seven Gables* as inappropriately jolly as the closing section of *Huckleberry Finn*. The denouement reminds one exasperated commentator [Von Abele, p. 58] of Artemus Ward's account of the 'Osowatomie Brown' show: 'Tabloo—Old Brown on a platform, pintin upards, the staige lited up with red fire. Goddiss of Liberty also on platform, pintin upards. A dutchman in the orkestry warbles on a base drum. Curtin falls. Moosic by the band.' "

FIVE

The Blithedale Novel

THE HOUSE OF THE SEVEN GABLES is a climactic moment in the progress to intimacy. The narrator joins with his narrative and with the culture narrative embodies. Self and other unite; purpose and genre are one. Conflict is resolved before it begins. Genre assimilated to purpose, purpose made genre, is a work with no direction in which to go, a work without beginning and without end. But *The House of the Seven Gables* must end; the book must come to a close. A technical problem, a necessity of printing that the work cannot integrate, stands as the ultimate limitation of the work's success. It is a limitation external to *House* and irreconcilable with the very limitlessness which the book otherwise achieves. It is the force of a world outside the work, a world unreconstructible in it. At the end of *The House of the Seven Gables*, as we have seen, Hawthorne attempts to assimilate this world, too. He would incorporate it in the work by regarding the end as the inevitable conclusion of tensions he now chooses to see as dominating the work. He would return to the dialectic of his career up to this point, reconstitute self and other as terms in an opposition which may seem to generate an end. Holgrave and Phoebe become the focus of the novel. Death and love—principles that are undifferentiated in an integrated world but that separate out in a world in which self and other are disunited—are resuscitated in conflict. But the story of Holgrave and Phoebe is forced, unbelievable. Such conflict as is possible in the work has been concluded, and any revival of it is but a rehearsal of action already successfully resolved. The assimilable world has been assimilated, the reconstructible self reconstructed. After such unity as *The House of the Seven Gables* has achieved, dialectic is no longer possible. The work as union of purpose and genre is complete, apart from a world with which it can never, in its own turn, unite.

Here is the abortive conclusion of Hawthorne's development, its ultimate boundary. To abandon *The House of the Seven Gables*, as Hawthorne must, is to enter a world in which intimacy may no longer be established. Literature itself, no longer the world entire, is but one object in a universe it can never comprehend. Accordingly, *The Blithedale Romance* is the start of writing in a different mode. Its author is a man whose purpose, fulfilled within its recently discovered limits, is non-existent in his present world. Here is the creation of a Hawthorne undirected toward, uninterested in, the very work he produces. It is the origin of a subjectivity free of the work that until now has in part defined it, a subjectivity defined, instead, by the author's very freedom from such definition. The author's work, neither any longer expressing, nor yet, since he has left it, coercing him, is an artifact he may disinterestedly observe. In *The Marble Faun*, indeed, disinterest itself becomes the means toward such intimacy as Hawthorne may again achieve. But the distinction of *The Blithedale Romance* is its lack, despite its serious moral and social concerns, of what we may term any "interest" at all.

Hawthorne leaves his space. As in the Preface to *The House of the Seven Gables* he invokes Scott. The invocation, however, is nostalgic. Conventions whose coercive pressure had to be familiarized in *House*, pass through the intimate area of the familiar to the distance of non-relatedness. Insofar as Hawthorne relates to Scott at all, he rather externalizes the relation in Scott's own words. The procedure of the Preface to *House* is reversed. So far from internalizing the coercion of convention, Hawthorne projects his refusal to be coerced onto the convention that is now dissociated from him. The conventions he uses, that is, declare both themselves and his non-reaction toward them. The "now a little more than ten years ago" imitates *Waverley*'s " 'Tis Sixty Years Since." The concern "to establish a theatre, a little removed from the highway of ordinary travel," recapitulates Scott's choice of the border country.[1] Scott is presented, but with, I would maintain, Hawthorne's distance from him. The writer of places far away and long ago is himself at a remove, no longer, as once, stirring Hawthorne's imagination.[2] A single code, as it were, carries a double message, as later, we shall see, an element of any one incident in *Blithedale* may be read as an element of any other. The Scott of *Blithedale*'s Preface, seizing upon a time and place that admittedly no longer exist, incorporates outside Hawthorne, Hawthorne seizing upon a Scott who no longer binds him. As the Preface continues more fully: "Among ourselves . . . there is as yet no such Faery Land, so like the real world, that, in a suitable remoteness, one cannot well tell the difference, but with an atmosphere of strange enchantment, beheld through which the in-

---

[1] " 'Tis Sixty Years Since" is *Waverley*'s subtitle. Cf., also, ch. 1: "By fixing, then, the date of my story Sixty Years before the present 1st November 1805, I would have my readers understand, that they will meet in the following pages neither a romance of chivalry nor a tale of modern manners; that my hero will neither have iron on his shoulders, as of yore, nor on the heels of his boots, as is the present fashion of Bond Street; and that my damsels will neither be clothed 'in purple and in pall,' like the Lady Alice of an old ballad, nor reduced to the primitive nakedness of a modern fashionable at a rout."

[2] Stewart, *Biography*, p. 8, quotes a letter of 1820 to his sister Louisa: "I have bought the Lord of the Isles and intend either to send or to bring it to you. I like it as well as any of Scott's other Poems. . . . I shall read The Abbott by the Author of Waverly [sic] as soon as I can hire it. I have read all Scott's Novels except that. I wish I had not that I might have the pleasure of reading them again." Years later, Hawthorne remarks: "The world nowadays requires a more earnest purpose, a deeper moral, and a closer and homelier truth than he was qualified to supply it with" (Stewart, p. 242).

habitants have a propriety of their own" (III, 2). Reluctantly, Hawthorne acknowledges the lesson of *The House of the Seven Gables*: The "Faery Land" is impossible, the "atmosphere" unreal.

And yet Hawthorne resurrects it, creates it in the face of the manifest failure the ending of *House* demonstrated it to be:

"This [Faery Land] atmosphere is what the American romancer needs. In its absence, the beings of imagination are compelled to show themselves in the same category as actually living mortals; a necessity that generally renders the paint and pasteboard of their composition but too painfully discernible. With the idea of partially obviating this difficulty (the sense of which has always pressed very heavily upon him), the Author has ventured to make free with his old, and affectionately remembered home, at BROOK FARM, as being, certainly, the most romantic episode of his own life—essentially a daydream, and yet a fact—and thus offering an available foothold between fiction and reality" (p. 2).

Hawthorne twists and turns. He presents two oppositions: the Faery Land is absent in America but exists in Brook Farm; in turn, in Brook Farm, the opposition of fact and fiction is resolved ("essentially a daydream, and yet a fact"). It is a mistake, however—though Hawthorne's complexity makes it difficult to see—to read the resolution of the second opposition onto the first, which cannot be resolved. As long as Brook Farm remains in America, fact and fiction united does and does not exist. In a sense Hawthorne creates his Faery Land, but its reality, fully admitted, is yet circumscribed. The reality of Blithedale is a reality discontinuous from that of the world outside. Hawthorne asserts it but, from his disinterested position, never confirms it. He speaks it, but in a way we shall explain more fully later, does not mean it. Blithedale exists independent of any authorizing power beyond itself. Indeed, it may even in places imitate what is beyond, but it remains at a discrete level. The characters of imagination "show themselves in the same category as actually living mortals," but presumably, the sentence implies, they are not the same. Thus even when Hawthorne goes so far as to project himself onto *The Blithedale Romance* the projection is externalized, cut off from the self which Hawthorne, outside his work, now is.

Consider Coverdale. On strictly biographical grounds, as a number of critics have pointed out, he is Hawthorne's most complete Hawthorne-figure, a poet uncharacteristically engaged in a transcendental enterprise in a socialistic community.[3] In terms of the literary career, we might add, Coverdale's failure enacts the turn from space Hawthorne begins at the end of *The House of the Seven Gables*. His immersion in and ultimate alienation from the Blithedale community recapitulate Hawthorne's progress. It has been argued, of course, that there are certain differences, that *The Blithedale Romance* is, after all, not an account of Brook Farm, nor Coverdale Hawthorne. *Blithedale* is art, not life, so the formalist criticism generally runs. And yet, I would maintain that such an argument concerns itself with the wrong parameters. *Blithedale* is art, not life, only because Hawthorne is apart from it. The similarity between the two worlds proves, precisely, their discontinuity: Hawthorne is beyond struggling to make them different. He need not define himself against a work which would coerce him. His purpose complete, at one with genre, he may simply dissociate himself from the completed world in its entirety.

On the one hand, Hawthorne may project himself on the work, but on the other, he asserts his separateness from his projection, declares it an other he now refuses to engage. Of course the process is reciprocal. As in *The House of the Seven Gables* we are faced with

[3] E.g., Von Abele, pp. 71 ff. The account in Stewart, *Biography*, pp. 59–60, is especially provocative.

the problem of linearizing a circle, with assuming a beginning that does not exist. The circle is comparable to the circle of projection and reaction we encountered before, but it inverts it. Here Hawthorne's "reaction" is to refuse to react. He attempts neither to integrate himself in his work nor to divide himself from it. Rather, he locates himself at a remove where both are impossible. The romance project is over. The book, for the first time in Hawthorne's career, is self-sustaining. Hawthorne no longer attempts to direct it, neither as a disembodied observer, everywhere in his material, as in *The House of the Seven Gables*, nor through a persona he carefully manipulates, like the pedant of "The Custom-House." The story, as it were, tells itself. The act of narration is included within the narrative. Hawthorne the writer becomes Coverdale the poet, a narrator within a book that may be analogous to, but stands in no active relationship with, the world outside.

Coverdale ruminates:

"I trod along by the dark, sluggish river, and remember pausing on the bank, above one of its blackest and most placid pools—(the very spot, with the barkless stump of a tree aslantwise over the water, is depicting itself to my fancy, at this instant)—and wondering how deep it was, and if any overladen soul had ever flung its weight of mortality in thither, and if it thus escaped the burthen, or only made it heavier. And perhaps the skeleton of the drowned wretch still lay beneath the inscrutable depth, clinging to some sunken log at the bottom with the gripe of its old despair. So slight, however, was the track of these gloomy ideas, that I soon forgot them in the contemplation of a brood of wild ducks, which were floating on the river, and anon took flight, leaving each a bright streak over the black surface" (pp. 207–208).

This is an important passage for the issue of narrative method. Critics have spent too much time over the question of Coverdale's reliability without considering it. Coverdale, it is often said, is an untrustworthy narrator. He misreports the events at Blithedale, filters them through a neurotic consciousness, which is Hawthorne's consciousness projected.[4] Once again, however, the wrong question is being asked. Such a reading flies in the face of the achievement of *The House of the Seven Gables*, an achievement of unity that *Blithedale*, rather than deny, merely severs from its author. As a result of *The House of the Seven Gables*, there is never a separation of self and other within *Blithedale*, whatever the case between *Blithedale* and Hawthorne. There is no distinction between event and report. Coverdale's fantasy of the suicide—the "overladen soul [that] had ever flung its weight of mortality in thither"—is potentially a vision of events outside him—Zenobia's death— but the vision is incorporated within his psyche as memory.[5] There is a continuity, here, of material and man. The observer is at one with what he observes. There is neither action existing independently outside him to which, as a prophet, he gives himself over, nor a psyche independent of events, misshaping them.

To consider the matter historically, Coverdale, far from being the unreliable narrator of material he is unable to accept, mediates through his so-called unre-

[4] See, especially, David L. Minter, "Definition of a Fictional Form: Hawthorne's *The Blithedale Romance*," in *The Interpreted Design as a Structural Principle in American Prose* (New Haven: Yale Univ. Press, 1969), pp. 137–60. Also Crews, *The Sins of the Fathers* and "A New Reading of *The Blithedale Romance*," *AL*, 29 (1957), 147–70; and Kelley Griffith, Jr., "Form in *The Blithedale Romance*," *AL*, 40 (1968), 15–26. All see Coverdale as an unreliable narrator struggling to subject reality—for Minter, the reality of failure; for Crews, the reality of sex; for Griffith, the reality of pure fact—to his imagination. William L. Hedges, "Hawthorne's *Blithedale*: The Function of the Narrator," *NCF*, 14 (1960), 303–16, on the other hand, is convinced of Coverdale's accuracy, but thereby, equally, with the others, sees a separation—admittedly overcome—that I would deny from the start.

[5] Crews, "A New Reading," p. 152, cites numerous other examples of Coverdale's premonitions.

liability the progress of the artist of "The Prophetic Pictures" towards the narrator of *The Sacred Fount.* Between the necessities of those two stories, vatic (the outside imposing itself on the inside) and psychological (the inside imposing itself on the outside) lies the narrative of *Blithedale.* Delicately, the book integrates the demands of opposite modes. Moreover, the integration occurs in such a way as to obviate Hawthorne's own existence. A complicated time scheme is involved. Coverdale, wondering about action that has taken place in the past, predicts action that will occur in the future. In turn, both past and future are alive in the present, while Coverdale reports his meditation to the reader, in the image "depicting itself to my fancy, *at this instant*" [my italics]. There is no room for an author, no time at which he stands. The interrelation of self and other in *The Blithedale Romance*, unlike the interrelation of *The House of the Seven Gables*, is unvalidated by Hawthorne's presence, nor need it be. The work validates itself, presents itself apart from any domination outside it.[6]

We must not, then, approach *Blithedale* as we have Hawthorne's earlier works. We will not offer a "reading" of it as we did, say, of *The Scarlet Letter.* We can discover in this way nothing to help us to understand Hawthorne's career. No purpose lies, here, between interpretations. The interpretations are their own purpose. We call such a work realistic. Indeed, I would define a work of realism as one in which the causes that validate romance—both cultural (generic) causes and authorial (purposive) causes—are reconstituted as necessities internal to the text.

Consider, once more, Coverdale reporting himself: "There can hardly remain for me (who am really get-

[6] Of course, in a sense a perfect romance is self-validating, too, but romance's self, so far from excluding the author, includes him and, indeed, the world. See below, pp. 191, on the inversion of *The House of the Seven Gables* in *The Blithedale Romance.*

ting to be a frosty bachelor, with another white hair, every week or so, in my moustache), there can hardly flicker up again so cheery a blaze upon the hearth, as that which I remember, the next day, at Blithedale" (p. 9). Here is the style of Hawthorne's earliest work transformed, narrative in the manner of Coleridge, Poe, Melville, become the manner of *Roderick Hudson* and *The Great Gatsby*. The "I" who "alone remain[s] to tell the story" in *Moby-Dick* is here the effete bachelor. The hair, suddenly turned snowy, of the descender into the maelstrom grows gray "another white hair, every week or so." The glittering eye of the tale-teller of *The Rime of the Ancient Mariner* is a hearth that "can . hardly flicker up again so cheery a blaze." The origin of realism is presented as a pragmatical appropriation of romance. By pragmatism I mean an attitude of demystification. The work, for Hawthorne, is no longer a force with which to contend, but an object outside contention.

Accordingly, the elements of the work are neutral and equally so. Coverdale exists at the level of his world. Discontinuous from Hawthorne, he is, as a consequence, continuous with the work. He is in a state of what we might call ontological equivalence with it. When he meets what in a romance sphere were coercive forces, energies—terror ("Descent"), vision (*Moby-Dick, Rime*)—that would seize him, he rather regards them according to the dimension of his own self, itself, from Hawthorne's point of view, discharged of energy. Hawthorne, that is, does not so much discard his old style, but his new stance redefines it as neutral. As he puts it at the end of the Preface: "Even the brilliant Howadji might find as rich a theme in his youthful reminiscences of Brook Farm, and a more novel one— close at hand as it lies—than those which he has since made so distant a pilgrimage to seek, in Syria, and along the current of the Nile" (p. 3). The Nile flows into the Charles, romance into the "novel." The old purpose, the "youthful reminiscences," remains but incorporated within the work as demystified object. As the pun suggests, romance, which "novel" historically signified,[7] is fully integrated into the newer mode.

Such transformation by inclusion is the program of *Blithedale*. Hawthorne reworks his entire career. On the narrative level, as we have already seen, the result is that the narration itself is included within the narrative. Purpose is assimilated to the realistic novel. The validating power that, in a different mode, lies outside the work, is incorporated, reflexively, within it. We are now in a position to elaborate more fully the way in which narrative is affected. We recall the circle of disinterest and observe its action on Hawthorne's act of disinterested narration. The work is separate from him, but projects him. In turn, he is separate from the work that is his image, and the work becomes an image of him separate from his image and so on. All this is instantaneous and, ideally, infinite. It is like two mirrors—Hawthorne and the work—facing each other, each projecting its multiple reflections on the other.

The result is a series of stories within stories, the narrator narrating no tale, but an image of himself telling a tale, as when Coverdale describes Zenobia as she recounts the story of "The Silvery Veil" or when he describes Moodie telling the story of his life. Coverdale, like Hawthorne, delegates authority. Of course it is important to realize that the discontinuity between Hawthorne and his work, though thus projected, at the same time implies the continuity that we have described of all elements of the work itself. The series of narratives is circular. It leads to no fixed point of reference, but backward into itself. For example, by way of contrast, we may note the story within a story as it appears in Hawthorne's earliest works, "Passages from a Relin-

[7] See Edith Kern, "The Romance of Novel/Novella," in *The Disciplines of Criticism: Essays in Literary Theory, Interpretation, and History*, ed. Peter Demetz, Thomas Greene, and Lowry Nelson, Jr. (New Haven: Yale Univ. Press, 1969), pp. 511–30.

quished Work," "Alice Doane's Appeal," "The Devil in Manuscript." In each of these cases the point of the tale is not the tale alone, as we are claiming it is in *Blithedale*, but its use in bringing together an audience and a vision. The narrator is the public's response to the tale, partially approving, more than a little skeptical, a projection of Hawthorne's social side reporting, bringing us closer to, the alienated writer ("Passages," "The Devil") or his mysterious fiction ("Alice Doane"). Coverdale, however, *is* the alienated writer. He is an image precisely of Hawthorne unconcerned with the work or its reception, dispassionately writing his novel. He represents us not at all, brings us closer to nothing, at best lets us see a story whose only significance is its telling.

In "Fauntleroy" Coverdale relates a story at least in part told to him by Old Moodie about Moodie's former self, "a man whom we shall call Fauntleroy." Here is a story of a story that leads to no elemental truth. Focus succeeds focus—Coverdale to Moodie to Fauntleroy—but no progress to some undistorted subject matter is made. Rather, the tale turns back to its teller. Its innermost kernel, Fauntleroy himself, is presented only as Coverdale sees him, a real man but with the name Coverdale assigns. That is to say, his ontological status is equivalent to Coverdale's own. He neither exists apart from him nor yet distorted by him, but at one with his self-validating narrative presence. Significantly, the series of projections continues. Moodie, even within his own story, has told Coverdale the story of himself telling yet another: "For Fauntleroy, as they sat by their cheerless fireside—which was no fireside, in truth, but only a rusty stove—had often talked to the little girl about his former wealth, the noble loveliness of his first wife, and the beautiful child whom she had given him. Instead of the fairy tales, which other parents tell, he told Priscilla this" (p. 186). The progress from "cheerless fireside" to "rusty stove" is much like Coverdale's progress from glittering-eyed mariner to barely flickering hearth. Moodie, like Coverdale, mediates the development from romance to realism. His past is romance ("fairy tale") converted, romance appropriated to his present existence, coexisting with it in the process of narration.[8]

Even more interesting is "The Silvery Veil." As in "Fauntleroy" Coverdale tells a story he has been told, and the series of projections is even longer. "Zenobia's Legend," the chapter in which "The Silvery Veil" is presented, opens as a repetition of the Preface. Coverdale sets the scene of the narrative and reports, on his own authority, Zenobia's words: " 'I am getting weary of this [tableaux vivants],' said she, after a moment's thought. 'Our own features, and our own figures and airs, show a little too intrusively through all the characters we assume. We have so much familiarity with one another's realities, that we cannot remove ourselves, at pleasure, into an imaginary sphere . . .' " (p. 107). And, continuing, in response to a request for a ghost story: " 'No; not exactly a ghost-story,' answered Zenobia; 'but something so nearly like it that you shall hardly tell the difference' " (p. 107).

Here, again, and in virtually the same language, are Hawthorne's remarks on the difficulties of establishing a sphere where his characters might act "without exposing them to too close a comparison with the actual

---

[8] A further extension is possible, too, if we consider that the story of Fauntleroy is a fleshed out "Feathertop": "The man had laid no real touch on any mortal's heart. Being a mere image, an optical delusion, created by the sunshine of prosperity, it was his law to vanish into the shadow of the first intervening cloud. He seemed to leave no vacancy; a phenomenon which, like many others that attended his brief career, went far to prove the illusiveness of his existence" (p. 183). Here is a consequence of *Blithedale*'s relation to Hawthorne, the fact that it so nearly is a projection of his disinterested being. Fauntleroy as Moodie, telling in order to appropriate the story of Fauntleroy, is a projection of Hawthorne as Coverdale, appropriating Hawthorne's romance to realism.

events of real lives," a "Faery Land, so like the real world, that, in a suitable remoteness, one cannot well tell the difference." Within "The Silvery Veil" itself—a story set off by a break in the type, a lack of quotation marks, and a special title—Zenobia on *her* authority now repeats what she had said earlier on Coverdale's: "Now, listen to my simple little tale; and you shall hear the very latest incident in the known life—(if life it may be called, which seemed to have no more reality than the candlelight image of one's self, which peeps at us outside of a dark window-pane)—the life of this shadowy phenomenon" (p. 108). "Now listen to my tale" enforces the point. Zenobia sets up a narrative that is to tell itself. Hawthorne's projection of his authority into the tale is repeated at every level. Coverdale projects the authority he receives from Hawthorne onto Zenobia, Zenobia projects what she receives from Coverdale onto the "tale," as if it existed independently. And, indeed, the independent tale seems to project from within it other independent tales. Thus "The Silvery Veil" itself begins with one character remarking on a "report" he has heard and Theodore on a "rumor." Everyone dissociates himself from his story, includes his narration within the narrative. On the other hand, the series remains circular, leading to no central reality. Coverdale, after all, admits that the story, presumably told in Zenobia's words, is really a "version of her story" from which he has left out certain "absurdities." There is no attempt, I think, at *bonafide* revision, here, no suggestion of an ultimate truth from which Coverdale veers away. Coverdale, evidently, has changed Zenobia's language, but in keeping with what Zenobia herself might have done, for Zenobia's own written productions, too, he tells us, are invariably less effective than the same material when she tells it orally. We have, once again, a case of ontological equivalence. In the same manner, the central character of "The Silvery Veil," though he exists, much like Fauntleroy, independently in the tale, receives his name from Zenobia, who "deem[s] it fit to call him 'Theodore.'"

The audience to which Zenobia addresses herself presents an interesting complication. "You have heard, my dear friends," she begins, "of the Veiled Lady, who grew suddenly so very famous, a few months ago" (p. 108). The "dear friends" to whom Zenobia is speaking are a group of listeners Coverdale has just carefully described in setting the scene. Here is a further example of the continuity we have been describing. Strictly speaking, however, it is not these listeners—indeed, not any of the members of Blithedale, as far as we know—who have heard of the Veiled Lady, but the audience Coverdale addresses in the first sentence of the book when he refers to the exhibition he has just witnessed. This audience is not us, although it may be our image. As Coverdale admits, he has "casually alluded" to the Veiled Lady as if his listeners knew who she were. The audience, instead, is one hypothesized by the narrative, included in the novel as united with it, the audience counterpart to the author's projection of himself into the work in the form of Coverdale. It is to such an audience that Zenobia speaks and yet, as well, to the audience Coverdale has prepared, and, perhaps further, to an audience we may suppose Zenobia within "The Silvery Veil" hypothesizes for herself. Here is an overloading of reference. Elements of one story may be elements of any other, too. To refine our mirror metaphor, one of the mirrors—the work—offers a flat projection. The series of Hawthorne's (non-) relation to his reflecting work we might call a three-dimensional series: the Hawthorne who disinterestedly observes the work exists at a level of reality different from the work. As the work reflects such disinterest, however, it reconstitutes it at its own level. A three-dimensional series is transposed to two dimensions. All the stories in *Blithedale* take place on a single plane.

The complexities of "The Silvery Veil" are best understood in this way. Like the story of Coverdale's failure in Blithedale and like Hawthorne's abandonment of a purposive art, either one of which or both it may reflect, Theodore's difficulties with the Veiled Lady represent the situation of pragmatical man in a romance world. Constitutionally unable to take a gothic lady on her own gothic terms, a man who "prided himself on his sturdy perception of realities," "whose natural tendency was toward scepticism," his reaction to the veil is to assume "the probability that her face was none of the most bewitching." The reflection of the problem of Coverdale and Hawthorne, complete in itself, becomes, from a wider perspective, however, but an element of yet another structure. The progress from narrator to projected narrator and so on is subject, by the continuity we have been describing, to be taken in reverse order. As a result, attention is deflected from the tale to Zenobia in the act of presenting it. The climactic episode, the moment when the magician arises, is muted, its intensity drawn off by Zenobia dropping a piece of gauze over Priscilla's head.

"At the word, uprose the bearded man in the Oriental robes—the beautiful!—the dark Magician, who had bartered away his soul! He threw his arms around the Veiled Lady; and she was his bond-slave, forever more!

"Zenobia, all this while, had been holding the piece of gauze, and so managed it as greatly to increase the dramatic effect of the legend, at those points where the magic veil was to be described. Arriving at the catastrophe, and uttering the fatal words, she flung the gauze over Priscilla's head; and, for an instant, her auditors held their breath, half expecting, I verily believe, that the Magician would start up through the floor, and carry off our poor little friend, before our eyes" (p. 116).

One story engrosses another. The end of the tale becomes the prelude to the climax of Zenobia's telling.

The story becomes action in a larger sphere, the means by which Zenobia punishes Priscilla. It is an assertion of worldliness against innocence and, as such, an inversion of the moral of the story taken alone. Theodore is condemned for his inability to live by the story's laws. But in the world of the frame, Zenobia judges the romance. Throughout, she, too, is a skeptic. Drawing on her own experience as a woman, she reacts to the veil precisely as does Theodore, conceiving, "considering the sex of the Veiled Lady—that the face was the most hideous and horrible, and that this was her sole motive for hiding it" (pp. 109–10). And now she subverts romance in the very act of telling it. As with Coverdale describing his moustache slowly turning gray, her narration reworks one mode into another.

It becomes difficult, at this point, to deal completely and convincingly with all of the incidents of the book. The relation of various reflections to each other is complex. Incidents, as we have said, are overloaded. Various elements participate simultaneously in different structures. Thus, for example, we may explain one problem that has been discussed often: why Coverdale claims to miss the crucial confrontation between Zenobia and Hollingsworth, remarks, despite his rendering of the substance of the meeting, that he arrives after the "crisis has just come and gone" (p. 215). Instead, we note, he focuses on a story of his own. Commenting on why he remains to watch a rejected Zenobia, now alone with her grief, he explains:

"But, so it happened, I never once dreamed of questioning my right to be there, now, as I had questioned it, just before, when I came so suddenly upon Hollingsworth and herself, in the passion of their recent debate. It suits me not to explain what was the analogy that I saw, or imagined, between Zenobia's situation and mine; nor, I believe, will the reader detect this one secret, hidden beneath many a revelation which perhaps concerned me less" (p. 222).

Zenobia's loss of Hollingsworth is an incident potentially too other. It exists apart from Coverdale, and he feels uncomfortable with it. By domestication of it to his own circumstances, however, Zenobia becomes an image of Coverdale, and her loss of Hollingsworth a reflection of Coverdale's loss of Priscilla. So conceiving it, Coverdale "never once dreamed of questioning my right to be there."

Appropriation of this sort may also work across different incidents rather than on the same one. Coverdale's method, applied to the book as a whole, provides a procedure for relating disparate events formally and a rationale for "interpretation" as well. We must read various actions in such a way as to find in them a common or "transformed" structure.[9] Thus "A Village-Hall" would constitute a reversal by assimilation of the second part of "The Silvery Veil." Hollingsworth, like Westervelt, asserts his will over Priscilla. But in place of the magician reasserting magical control, we have Hollingsworth rescuing Priscilla from a life of magic.

Such a procedure, of course, is applied by formalist critics to all works. But the very circularity of our argument, here, is in keeping with the circularity of *Blithedale* as a whole, *Blithedale*'s redefinition of itself as a new kind of literature. Ideally, we should read every incident of *Blithedale* as a transformation of every other. We may perform, that is, a formal analysis on it precisely because of that equality of all its elements which we have discussed. Here alone no purpose external to the work, struggling to impose itself on it, invests some incidents with special significance, contests others, fails to consider still more. Here alone, in Hawthorne, the book exists independently *as* a form.

[9] This is not to say, however, that we must read them as signifying messages concealed or "coded." The process of interpretation, here, may be strictly formal, a matter of noting structural similarities without references to messages. See pp. 180 ff. on the elimination of signification in realism. Once again, we do not offer a "reading" of *Blithedale* in the way we did of *The Scarlet Letter*.

We have called such a work realistic. It is a work that subsumes the forces that might otherwise impinge on it from the outside into its own neutrality. In Hawthorne it swallows even its beginnings, incorporates within itself the very influences that give rise to it, transforms, in other words, its history into an ontology. Within its own compass *Blithedale*, therefore, must stake out afresh ground already broken in England and elsewhere. Indeed, it plays out in itself—because it absorbs its tradition into itself—the development of English realism from English realism's own beginnings.

Blithedale's characters, for example, emerge from the eighteenth-century "Character": "The self-concentrated Philanthropist; the high-spirited Woman, bruising herself against the narrow limitations of her sex; the weakly Maiden, whose tremulous nerves endow her with Sibylline attributes; the Minor Poet, beginning life with strenuous aspirations, which die out with his youthful fervor" (pp. 2–3). It is filled with the sort of justifying quasi-biographical material Defoe used: "Doctor Griswold—as the reader, of course, knows—has placed me at a fair elevation among our minor minstrelsy" (p. 246). Here is an absorption of a potential external cause—the writer: why he wrote the book or, in this case, his ability to write—within the fiction. Hawthorne must invent the mode all over again.

There is a manifest concern with names. Hawthorne rationalizes anew the realistic use common in eighteenth-century novelists, of names' symbolic meanings, as Ian Watt has demonstrated.[10] We note Hawthorne's own difficulty in finding a title for his book.[11] How may he give it a name yet withdraw purpose, maintain disinterest in the face of valuating the book with a name? The problem is projected onto the work. The commun-

[10] *The Rise of the Novel: Studies in Defoe, Richardson and Fielding* (1957; rpt. Berkeley: Univ. of California Press, 1967), p. 19.

[11] Pearce, *Centenary Edition*, p. xix.

ity considers "Sunny Glimpse," "Utopia," and "The Oasis," manifestly allegorical designations, so that when it settles on the equally allegorical "Blithedale," it seems in contrast, as Coverdale says, "neither good nor bad" (p. 37). Or, alternatively, a natural name is forced to project mystic significance: "Priscilla! Priscilla!" says Coverdale, "I repeated the name to myself, three or four times; and, in that little space, this quaint and prim cognomen had so amalgamated itself with my idea of the girl, that it seemed as if no other name could have adhered to her for a moment" (p. 29). The symbolic name, the name that seems to suit the character of its bearer, while present and in no need of justification in novelists writing after the early 1700's, must be brought in, here, by the back door.

What has been taken as Hawthorne's occasional clumsiness, then, so far from exemplifying the comparative inability of a romancer in the territory of Richardson, Austen, and Eliot, is precisely a measure of his originality.[12] James was right about the alienation of the American artist, the absence in America of artistic community. Hawthorne, despite the availability to him, indeed even the influence on him, of the British models James, for one, not only drew upon but frankly acknowledged, by the very nature of his artistic endeavor must move towards a reinvention of realism on his own. He is forced back on, in order to rework, the conventions of his own books. It is his contribution to the founding of a new line, of which James himself was the illustrious successor, to have "realized" in *Blithedale* the pragmatical possibilities of American romance. In

[12] This has been a common criticism. See, e.g., the representative view of Robert C. Elliott, *"The Blithedale Romance,"* in *Hawthorne Centenary Essays*, p. 117: "Hawthorne's situation once again runs parallel to that of the poet he created. He was by no means the man by conviction or temperament to write the epic of Brook Farm. Nor was he prepared to write a novel (to say nothing of a satirical novel) grounded in range and depth in his own experience. . . ."

a characteristic projection—Hawthorne discussing his art in the form of Coverdale discussing his own in the form of describing Westervelt performing his magic—the history of the novel as a history of spiritualism is recounted:

"Now-a-days, in the management of his 'subject,' 'clairvoyant,' or 'medium,' the exhibitor affects the simplicity and openness of scientific experiment; and even if he profess to tread a step or two across the boundaries of the spiritual world, yet carries with him the laws of our actual life, and extends them over his preternatural conquests. Twelve or fifteen years ago, on the contrary, all the arts of mysterious arrangement, of picturesque disposition, and artistically contrasted light and shade, were made available in order to set the apparent miracle in the strongest attitude of opposition to ordinary facts" (pp. 5–6).

"Twelve or fifteen years ago" the preternatural was exhibited as a challenge to rationalism. As R. B. Heilman has pointed out, the gothic's historical function was to open us to the "extra-rational," to "enlarge the sense of reality and its impact on the human being."[13] Now the situation is reversed. The extra-rational is brought back to reality. Significantly, the "subject," the "medium" of the new mode remains the same. The enlargement has been successful. The preternatural is never eliminated, simply pragmatized. As Coverdale later remarks: "It was a period when science (though mostly through its empirical professors) was bringing forward, anew, a hoard of facts and imperfect theories, that had partially won credence, in elder times, but which modern scepticism had swept away as rubbish. These things were now tossed up again, out of the surg-

---

[13] "Charlotte Brontë's 'New' Gothic," rpt. in *Victorian Literature: Modern Essays in Criticism*, ed. Austin Wright (New York: Oxford Univ. Press, 1961), pp. 71–85. Quoted by Francis Russell Hart, "The Experience of Character in the English Gothic Novel," in *Experience in the Novel*, p. 86.

ing ocean of human thought and experience" (p. 187).
The old paradise of rationalism is fallen. Gothicism,
proceeding out of the "ocean of human experience," is
not discarded, but empirically reconceived.

All this has interesting cultural consequences. It is
usual for historical critics to see *Blithedale* as a serious
social critique unfortunately marred by the persistence
of certain habits of Hawthorne's earlier writing. And
yet, it is precisely those habits which make the social
critique possible. Consider, for example, the sexual
content latent in Hawthorne's gothicism. We have
hardly discussed the Oedipal interest, say of "Rappaccini's Daughter," and only briefly that of "The Artist
of the Beautiful," an interest Crews, for one, has uncovered elaborately. Similarly, we have bypassed the
primal scene at the heart of *The Scarlet Letter*, as
Fiedler would have it.[14] It is our position that such interests do not necessarily implicate the author. They
inhere in the very nature of the genre, are representative fantasies of the culture gothic novels embody. The
pragmatization of gothicism, however, its assimilation
into a realistic mode, brings what was latent to its social
surface. Fantasy becomes sociology. Chillingworth's
demonism, his pursuit of the copulating couple by
mystical signs and magical stratagems, becomes Coverdale's prurience, his establishment of social relationships on a voyeuristic base. There is no question of
latency here. In realism all content is manifest. Nothing
is latent, because disinterest destroys ulterior motiva-
tion. The work is a surface, as we have said, a mirror
reflecting the world it supposes to be outside it. When
content is hidden from a character, for example, it is
the hiding, too, that the realistic book as a whole portrays. Coverdale thus reports Hollingsworth's prayers:

"My sleeping-room being but thinly partitioned from
his, the solemn murmur of his voice made its way to my

---

[14] Crews, *The Sins of the Fathers*; Fiedler, p. 230.

ears, compelling me to be an auditor of his awful privacy with the Creator. It affected me with a deep reverence for Hollingsworth, which no familiarity then
existing, or that afterwards grew more intimate between us—no, nor my subsequent perception of his own
great errors—ever quite effaced. It is so rare, in these
times, to meet with a man of prayerful habits (except,
of course, in the pulpit), that such an one is decidedly
marked out by a light of transfiguration, shed upon him
in the divine interview from which he passes into his
daily life" (pp. 39–40).

Manifestly, religion is Coverdale's smokescreen. It is
a psychic construction. The claim of increased reverence and the theological peroration in which the passage culminates are lame concealments that all the
more clearly demonstrate the essentially voyeuristic
nature of Coverdale's listening.[15] Nor, once more,
should we speak of Coverdale as distorting the true
nature of his action. Distortion itself, like Coverdale's
prophetic memory in the passage quoted towards the
beginning of this chapter, mediates between a psyche
and an event equally true, between inner and outer
realities, locating them at a single level. Again, compare *Blithedale*'s treatment of sex with the reticence,

[15] Similarly: "For, was mine a mere vulgar curiosity? Zenobia
should have known me better than to suppose it. She should
have been able to appreciate that quality of the intellect and the
heart, which impelled me (often against my own will, and to the
detriment of my own comfort) to live in other lives, and to
endeavor—by generous sympathies, by delicate intuitions, by
taking note of things too slight for record, and by bringing my
human spirit into manifold accordance with the companions
whom God assigned me—to learn the secret which was hidden
even from themselves" (p. 160).
Also: "It is really impossible to hide anything, in this world,
to say nothing of the next. All that we ought to ask, therefore,
is, that the witnesses of our conduct, and the speculators on our
motives, should be capable of taking the highest view which the
circumstances of the case may admit. So much being secured,
I, for one, would be most happy in feeling myself followed,
everywhere, by an indefatigable human sympathy" (p. 163).

which some have claimed is Hawthorne's own, in *The Scarlet Letter*.[16] The word "adultery," the subject of the book, is never used. The sexual act occurs before the book begins. But Coverdale unabashedly speculates on the state of Zenobia's virginity (pp. 46–47). The word "effeminacy" appears for probably the first time in Hawthorne (pp. 58, 145), and nudity is discussed on two occasions (pp. 17, 64). Gothicism pragmatized brings to consciousness the sexual component of social relationships, brings sex into society as one with it. We even get, as it were, a kind of sexual politics, an awareness of the female position in nineteenth-century America:

"Now, as I looked down from my upper region at this man and woman [Westervelt and Zenobia]—outwardly so fair a sight, and wandering like two lovers in the wood—I imagined that Zenobia, at an earlier period of youth, might have fallen into the misfortune above indicated [submission to Westervelt]. And when her passionate womanhood, as was inevitable, had discovered its mistake, there had ensued the character of eccentricity and defiance, which distinguished the more public portion of her life" (p. 103).

The child watching the violation of his mother sees the woman retaliating. In social terms, Hawthorne sees the rise of feminism. Here is the etiology of what will later be called the great American bitch.

Critics have often noticed, in America, the persistence of romance in realism.[17] Its presence may now be seen as far more thoroughgoing than has generally been imagined. The first person narrative itself, common to some of the best works of American realism (*Huckleberry Finn*, *The Sun Also Rises*, *The Great Gatsby*), is but gothicism transformed, the primal scene assimilated. "Call me Ishmael," with all its exhibitionistic

[16] E.g., Fiedler, p. 228.

[17] The classic statement is Chase, *The American Novel and Its Tradition*.

overtones, remains a dominant American voice. James's technique of "point of view," in this light, is voyeurism raised to an ontological principle. It is the first person narrative conceptualized, initiated by a persona no longer necessary to maintain it. One notes, for example, *The Ambassadors'* Lambert Strether, investigating the liaison between Chad and Mme. de Vionnet. Even if, as has been charged, the voyeurism is James's own and not, originally, that of the form,[18] then the form it naturally takes is nevertheless a progress of voyeurism similar to Coverdale's. In *The Bostonians*, feminism and sexual speculation, particularly of a perverse nature, are the very substance of James's social critique.

It is of course true that elements of romance seem to persist in the new mode unregenerated. At least in *Blithedale*, however, it is well to consider such elements more closely. What Irving Howe, in some disparagement of *Blithedale*, calls "Gothic flim-flam"[19] is, rather, gothicism re-emerging with a difference after assimilation has taken place. "A Village-Hall," the only chapter in which we actually see the Veiled Lady perform, is perhaps the best place to begin. Coverdale describes Westervelt's invocation:

"The Professor began his discourse. . . . It was eloquent, ingenious, plausible, with a delusive show of spirituality, yet really imbued throughout with a cold and dead materialism. . . . He spoke of a new era that was dawning upon the world; an era that would link soul to soul, and the present life to what we call futurity, with a closeness that should finally convert both worlds into one great, mutually conscious brotherhood. He described (in a strange, philosophical guise, with terms of art, as if it were a matter of chemical discovery) the agency by which this mighty result was to be effected;

---

[18] E.g., Maxwell Geismar, *Henry James and the Jacobites* (Boston: Houghton Mifflin, 1963).

[19] *Politics and the Novel* (New York: Horizon Press, 1957), p. 174.

nor would it have surprised me, had he pretended to hold up a portion of his universally pervasive fluid, as he affirmed it to be, in a glass phial" (p. 200).

Here, as we have seen before, is fantasy presented as reason. Transcendentalism, the old idealism behind "an era that would link soul to soul," has become a "chemical discovery." "Spirituality" is "a cold and dead materialism." Indeed, the erstwhile magician is, rather, a "Professor," no doubt of the class of the itinerant professor of physiology who also exhibits in the Village-Hall (p. 196). More significant, however, is Coverdale's fright at the change that has taken place. Westervelt may be perfectly rational, but the rationalization of the soul is as dangerous as the demons rationality dissipates. We are converted into a physiological machine. Mysticism becomes mechanism, the Virgin, in Henry Adams' terms, the Dynamo. In a sense, pragmatism, exorcizing romantic demons from the universe, generates, instead, a pragmatic demonology of its own. Romance, passing through a neutral realism, becomes what will later be called naturalism. Coverdale reacts to the stories he overhears while waiting for Westervelt to speak:[20]

"At the bidding of one of these wizards, the maiden, with her lover's kiss still burning on her lips, would turn from him with icy indifference; the newly made widow would dig up her buried heart out of her young husband's grave, before the sods had taken root upon it; a mother, with her babe's milk in her bosom, would thrust away her child. Human character was but soft wax in his hands; and guilt, or virtue, only the forms into which he should see fit to mould it. The religious sentiment was a flame which he could blow up with his breath, or a spark that he could utterly extinguish. It is unutterable, the horror and disgust with which I lis-

[20] Compare Hawthorne's reaction to Sophia's suggestion that she submit to hypnotism to cure her neurasthenia, in *Love Letters*, p. 126.

tened, and saw, that, if these things were to be believed, the individual soul was virtually annihilated, and all that is sweet and pure, in our present life, debased, and that the idea of man's eternal responsibility was made ridiculous, and immortality rendered, at once, impossible, and not worth acceptance" (p. 198).

Once again, we may note, a latent concern with sexuality is socialized. Violation of the human body—lurking, still, in the ghoulish metaphor of the widow who "would dig up her buried heart out of her young husband's grave"—passes over, as the paragraph continues, into a violation of family ("a mother, with her babe's milk . . ."), morality ("and guilt, or virtue . . ."), and religion ("and immortality rendered . . . impossible"). Gothicism, projecting itself onto the pragmatic consciousness, becomes a critique of manners and morals. Once again, too, however, Coverdale's "horror and disgust" resuscitates a ghoulishness previously assimilated. The demon demystified is born again as a machine. Humanity is "soft wax." Society, that is, is but the wax museum, one more of the exhibitions at the hall, on a larger scale. It is an indiscriminate collection of "murderers and beautiful ladies," soulless figures ranked side by side. Its scenes are but the clockwork of the diorama extended (p. 196). Here is an inversion of the miniaturization we noted in *The House of the Seven Gables*. Miniatures in *Blithedale* do not contain super-rational forces, but replace them. The universe, mechanized, is romance in an opposite mode.

Perhaps, at this point, we should systematically re-define the three major types of American fiction in light of the turn they take in Hawthorne's *Blithedale*. Consider the diagram on page 175. The co-ordinates, here, should be seen as dynamically related. Strictly speaking, neither x, genre, nor y, purpose, exists except as it acts on the other. They call each other into being, are meaningless except as interanimating forces, so that, for example, the approach of either

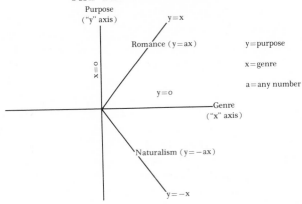

to zero is not its disappearance, but its submission to the other, which overpowers it. With this proviso we may proceed.

Romance, as we have said, is the interplay of purpose and genre, a mutual coercion. The work inflicts itself on the writer, provides the only language in which he may write. The writer, in turn, imposes himself on his material, attempts to reform an audience reflected in the work. In its most perfect form purpose and genre are joined ($y=x$). The work is the product of an audience and an author united. The voice of the novel is the voice of the novelist, the voice of a collective psyche. Interanimation, however, may not be mutual ($y=ax$: any line in the upper quadrant). In such cases purpose or genre may dominate (a is greater or smaller than 1). If purpose is large enough (as a approaches infinity) the result is pure fantasy, the reformation of genre as personal. If it is small enough (as a approaches zero) the writer submits himself to the work: we have pure sentimentality, giving the audience what it expects.[21]

[21] The definition of sentimentality is from Frye, *A Natural Perspective*, p. 130: "It is possible, of course, to bring into the theater with us a more or less definite notion of what is desirable and demand that the action lead simply to reproducing it. This demand is the core of the conception in the arts that we call the sentimental, the movement that leads back, not to the beginning of the action of the play, but to a state of our minds

As we noted in the first chapter, of course, our own practice of criticism is largely an attempt to discover in any particular work precisely the degree of such reformation and submission. But in a strictly hermeneutic context, from the standpoint of interpretation as it is usually performed, without such prior investigation, it is easy to see which terms most interpreters will find especially appropriate. Works which lie above the $y=x$ line—for example, those of Brockden Brown and Poe—will be most generally interpreted psychoanalytically. The elements of the work appear, at least on the surface, as projections of the writer's psyche. Often we find a character who seems to *be* the writer. Works below $y=x$, such as the novels of Cooper, have generally been analyzed from an ethical or social point of view. The progress of events is the myth of a nation. As long as ordinate and abscissa remain, however, interpretations of both sorts are possible. In either case, too, a certain energy or animation must be accounted for. The two levels of interpretation interact, are, in both ordinary and mathematical terms, functions of each other. The work is never static, but a resolution of interdependent forces. It is alive, informed by the presences of author and audience. Characters are no objects, but subjects possessed, angelic or demonic. Events are not historic, but in the vital, almost animistic sense in which the word is generally used, mythologic.[22]

---

before the play which remains unchanged by its action." Hence, too, in *Anatomy of Criticism*, p. 35, he says that " 'sentimental' refers to a later recreation of an earlier mode." What the readers want, the "state of our minds before the play," is the genre that embodies them.

[22] See, for the classic definition, Henri Frankfort and Mrs. H. A. Frankfort, "Myth and Reality," in *Before Philosophy: The Intellectual Adventure of Ancient Man; An Essay on Speculative Thought in the Ancient Near East* (1946; rpt. Baltimore: Penguin Books, 1949), pp. 11–36. History is what has happened to a nation, events considered objectively; myth is what has happened perceived as a living, personal entity, an "I-Thou" relation between event and people, or, in our terms, between genre and purpose.

Naturalism is the inverse of romance. The writer turns back the work's coercive power. His purpose is to assert himself as free of its necessities. Rather than attempting to reform them, he becomes superior to them. In a balanced naturalism $(y=-x)$, purpose and genre are precisely opposite. The voice of the writer is a constant rebuke to the world of the work, an assertion of the freedom of the novelist as one able to describe a necessary world. His voice is a fate by which the characters are bound, but from which he escapes. He is an experimenter uncovering the laws of the novel, whose very experimentation shows he stands on the novel's outside. If he projects himself inside, his projection is generally powerless to reform anything. No character is ever the writer except, like Ames in *Sister Carrie*, insofar as he stands in ineffectual opposition to the action of the rest of the work. Rather, characters in naturalism, as we have said, are automatons. The work is a machine, whose very inexorability affirms the writer's liberty.

Below the $y=-x$ line, as the force of genre diminishes, the assertion of freedom begins to dominate the description of fatality. The book becomes talky, polemical, announcing the movers behind the naturalistic movement. The experimental novel becomes "The Experimental Novel," as Zola called his essay, a description of why the novelist chooses to write what he does. Interestingly, in "The Experimental Novel," the artist's sense of his freedom becomes so strong that he begins to describe ways in which his writing may reform the world. Naturalism, inverting romance, is inverted again and becomes romance. In a proper naturalism, however, reformation is impossible. The writer's freedom is never freedom to act, but freedom from being acted on. The work, as in romance, is still no object, is never independent of the writer. But the presence it is subject to, this time, is presence of a negative sort. The work remains never static, but a tension of forces moving away from resolution, tied together by the artist striving to set them apart.

Realism is the place between naturalism and romance ($y=0$). It is a work in which purpose is wholly dissolved or, rather, in which the work is its own purpose. Genre, with no longer anything to coerce, exists on its own, cut off from its author. Realism is, if we use the word in a qualified sense, an "objective" report, like newspaper writing, in fact, except that in fiction the object reported is always hypothetical. It may be hypothesized for any number of psychic and social reasons, but the reasons are reborn in the object as internal necessities. They are fully adopted, neutralized as a coercive pressure.

Accordingly, our diagram allows for a full range of historical relativity. It maps a relation only, a ratio. Its axes may be redrawn in any given period of time. Realism is never a description of what is, but what, to the writer, is neutral, free of subjectivity, whether positive or negative. As the diagram shows, realism is but a line. It is liable at any moment to become one or the other of the modes that bound it. And, in fact, where *Blithedale* is not the line itself, it is constantly playing off one against the other to establish a middle voice in effect. We have seen already the "wizard" as "Professor" of physiology. Westervelt the devil is also Westervelt the scientist and perhaps, finally, a simple mountebank, negating the claims of both. His false teeth are the mask of the demon, concealing the "wizened little elf" behind the mask, or there is no Westervelt at all, "nothing genuine about him," save soulless parts pieced together. His body is "a necromantic, or perhaps a mechanical contrivance" (p. 188): the two are the same. In much the same way Hollingsworth "is a man after all . . . his Maker's own truest image, a philanthropic man!—not that steel engine of the Devil's contrivance, a philanthropist!" (p. 71). Here, overtly, the demonic and

peace, and, perhaps, even God (by analogy to "pigeon"). We are likely to remember that Hawthorne called Sophia "dove," that personally and in society at large it is a term of endearment. It is an agency of intimacy, that is, a term in which the speaker meets the spoken, asserts his relation to an object that is itself the form in which he speaks it. It is what Roland Barthes calls a myth, a second-order sign in which the arbitrary relation signifier/signified becomes itself the signifier in a humanized relation to another, more inclusive signified.[25]

For example, to extend Barthes to an analysis of novels, in *Moby-Dick* the sound "whale" signifies a particular kind of animal, but "whale"/animal comes to signify, say, sexual potency, something essential in Ahab that he sees outside him in the whale as well. Nor can the process, once started, end here. Once begun, it continues infinitely. "Whale"/animal//sexual potency soon comes to signify, say, God, and so on until the whale engrosses the universe. A true symbol, that is, ultimately takes over the book; the end of its signification is nothing short of some universal principle, as Christian allegorists well knew, a wholly valuated, wholly humanized world. In the more limited case of *Blithedale*, "dove"/dove becomes "dove"/dove//gentleness or innocence, which becomes "dove"/dove//gentleness///Priscilla. Coverdale, eschewing language as arbitrary, forsaking description of what exists unrelated to him (a bird outside his window), speaks "dove" to assert a relation. He affirms his attachment to Priscilla. Purpose, informing his use of the sign, pushes it up the ladder of signification. The dove in the dormer is a symbol, and the naive reader has not read deeply enough.

And yet, curiously, even the sophisticated reader must admit that as the image continues over the length

[25] *Mythologies*, trans. Annette Lavers (New York: Hill and Wang, 1972), p. 115.

182

the mechanical are again equivalent: the devil-created philanthropist is a steel engine. Moreover, as the noun "philanthropist" becomes an adjective in "philanthropic man," demonism-mechanism becomes a simple qualifier of a general mankind, is familiarized into a neutral humanity.[23]

It is not, however, the difficulty of maintaining neutrality that is *Blithedale*'s problem. By and large it establishes a balance, and it is its very success in achieving it that is its larger failure. The negative side of neutrality is emptiness. There is a valuelessness about *Blithedale*, a deadness that replaces significance and that threatens every word written. Valuelessness is more than the theme of the book. It is a quality of the way in which the themes are perceived. We should elaborate on our previous brief distinction between significance and signification.[24] Significance is a function of the use of the work, of the relation of author to the audience the work embodies. It is what generates meaning, as we have been using that term. Signification is a function of the message the work encodes. It is the relation, in linguistic terms, between Saussure's signifier and signified. Of course, code and use act on each other as a means delimiting an end, an end informing a

[23] Possibly we might enlarge our diagram to include the two neglected quadrants. Quadrant III, for example $(-y = -ax)$, would represent a demonic romance that inverts the transcendentalism of Quadrant I. Union of purpose and genre, here, would be the opposite of the oceanic feeling, a union in death, not love. Quadrant II, in which genre is negative but purpose positive $(x = -ay)$, might represent a sort of naturalism in which, rather than the author asserting his freedom in opposition to genre, genre would assert its freedom in opposition to the writer. Thus, for example, in *Sister Carrie*, all Dreiser's attempts to explain Carrie, his kata-states and chemisms, fail before the utter blankness, the inarticulateness of her nature. *Blithedale*, it might be shown, plays off not only romance against naturalism, but positive romance against negative romance and positive naturalism against negative naturalism.

[24] Cf. ch. one, esp. p. 16.

179

means. But they may, and in realism do, come close to dissociation. Valuelessness, in effect, results when the message has no use.

Now in *Blithedale*, Hawthorne does not attempt to open an intercourse with the world. He is disinterested in it, and, therefore, *Blithedale* is a message with no meaning, so to speak, content reduced to form. Whatever *Blithedale* may say, it never says it to affect us. Coverdale, as we have seen, may address an audience, but Coverdale and Coverdale's audience are a projection of Hawthorne and us readers from whom, with Hawthorne, we have become dissociated. The author, excluding himself from the book, excludes the reader as well. The work is an object, self-contained, a world apart from the world in which Hawthorne and his readers now find themselves. Of course, some analogy between the worlds exists. Some idea, such as the world being valueless, is part of the message of *Blithedale*, as when Coverdale proclaims, "As regards human progress . . . let them believe in it who can . . ." (p. 246). There would seem to be, that is to say, some connection between message and meaning. The connection, however, is strictly formal, never substantial. It results from the projection of Hawthorne's disinterest, a reconstitution of it internally at a level however like, yet qualitatively different from, the level of significance. Message, in *Blithedale*, never quite becomes meaning, and, in fact, the meaninglessness of the work projected onto the message reduces and in places even eliminates signification.

We will cite examples in a moment, but, by way of preliminaries, consider a modern reader's approach, say, to medieval Christian allegory. The text has lost its significance for him—he has no interest in it—and, as a result, he will be unable to uncover its signification. Of course, the text itself is not altered by the reader. Its message remains and may, with some effort, still be decoded. But in *Blithedale* Hawthorne's disinterest, as

we have seen, is projected back onto the book. The result, as the cycle of dissociation and projection continues, is that signification itself is attacked. *Blithedale* is a system of signs whose message is self-contained and which, because of its isolation, soon comes to signify nothing.

There is a remarkable "sign" that appears two or, perhaps, three times in the book and to no immediately evident end. As Coverdale looks across from his hotel room to the neighboring boarding-house in which Zenobia and Priscilla will shortly take up residence, he notices a dreary and forlorn dove in one of its dormer-windows:

". . . I wondered why she chose to sit there, in the chilly rain, while her kindred were doubtless nestling in a warm and comfortable dove-cote. All at once, this dove spread her wings, and launching herself in the air, came flying so straight across the intervening space that I fully expected her to alight directly on my window-sill. In the latter part of her course, however, she swerved aside, flew upward, and vanished, as did likewise the slight, fantastic pathos with which I had invested her" (p. 152).

To the naive reader the dove poses no problem. He looks for signification, not significance. If there is a phrase he cannot understand, he turns to the dictionary. He takes the word as a "sign": a relation, wholly arbitrary, of a signifier, the sound "dove," and a signified, a particular kind of bird. The dove Coverdale sees out the window is a dove Coverdale sees outside the window. As critics, however, sophisticated readers trained in Hawthorne's more usual methods, we are likely to look for meaning. "Dove" is no simple sign, but a symbol, which I would define as a valuated sign or a meaning continuous with its ends. It is the very opposite of arbitrary. It is pregnant with purpose, rich with the presence of culture. In Western civilization it is associated, variously, with the idea of love (turtled-

of the passage, a certain arbitrariness creeps back into it. If the dove is Priscilla, then some such interpretation as this is necessary for the whole of Coverdale's observation: the "comfortable dove-cote" is Blithedale farm; the dove spreading her wings, Priscilla leaving Blithedale or, perhaps, blossoming into a young woman, as Coverdale earlier describes; the expectation that it will alight on Coverdale's windowsill, Coverdale's fantasy that Priscilla will fall in love with him; its vanishing, Priscilla's failure to love him; and the vanishing of its "slight, fantastic pathos," the disappearance of Coverdale's involvement with her. Surely the fit, here, is too easy, too shallow. It is so unproblematic, so static in its failure to expand itself in the way Moby Dick expands himself, that, whatever the original meaningful connection, it becomes virtually arbitrary once again.

Indeed, there is practically no dove imagery elsewhere in *Blithedale*. In no society that *Blithedale* creates does it resonate like the "A" in the Puritan world of *The Scarlet Letter*. In "The Artist of the Beautiful" the butterfly over Owen's head is charged with a delicacy and beauty designed especially to enlist our sympathy for him. It signifies more than a butterfly, more even than Owen, but the aesthetic of the audience written into the Owen the audience observes. Even in *The Marble Faun*, in many ways a realistic work like *Blithedale*, the doves surrounding Hilda are fully sustained as symbols of a Christian mythology uniting the faith of the reader and the innocence of the maiden. We need, rather, to combine sophisticated and naive readings, to explain why we feel the necessity and yet inadequacy of each. The dove in *Blithedale*, I would maintain, is a symbol on the way to becoming a sign. It is a message from which meaning is in the process of dissipating. Coverdale *is* asserting a relationship to Priscilla, but it is a relationship with fewer and fewer points of contact to the man. There is a contracting circle of reference, here: an innocent dove affirms an esteemed Priscilla; dove equals

Priscilla; "dove" is a dove. Perhaps we might say that once again romance is converted to realism; one mode becomes another. Our method in approaching the former is postulated only that it might be reduced to an approach proper to the latter. For Coverdale the dove serves as a kind of transitionary language, a term appropriate to Priscilla in a non-existent model, but now largely neutral. It is a language in which Coverdale may express potentially interested feelings in a disinterested way. It is a principle, as it were, for organizing without valuating his attention.

The chief action of the dove, indeed, would seem to be to serve as a connective. It links two chapters. The remark quoted, the last words in "The Hotel," introduce the first words in "The Boarding-House": "The next day, as soon as I thought of looking again towards the opposite house, there sat the dove again, on the peak of the same dormer-window!" (p. 153). And again, the dove appears at the end of "The Boarding-House" as a kind of coda, the final, summarizing notes of Coverdale's meditation: "Priscilla had disappeared from the boudoir. But the dove still kept her desolate perch, on the peak of the attic-window" (p. 159). The dove, here, is not the sign of an end. The musical metaphor we have used is deliberate. Notes, except in cases of program music, or other special kinds, signify nothing. Musical "themes" relate only to each other, and the coda does not represent the end, but is the end itself. Even the openness of "the dove still kept . . ." should not be read as signifying that Coverdale will continue to think about Priscilla, though of course he will. Rather, it is a particular kind of musical end, a close on the dominant rather than on the tonic.

The situation is not unlike what we find in later works of American literature, called naturalistic but that we would term realistic, the stories of Crane and certain parts of the early novels of Norris. For Crane and Norris the progress of history neutralizes the work in much the same way that the progress of Hawthorne's art neutralizes it for him. With theology discredited and Darwinism not yet completely found, they adopt, for purely formal reasons, an imagery that only secondarily may develop thematic resonance. Such is the blueness of the hotel in "The Blue Hotel." Its garishness attracts attention, serves as a focus for otherwise unrelated actions that, indeed, occur outside in the street or in a neighboring bar. Unlike Hawthorne's House of the Seven Gables, the unity it gives is factitious. As Crane remarks, "Such scenes often prove that there can be little of dramatic import in environment. Any room can present a tragic front; any room can be comic. This little den was now hideous as a torture-chamber. The new faces of the men themselves had changed it upon the instant." When the Easterner assigns each guest at the hotel a causal role in the gambler's murder, he attempts to affirm an organicity that the Blue Hotel, however, does not have. Similarly, when McTeague packs a cavity in Miss Baker's tooth with pieces of gold, he is filling one hollow symbol with another. Gold and teeth resonate purely reflexively. They are points of order on which a story may be constructed, but useless except insofar as a story does result as characters pursue them. Signification itself—that is, any allegorization we choose to perform on the symbol, pursuing it with interpretation, as it were, so as to generate between repetitions of the symbol the progress of a theme—is simply the product of organization. Theme, content, as we have said, is reduced to a pure form. The symbol is no symbol, is hardly even a sign. Or, perhaps, it is a sign which signifies only itself.[26]

[26] The situation of Hemingway presents an interesting test case. Living in a world whose gods, he feels, have been destroyed, he has no ready means of organizing his novels. Accordingly, he begins with burnt-out symbols (the death and rebirth motifs of *The Sun Also Rises*, for example), using them largely as but counters on which to string otherwise random action. As his career progresses, however, he begins to take his

The same point is made in an opposite way by the image of the "pale man in blue spectacles" (p. 198), who tells Coverdale various instances of the mesmerist's power. If the dove is a seeming symbol that is no more than a sign, the spectacled man is a seeming sign that is actually a pure symbol. Coverdale presumably describes the source of his information. His description, though brief, would seem to be based on close observation, as he is able to tell us even the shade of the man's complexion and the color of his eyeglasses. Here is no overloaded dove, but a particular man with particular stories to tell. And yet, the specificity is surely an illusion, the detail pseudo-detail. "Pale man in blue spectacles" hardly describes anyone. In contrast, the other minor characters in the book are rendered quite clearly, the details serving to paint a genuine picture. Our first glimpse of Moodie is as an "elderly-man of rather shabby appearance" (p. 5). Silas Foster is "stout"; his wife has "a back of generous breadth" (p. 13). There is not much here, perhaps, but surely enough to begin to suggest what the figures look like. As for the man in spectacles, then, I would maintain we are for no more than a moment asked to suppose that he exists. Our tendency to read as if words always signified something is used, rather, for the purpose of significance. Much as the meaning of the dove was conventionalized, reduced to mere message, so, here, a message is elevated to pure meaning. Specifically, the "as told by" habit of writers such as Defoe and Poe—the claim, for example, that *Moll Flanders* is a modest revision of an original written in the style of Newgate—designed to authenti-

---

symbols too seriously. The themes inevitably generated from too much brooding upon them gradually get the better of their primary aesthetic function. By the time of *The Old Man and the Sea*, the balance is hopelessly upset. A Christ symbolism impossible in the godless world in which he began to write in the first place becomes the meaning of the book and, accordingly, has been felt by most readers as obtrusive and even false.

cate the narrative, is refined to its action. What exists is not a source of the narrative, but the force of the convention of a source. The "man" is the vehicle of a determining energy, "terribly efficacious in compelling the auditor to receive them [the stories] into the category of established facts" (p. 198). Of course, "reading down" from value, much as we "read up" from message when we looked at the dove, we are likely to provide a message suitable to its meaning. The man's "pale" color we will take as the "simple, unimaginative steadfastness" of his speech, the blue spectacles as the exotic nature of what he claims to have observed, "stranger stories than ever were written in a romance" (p. 198). Even so, we never read down all the way to the man. As signs, spectacles and paleness are of the second order, but without a first order ever having been established. They are symbols virtually pure. And, indeed, just as signs unvaluated come, ultimately, to signify nothing, so symbols that signify nothing come to have no value. They are the presence of Hawthorne's absence, the attitude of disinterest that establishes the independence, the self-validation of the realistic novel. They bespeak the speech of the book itself, the existence of the stories, but as stories that exist in the book. They are *kosmoi*, as Angus Fletcher calls them,[27] symbols locating character in a cosmos, but whose cosmos they themselves constitute.

Admittedly, of course, the dove and the spectacles are radical cases. It is their very anomalousness, however, that tests to the limit our reading of *Blithedale* as self-contained. They are all that is left of a literature once widely engaging. The dove would claim the existence of meaning in *Blithedale*, the spectacles of message. Both

[27] Fletcher, p. 109, defines "kosmos": "It signifies (1) a universe, and (2) a symbol that implies a rank in a hierarchy. As the latter it will be attached to, or associated with, or even substituted for, any object which the writer wants to place in hierarchical position."

claims are spurious, and there are virtually no other images in the book that even make such a claim. The veils that appear scattered throughout the novel, for example, are not, I would maintain, even seeming symbols. It is quite wrong to read them as a metaphor for alienation, for the separation of one character from another. Indeed, it is like the word "separation" itself. Here is no metaphor, no physical displacement employed as vehicle for conceptual displacement. By virtue of its conventional usage, rather, we read separation as the concept itself. So "veils," in the context of *Blithedale*'s usage—indeed, perhaps, even the usage of Hawthorne in general—are the concept of separation. They are virtually in no need of interpretation. They are signs of the first order, perhaps, sounds signifying an idea. But robbed, like the dove, of greater depth, their chief function is as a connective. To analyze veil imagery is, properly, only to note its recurrence—never to engage the text, merely to repeat it. *Blithedale* is a work that, by and large, presents only itself and presents it *to* itself as well.

As in *The House of the Seven Gables*, there is a certain redundancy, a replication in *Blithedale*. Its function, however, far from *House*'s celebration, may now be seen as sterile self-preservation. The chapter titles are examples. They are spoken by no one, addressed to no one. Such headings as "Coverdale's Sick-Chamber," "The Convalescent," "Coverdale's Hermitage" are written in a voice distinct from the first-person narrative that otherwise predominates. They are not the words of Coverdale, but the voice of the book itself, the chapter that is to follow caught in a phrase that is neither sign nor symbol. Similarly, Coverdale discovers his bower. He projects outside himself an image of himself into which he then retreats. "It symbolized my individuality, and aided me in keeping it inviolate. None ever found me out in it. . . . I brought thither no guest . . ." (p. 99). The bower's only purpose is self-enforcement. It is a reminder *to* Coverdale *of* Coverdale and one that he shares with no one else. Even Zenobia's hot-house flower should be seen in this way. There is, of course, a good deal of flower imagery throughout the book, and Coverdale would make much of it. He allegorizes it, takes Zenobia's flower, for example, as "indicative of the pride and pomp, which had a luxuriant growth in Zenobia's character" (p. 15). He deems that she "scorned the rural buds and leaflets" (p. 59), the purity and naturalness with which she decks out Priscilla, and even that she is dressing herself for effect (p. 15). Zenobia's dress, however, flower and all, is but one more such reflexive projection as Coverdale's bower. Despite himself Coverdale must give over interpretation. The things Zenobia wears, the furnishings of her apartment, "the gorgeousness with which she had surrounded herself" are a "redundance of personal ornament," as he puts it. Though Coverdale would "malevolently" interpret them as her incapacity for "pure and perfect taste," yet, ultimately, "I saw how fit it was that she should make herself as gorgeous as she pleased" (pp. 164–65). The standard for Zenobia's behavior is Zenobia's behavior. The flower reiterates her, is beyond judgment. Unlike the "A" of *The Scarlet Letter*, which takes Hester outside herself, gives her actions a larger social, even theological consequence, unlike the rose-bush that relates Pearl to nature, Zenobia's flower is Zenobia. It enacts her without expanding her.

Indeed, enaction is the only kind of action that there is in *Blithedale*. Throughout the book, as Coverdale notes, the characters are performing a vast charade. Tableaux vivants, playlets, Arcadian masquerades are their entertainment: ". . . the presence of Zenobia caused our heroic enterprise to show like an illusion, a masquerade, a pastoral, a counterfeit Arcadia, in which we grown-up men and women were making a play-day of the years that were given us to live in" (p. 21). This is not to say, though, as is often said, that the characters are hypocritical, insincere in their attempts at Utopia. It is rather that performance, in *Blithedale*, is always to no purpose. As Coverdale continues, "I tried to analyze this impression, but not with much success." Quite simply, there is nothing to say about what the characters do, because what they do has no significance beyond itself. Action is what Angus Fletcher calls "mimetic self-projection."[28] It is a kind of reflexive method-acting in which the character the actor enters is the character of an actor entering a character which, however, does not exist. It is the imitation of a non-existent model, the opposite of celebration, as we have said, celebration of an absence rather than a presence.[29]

Consider Zenobia once again. She is, of course, a consummate actress. But her acting is no mere pretense. Coverdale thinks about Zenobia's city appearance: "To this day, however, I hardly knew whether I then beheld Zenobia in her truest attitude, or whether that were the truer one in which she had presented herself at Blithedale. In both, there was something like the illusion which a great actress flings around her" (p. 165). And again, in response to Coverdale's suggestion that life at Blithedale appears, from the city, "like a dream," Zenobia answers: " 'I should think it a poor and meagre nature, that is capable of but one set of forms, and must convert all the past into a dream, merely because the present happens to be unlike it' " (p. 165). Neither role conceals her. Each presents her. There is neither contradiction nor attempt at resolution. Zenobia does what she does, is what she is, and there is nothing more to be said about it. She is like God, in a way, the God "I am that what I am," except—and here is the crucial difference between value and valuelessness, the speech that is prophecy and the speech that is real-

---

[28] "The Liminal Riddle," a lecture presented on January 29, 1973 at the State University of New York at Buffalo.

[29] Note that in the masquerade, Zenobia plays the part of the Princess Zenobia, who seems to exist, in *Blithedale*, simply to give Zenobia her name.

ism—where God is the author of the world, Zenobia's only world is herself.

Here, most importantly of all, *Blithedale* inverts *The House of the Seven Gables*. There everything is present in anything; here nothing relates to nothing. Fullness of action becomes emptiness of enaction. In other terms, as we have noted, *The House of the Seven Gables* would continue indefinitely. Resolution is impossible because everything is already resolved. Purpose is complete, present throughout in the work, and any end must be palpably false. But *Blithedale is* an end. Resolution is impossible because there is never anything *to* resolve. *Blithedale* closes by enacting itself one last time and then stopping. Dramatization ceases and no drama remains. Zenobia dies by giving a final performance. There is "Arcadian affectation" in her drowning, which, however, takes nothing from the "tragedy" (p. 237). Similarly, the "Veiled Lady" dies. Her "performing" days over, so too is she. Interestingly, what remains is the Priscilla who "had kept . . . her . . . sanctity of soul, throughout it all" (p. 203). Insofar as she preserves herself from the drama she remains alive as the one value—albeit not very believable—on which the book may come to rest. Even Hollingsworth, whose actions, perhaps, are more than dramatization, simply works himself up to where Zenobia has been all along. His scheme for the reformation of criminals becomes a scheme to reform himself, now, too, a criminal, a "murderer," as he says. The "grand edifice" becomes "a very small one," the small cottage he inhabits and which "answers all my purposes" (pp. 242, 243). Action with a purpose outside Hollingsworth bends back on itself, presents a self who previously had resisted self-presentation.

The career of Coverdale sums it up best. An observer, an interpreter, neither actor nor enactor, he neither dies nor wishes to live. He gives up poetry, however, gives up interpretation. There is, simply, nothing to interpret. "I—I myself—was in love—with—Priscilla!" is the novel's final line. Few of *Blithedale*'s critics fully believe this. But it is quite wrong to say that Coverdale is attempting to conceal his real interest, his attraction for Zenobia. *Blithedale* has nothing to conceal, and that, precisely, is its problem. It stands openly and emptily as *Blithedale*. Coverdale, then, would assert a self beyond himself, a relation with the only thing that remains in the book. He would stay the inevitable descent to non-existence down the ladder of signs. In the absence of such relation, as the first part of that sentence tells us, "I," iterating itself, is reduced to a stutter. "As I write it," Coverdale says, the audience "will charitably suppose me to blush, and turn away my face" (p. 247). There is a suggestion, here, that the reader may yet redeem, by himself engaging in, a work that cannot on its own engage him. We shall follow this, in fact, in *The Marble Faun*.

SIX

The Novelist as Critic

THE MARBLE FAUN recommences the progress to intimacy. *The House of the Seven Gables* carries purpose to its problematical end. *The Blithedale Romance* neutralizes it. In *The Marble Faun*, therefore, Hawthorne, so far as is now possible, would begin again. He would re-establish intimacy in accordance with the lessons of his latest fiction. The Preface reconsiders the introductions to *Twice-told Tales* and *The Scarlet Letter*. It recapitulates the first paragraphs of "The Custom-House" in light of the disinterest that now dominates Hawthorne's work.

Once more Hawthorne announces his intention to open an intercourse with the world. But the direct appeal of "The Custom-House" has here "grown to be a custom." It is an "antique fashion of Prefaces" to address what formerly was the "indulgent reader" (I, 3) as the " 'Indulgent Reader' " (IV, I). Hawthorne must "stand upon ceremony, now."[1] He can no longer attempt to assimilate convention, to appropriate it as his own. He must work not purposively, but through a purpose itself appropriated—as it were, conventionalized. He must work through a "familiar *kind* of Preface" (my italics), as, since *Blithedale*, it has become. The alienated observer observes himself seeking intimacy, and it is by turning from the work to observation of it that he would now reach his reader.

[1] Cf., for example, Hawthorne's emphasis in "The Custom-House" on the impropriety of his overture: "It is a little remarkable, that—though disinclined to talk overmuch of myself and my affairs at the fireside, and to my personal friends—an autobiographical impulse should twice in my life have taken possession of me, in addressing the public" (I, 3).

Hawthorne, unable to overcome disinterest, then, seeks to employ it. He places the reader at an equal remove from the book. The Preface presents a "prim old author" who "seven or eight years" ago, in the days of his "literary fashion," used to make his appeal to a reader as antiquated as he, now "under some mossy grave-stone," "withdrawn to the Paradise of Gentle Readers." As at the end of "The Custom-House," Hawthorne resigns one self—here, the interested self and its responding reader both—to his art, saving the other for action in a sense outside art altogether. A new familiarity is created. Writer and reader join in a criticism of Hawthorne's work.

This stance cannot be sufficiently emphasized. We may call it "criticism" insofar as the text is engaged without being "informed"—read, discussed as an object outside subjectivity. It accounts for the major differences that distinguish *The Marble Faun* from Hawthorne's earlier novels. The work is simply not the same animated article. On the one hand, Hawthorne's proper voice may be heard, as it is not at all in *Blithedale*. On the other, it may be heard remarking on a work which, unlike *The House of the Seven Gables*, fails to articulate him. Thus he may comment on the productions of American artists living in Rome: "What he has said of them, in the Romance, does not partake of the fiction in which they are imbedded, but expresses his genuine opinion, which, he has little doubt, will be found in accordance with that of the Public" (p. 4). Hardly any comment in the three earlier novels "does not partake of the fiction," whether as an element of Hawthorne's psyche continuous, however, with a subjectivized fiction, as in *House*, or as a disinterested remark continuous with a fiction dissociated from its author, as in *Blithedale*. Here Hawthorne announces, however, there is a voice outside the work, remarking on the work, that finds communion in critical consensus. The work, no longer a communal space itself, becomes, as alien object, the focus of community. Hawthorne, no longer able to create his world, becomes the critic to his nation of other related, but different, worlds, in this case the world of American expatriates.

It is precisely in this relation that Hawthorne stands to Italy. As former official representative of the United States government in Europe and as author of *The Scarlet Letter* he is the perfect tourist to the American artists' colony, just the American public's man in Rome. He is New England's best, to be trusted to react as a cosmopolitan, but nevertheless thoroughly New England, observer might. Italy provides a new and totally different ground for intimacy. Unlike even England, the scene of the recently failed *The Ancestral Footstep* —distant, to a degree, yet still too present to the American mind to serve, after *Blithedale*, the needs of a disinterested observer[2]—Italy demands just the critical stance into which Hawthorne has been forced. No wonder he abandons America and chooses "as the site of his Romance" a "poetic or fairy precinct" ready-made, as he finds Italy to be, providing "congenial and easily handled themes." No wonder he acknowledges, too, that "actualities would not be so terribly insisted upon, as they are, and must needs be, in America." Growing increasingly familiar as the nineteenth century progressed, but still ineradicably foreign,[3] Italy is a space unlike any Hawthorne has ever known and that he is not likely ever to know: "He has lived too long abroad, not to be aware that a foreigner seldom acquires that knowledge of a country, at once flexible and profound,

[2] See, however, *Our Old Home*, where even England is an impenetrable conventionality, a pretty picture of the picturesque: "In their humble way, they [the sketches] belong entirely to aesthetic literature, and can achieve no higher success than to represent to the American reader a few of the external aspects of English scenery and life, especially those that are touched with the antique charm to which our countrymen are more susceptible than are the people among whom it is of native growth" (v, 3).

[3] See Pearson, pp. i–civ; Wright, pp. 138–67.

which may justify him in endeavouring to idealize its traits" (p. 3).

Hawthorne's audience is no longer reflected in his materials. The possession of a reader by reformation of the work that embodies him is impossible when such embodiment is absent. The reader is expelled from the work, excorporated. He never reads himself in *The Marble Faun*. Interpretation is not self-discovery, but a sterile hermeneutics. It is a hermeneutics in which Hawthorne himself participates, however. He engages the social side of allegory that we discussed in the first chapter. The community of interpreters that interpretation assumes is the ready-made community he too easily joins. Italy remains alien, as critics have noted, and must remain so to establish the intimacy for which Hawthorne will now settle.

The first sentence of the first chapter extends the neutral style of Coverdale's narrative, adumbrating the beginning of James's *The American*:[4] "Four individuals, in whose fortunes we should be glad to interest the reader, happened to be standing in one of the saloons of the sculpture-gallery, in the Capitol, at Rome" (p. 5). Unlike the familiar openings of *The House of the Seven Gables* ("On my occasional visits . . ."), beyond even that of *The Blithedale Romance* ("The evening before my departure . . ."), the narrator's polite tones suggest a certain decorous separation from the action. Together, reader and writer then apply themselves to overcoming the separation, as they observe a story being played out on a scene Hawthorne now begins to set:

"It was that room (the first, after ascending the staircase) in the centre of which reclines the noble and most pathetic figure of the Dying Gladiator, just sinking into

---

[4] Cf. Henry James, *The American*: "On a brilliant day in May, in the year 1868, a gentleman was reclining at his ease on the great circular divan which at that period occupied the centre of the Salon Carré, in the Museum of the Louvre."

his death-swoon. Around the walls stand the Antinous, the Amazon, the Lycian Apollo, the Juno; all famous productions of antique sculpture, and still shining in the undiminished majesty and beauty of their ideal life, although the marble, that embodies them, is yellow with time, and perhaps corroded by the damp earth in which they lay buried for centuries. Here, likewise, is seen a symbol (as apt, at this moment, as it was two thousand years ago) of the Human Soul, with its choice of Innocence or Evil close at hand, in the pretty figure of a child, clasping a dove to her bosom, but assaulted by a snake" (p. 5).

An entire novel, the novel as elaboration of dissociation, is contained in this one paragraph. To objective description, detail serving, presumably, simply to set the scene—"that room (the first, after ascending the staircase)"—accrues, by a repetition we meet later in the work, a kind of latent theme—"ideal life . . . yellow with time, and perhaps corroded by the damp earth in which they lay buried for centuries"—and of the sort that Hawthorne himself ultimately chooses to articulate in the allegorization at the close—"a symbol of the Human Soul, with its choice of Innocence or Evil. . . ." Here is the progress noted in connection with *McTeague* or "The Blue Hotel," the development of second-level messages by extension of imagery that is at first self-contained. Content has become an accident after form, what a man makes of material that fails to speak to him. The artist, so far from meaning anything, translates a work that is never his into the language of his community. The voice of the teller of *The Marble Faun* is the voice not of a creator, but of a critic, from the very first paragraph interpreting the novel. Indeed, the action which Coverdale berates himself for watching as though it were a drama is here interpreted, as we shall see, exactly as if it were.

Hilda, commenting on the reliefs of Trajan's monument, states the case epigrammatically: "There are

sermons in stones . . . and especially in the stones of
Rome" (p. 151). Shakespeare's verse suggests the
equality of nature with art. It holds out the possibility
of understanding unmediated by books, knowledge of
the nature of things by direct apprehension.[5] Hilda's
reversal indicates how thoroughly art has usurped the
place of nature in *The Marble Faun*. Rather than mediating the world outside it, it rather objectifies it, even
takes its place. Life has become an object for what we
have called criticism. Instead of Donatello, Hawthorne
describes the Faun of Praxiteles, the "marble image"
of Donatello (pp. 9–10), going so far as to project a
hypothetical biography for it. Instead of Miriam's features, he rhapsodizes over Miriam's self-portrait: "we
forbore to speak descriptively of Miriam's beauty earlier
in our narrative, because we foresaw this occasion to
bring it perhaps more forcibly before the reader" (pp.
48–49). Kenyon's interest in Donatello's character is
attributed to Kenyon's passion for his sculpture: "Kenyon, it will be remembered, had asked Donatello's
permission to model his bust. The work had now made
considerable progress, and necessarily kept the sculptor's thoughts brooding much and often upon his host's
personal characteristics" (p. 270). Hawthorne's often
noted reluctance to violate, as he phrased it, "the sanctity of a human heart"[6] is here positive alienation. He
will not engage character, refuses to know anything he
cares about knowing, but instead investigates only an
image of his concerns, a world that, even when it is
like his own, is discontinuous from it. He is the inves-
tigator he mocked in "The Custom-House," struck by an
artifact whose reality, he now knows, is the only reality
he may ever decipher.

Interestingly, in this connection, there is no pretense
to authenticity in the Preface to *The Marble Faun*. The

---

[5] *As You Like It*, II. i. 1–17.

[6] The locus classicus is Dimmesdale's remarks to Hester concerning Chillingworth, *The Scarlet Letter*, p. 195.

fiction, as we have seen, is freely admitted.[7] But Hawthorne's now critical attitude demands a manuscript to ponder. A claim for the book's documentary origin slips suddenly into the middle of the story not, I would maintain, as authorizing it, but because the document—or, in this case, the picture—is all that Hawthorne chooses to see: "It was the contemplation of this imperfect portrait of Donatello that originally interested us in his history, and impelled us to elicit from Kenyon what he knew of his friend's adventures" (p. 381). This is the Hawthorne of Robert Lowell:

> Leave him alone for a moment or two,
> and you'll see him with his head
> bent down, brooding, brooding,
> eyes fixed on some chip,
> some stone, some common plant,
> the commonest thing,
> as if it were the clew.[8]

The "clew," however, is no clue to anything except itself, the portrait no imitation of a life outside, but itself the only life that Hawthorne will consider. It is the process of brooding, not what is brooded upon, that is of interest.

Hawthorne makes of his "brooding," then, the basis of community. His role as the "one observer in a thousand" he praises who sees the ostensibly deeper significance of the Faun of Praxiteles is as a publicist. Insofar as he is an artist, his art, like Hilda's copying, is a socialization of other works. Hilda "multiplied it for mankind. From the dark, chill corner of a gallery . . . she brought the wondrous picture into daylight, and

---

[7] Consider, further, Hawthorne's disavowal of the Monte Beni records in favor of folklore, p. 236: "But, to confess the truth, the information afforded by these musty documents was so much more prosaic than what Kenyon acquired from Tomaso's legends, that even the superiour authenticity of the former could not reconcile him to its dulness."

[8] "Hawthorne," in *Hawthorne Centenary Essays*, p. 4.

gave all its magic splendour for the enjoyment of the world" (p. 60). As he does with Holgrave, Hawthorne praises her disavowal of a self-assertive art and asks the reader for intimacy in return: ". . . let us try to recompense her in kind by adducing her generous self-surrender, and her brave, humble magnanimity in choosing to be the handmaid of those old magicians, instead of a minor enchantress within a circle of her own" (pp. 60–61). Hilda's art is a renunciation of the egocentric. It is submission, a denial of self for a work allowed to dominate the self. And yet, unlike Hilda, Hawthorne does not quite give himself over, either. He is appreciative and skeptical simultaneously, admiring the art of Rome but not too much. His desire to understand it is sufficient to start him asking questions, yet insufficient for him ever to care about the answers. He avoids the "negative capability" of Hilda as simply the obverse of the "egotistical sublime." Neither imposing himself on the work nor being imposed on by it, he keeps up the attitude of Lowell's brooding only to enlist the reader in a communal process.

The transformation into plot of such an attitude produces mystery, but a mystery that remains impenetrable: the mysteries of Miriam's family and Donatello's race, particularly as they are set forth in the "Postscript." Separate from his work, but still able to use his very separateness, fearful that he has lost touch with his audience, yet even at this late stage willing to try to establish contact once again, Hawthorne appends the only afterword of his career. It marks his last working understanding of his art, as the subsequent fragments, filled with interpretation taken seriously, littered with symbols and their interpretation after rejected interpretation, show. The "Postscript" defines the significance of the novel. It sets aside thematic concerns, summing up the book as a detective story in the manner of Poe or Conan Doyle. Hawthorne becomes a Watson to Kenyon's Sherlock Holmes:

" 'Yes; it is clear as a London fog,' I remarked. 'On this head no further elucidation can be desired.' . . . 'Ah! quite a matter of course, as you say,' answered I. 'How excessively stupid in me not to have seen it sooner! But there are other riddles.' . . . 'The atmosphere is getting delightfully lucid,' observed I, 'but there are one or two things that still puzzle me' " (pp. 465–66).

Kenyon answers: " 'You must recollect,' replied Kenyon, with a glance of friendly commiseration at my obtuseness. . . . 'Is it possible that you need an answer to these questions?' exclaimed Kenyon, with an aspect of vast surprise" (pp. 465–66).

The "Postscript," as Hawthorne notes, is a response to the demands of his still unsympathetic audience.[9] The "Kind" or "Gentle" or "Beloved" reader does not, as he foresaw in the Preface, exist for him. The reader has taken the mystery too much to heart, lost sight of the detective process in his insistence that it produce results:

"He [the author] had hoped to mystify this anomalous creature between the Real and the Fanastic, in such a manner that the reader's sympathies might be excited to a certain pleasurable degree, without impelling him to ask how Cuvier would have classified poor Donatello, or to insist upon being told, in so many words, whether he had furry ears or no. As respects all who ask such questions, the book is, to that extent, a failure" (pp. 463–64).

Hawthorne, undaunted, however, shifts ground. Reluctantly, he enters the work as a character, courts intimacy by assuming the identity of the very reader he berates for asking unanswerable questions: " 'Only one question more,' said I, with intense earnestness. 'Did Donatello's ears resemble those of the Faun of Praxiteles?' 'I know, but may not tell,' replied Kenyon, smil-

---

[9] The "Postscript" was added after the initial printings. For a complete account of its history see the Introduction to the *Centenary Edition*, pp. xxx–xxxii.

ing mysteriously. 'On that point, at all events, there shall be not one word of explanation' " (p. 467). Hawthorne as Kenyon might explain all that is forever alien to Hawthorne as Hawthorne the character. The division of himself into alternative egos enables explanation in the face of irrevocable disinterest. It exposes the nature of a book improperly defined by either of its two spokesmen—a criticism that expresses how much need not, to establish intimacy, be understood.

The Marble Faun, therefore, alternates between elaborate interpretation and confession of the poverty of interpretation. On the one hand, nearly everything described is promptly moralized by Hawthorne himself or one of the characters. Thus, selecting at random:

" 'As these busts in the block of marble,' thought Miriam, 'so does our individual fate exist in the limestone of Time' " (p. 116).

" 'Ah, how exquisite!' said Kenyon . . . 'this fragrance, which is like the airy sweetness of youthful hopes, that no realities will ever satisfy!' " (p. 223).

"Hilda wondered if it were not possible, by some miracle of faith, so to rise above her present despondency that she might look down upon what she was, just as Petronilla in the picture looked at her own corpse" (pp. 352–53).

On the level of style moralization flourishes as epigram, which, in at least one place, Hawthorne himself admits creates but an illusion of understanding: "Thus it would be easy to go on, perpetrating a score of little epigrammatical allusions, like the above, all kindly meant, but none of them quite hitting the mark, and often striking where they were not aimed" (p. 134). On the level of incident moralization becomes replication. Replication would fix firmly a subject matter never properly defined. The dove-like Hilda must be surrounded with actual doves, must be called by her friends, the "Dove." Miriam's conscience is a daimon, appears bodily in the shape of the model, who, moreover, incarnates the "spectre" of Guido. At the first carnival Donatello dresses as a faun and Miriam as, alternately, the lady she was and the peasant she becomes. At the second carnival, Kenyon's daymare is actualized in the parade of costumed monsters that physically assault him. As Hawthorne says of the "Sylvan Dance" at the gardens of the Villa Borghese, "it seemed the realization of one of those bas-reliefs, where a dance of nymphs, satyrs, or bacchanals, is twined around the circle of an antique vase . . ." (p. 88). The "Transformations"[10] of *The Marble Faun* are, as it were, the word made flesh. No wonder the reader asks, and quite legitimately despite Hawthorne's objections, whether Donatello has furry ears. The meaningless word inevitably cannot be understood, and the flesh is offered as its substitute.

On the other hand, then, Hawthorne acknowledges the failure of moralization. Artists may merely transcribe their subjects. Praxiteles "diffused throughout his work" the "mute mystery which so hopelessly perplexes us, whenever we attempt to gain an intellectual or sympathetic knowledge . . ." (p. 10). An idea has a "nameless charm" (p. 13), a painting "that indefinable nothing" (p. 60), the Italian weather "an indescribable something" (p. 422). Hawthorne would even pretend failure is success: "Unless words were gems, that would flame with many-coloured light upon the page, and throw thence a tremulous glimmer into the reader's eyes, it were vain to attempt a description of a princely chapel" (p. 345). The gaudiness of the metaphor substitutes for the splendor of the church. Linguistic flourish would make a virtue of inarticulateness.

Hawthorne's basic strategy, however, is to subsume both moralization and avowal of its failure within the larger attitudes of the reader. The book's mostly American point of view, the criticism of Italian art and culture

---

[10] *Transformation*, of course, was the English title of *The Marble Faun*.

from the standpoint, as Roy Harvey Pearce notes, of New England,[11] serves, as Hawthorne's allegory had earlier, to affirm a community of interpreters regardless of the validity of interpretation. The "nature" of Italy is judged by the nature of the United States. Often this amounts to no more than a rejection of Tuscany peaches for the "rich reminiscences of that fruit in America" (p. 274), or the Monte Beni sunset, which, compared to the Western sky, "looked airy and unsubstantial" (p. 266). Nature, simply, would seem to be less fully natural in Europe. Strictly speaking, however, sunset is a "spectacle," and its colors brighter than those of poets and painters (p. 266). Here is no observation of sunsets, but the imposition of a transcendental aesthetic as a tool for easy schematization. The comparison is once removed from its ostensible object. So far from judging watery peaches against juicy, it measures one standard of art against another:

" 'Nay; I cannot preach,' said Kenyon, 'with a page of heaven and a page of earth spread wide open before us! Only begin to read it, and you will find it interpreting itself without the aid of words. It is a great mistake to try to put our best thoughts into human language. When we ascend into the higher regions of emotion and spiritual enjoyment, they are only expressible by such grand hieroglyphics as these around us' " (p. 258).

This, of course, is the "hieroglyphic" language of Emerson. It is through "Nature" that nature is approached. As Kenyon puts it once more, this time from the opposite vantage point, defending sculpture against Miriam's claim that all statuary groups imitate forms set out in antiquity, "as long as the Carrara quarries still yield pure blocks, and while my own country has marble mountains, probably as fine in quality, I shall

[11] Pearce, "Hawthorne and the Twilight of Romance," *Yale Review*, 37 (1948), 487–506. See, also, Gary J. Scrimgeour, *"The Marble Faun:* Hawthorne's Faery Land," *AL*, 36 (1964), 271–87.

mother and to her Italian father (pp. 23, 429–30). The very air of Rome "instils poison into its very purest breath" (p. 100), and, in a personification that demonstrates Hawthorne's racial approach to the city as well as to its people, Rome's malarial effusions are said to be one aspect of its pestiferous "life-blood." In contrast, an American community of the racially innocent is preserved. The dark lady aspect of Hawthorne's New England ancestry is cast out in *The Marble Faun* and embodied in European types. Goodness reposes in the New England stock alone. Even Hilda's priest was born and lived for many years in New England. Hawthorne has it both ways. Insofar as the priest is benevolent, avuncular, he is Hilda's own. But such seductiveness as he shows is one more Jesuitical—that is to say, European—snare (p. 344). At its worst this is racism. At its best it promotes the sort of community Tolkien talks about in reference to *Beowulf*, the healing of internecine divisions in the face of an evil externalized for precisely that purpose.[12] In any case, it demonstrates Hawthorne's increased desperation, his need, in the face of alienation, of a communal identity so firm that only one that may be defined "scientifically" will do.

We have spoken of an official point of view in *The Marble Faun*, a transcendental interpretative stance the author takes from the beginning of the book. The point is assumed, in effect, before the book begins. The work does not establish community, but, providing a focus for interpretation, allows a community of interpreters to form around it. Hawthorne's readers do not discover themselves in the work; they join with him in observing a work powerless to engage them on its own. Repeatedly, indeed, whenever a more direct involvement threatens, Hawthorne frustrates it. He prevents us

[12] J. R. R. Tolkien, "Beowulf: The Monsters and the Critics," *ceedings of the British Academy*, 22 (1936), rpt. in *The wulf" Poet: A Collection of Critical Essays*, ed. Donald K. (Englewood Cliffs, N.J.: Prentice-Hall, 1968), pp. 8–56.

steadfastly believe that future sculptors will revive this
noblest of the beautiful arts, and people the world with
new shapes of delicate grace and massive grandeur"
(pp. 124–25). Statues are natural, for their origins are
in quarries. Moreover, American quarries, as good as
any in Italy—as American peaches and sunsets are as
good or better—will ultimately produce better statues.

Interestingly, we have, here, a version of art exactly
the opposite of Hawthorne's bitter prefatory note—"Romance and poetry, like ivy, lichens, and wall-flowers,
need Ruin to make them grow" (p. 3). There is a progressive contraction of his poetics at work. Elements of
the gothic that, in *The Scarlet Letter*, he had engaged
as embodiments of a New England he would reform
are, in the Preface, reluctantly cast out onto Europe,
And now, in Kenyon's statement, even the reluctance is
gone. New England is radically simplified, transcenden-
talized. Rome, its opposite number, is gothicized. This
perspective bespeaks neither Hawthorne's culture as he
has ever perceived it before, nor Europe as he perceiv
it to be. Limited and coherent, it provides but a grou
for interpretation, certainty in the face of ambig
As he does in "The Gray Champion," Hawthorne
time, however, renouncing, where formerly he h
sufficiently developed, a reforming art—puts on
tious identity, the identity purified, even em?
of the only audience he is willing to address.

The racial undertone of *The Marble Faur*
able. Hilda's radiance, so far from "the che
active temperament" that in *The House*
Gables is Phoebe's "New England trait"
to say her geographical inheritance, i
even in her angelic tower, of "the fair·
(p. 56). More significantly, in contr
but nevertheless Puritan, Hester P
her darkness, her "Jewish aspect
it—commingled as well, it may
drop of African blood in her ve;

from becoming too seriously concerned. Characters to whom the audience might too closely relate are shielded from the chief development of the action. The book is reduced by half. The story of the "Four individuals in whose fortunes we should be glad to interest the reader" becomes a story of two individuals as two others observe it.

As the progress of evil continues, Donatello and Miriam take center stage in the drama. Kenyon, heretofore a character inside the narrative frame of the book, is separated out and emerges as point of view. It is through him we first see the castle (p. 214). It is he who now begins to epigrammatize (p. 223).[13] It is his own investigation, not the elucidation of an omniscient author, that uncovers the Monte Beni history (p. 231). At one point Kenyon has so completely become the validator of events that Hawthorne may not attribute to him a point he characteristically wishes to suggest yet personally disown. It is Kenyon, instead, who attributes the rumination to yet a third party. There is a movement in the course of the novel from " 'She has been in some sad dream or other, poor thing!' said Kenyon, sympathizingly; 'and even now, she is imprisoned there in a kind of cage' " (p. 112) to "It occurred to Kenyon, that the enemies of the vine, in his native land, might here have seen an emblem of the remorseless gripe, which

---

[13] For example, "Whether so intended, or not, he understood it as an apologue, typifying the soothing and genial effects of an habitual intercourse with Nature, in all ordinary cares and griefs; while, on the other hand, her mild influences fall short in their effect upon the ruder passions, and are altogether powerless in the dread fever-fit or deadly chill of guilt" (p. 246). Similarly, Kenyon remarks directly: "Or, let us rather say, with its difficult steps, and the dark prison-cells you speak of, your tower resembles the spiritual experience of many a sinful soul, which, nevertheless, may struggle upward into the pure air and light of Heaven, at last" (p. 253); "And this . . . is a most forcible emblem. . . . Christian Faith is a grand Cathedral, with divinely pictured windows. Standing without, you see no glory, nor can possibly imagine any; standing within, every ray of light reveals a harmony of unspeakable splendours!" (p. 306). Etc.

the habit of vinous enjoyment lays upon its victim" (p. 292). We have here a progression from Kenyon as Coverdale, observing in his own person the characters of others, to Kenyon as reader, observing even the observing Kenyon, attributing the conception of the emblematic signification of the vine to someone else. It is a reverse development in which, rather than the audience identifying with the character in his own right, the character loses his independent involvement in the action to become one with the audience. Increasingly, Kenyon, as the audience is from the start, is cut off from direct participation in the novel.

Similarly, Hilda must literally be kidnaped into a plot whose gothicism assures that her transcendent and transcendental nature may never become involved. Her brush with evil is twice removed. Early on she, in effect, observes Miriam watching Donatello performing a murder. Later, abducted by a positively Medician papacy, she is yet in the "kindly custody of pious maidens, and watched over by such a dear old priest" (p. 466). What she sees never touches her, uncovers no hidden part of herself, never changes her at all. As Miriam notes, she hardly experiences the evil which is all around her: ". . . for the sake of the piety with which she keeps the lamp a-light at her shrine . . . [she] is just as safe, in these evil streets of Rome, as her white doves, when they fly downward from the tower-top, and run to-and-fro among the horses' feet" (p. 180). We are in no danger, should we identify with her, of ever engaging that evil whose progress more and more comes to dominate. Properly speaking, indeed, she is not even a character, and so no identification is possible. Like Coverdale's dove imagery, rather, she is a language that maintains separateness in the face of interest. She is a terminology in which potentially engaging material may be couched without trouble to reader or writer.

At this point we should, perhaps, resolve two seemingly contradictory statements we have made: that the novel is foreign, that it cannot reform because the American reader cannot "interest" himself in it, and yet that Hawthorne's strategy is to present an American view of Rome. I do not mean to separate the material of the novel from the novel itself, the matter of Italy from the way in which Italy is perceived. The one exists only within the context of the other. As Hawthorne interprets, however much in an American vein, his interpretation, too, becomes a part of the novel from which the reader is separated. I would distinguish, however, between what interpretation says and the community from which it proceeds. Words in *The Marble Faun* do not quite, as they did in *The Blithedale Romance*, signify nothing. As we have seen in the last chapter, such a state would preclude a reader, would prevent even that engagement in the process of interpretation with which *The Marble Faun* is concerned. To the neutrality of *The Blithedale Romance* interest is reintroduced after all, but, as we have said, at a secondary level, only in the face of inescapable disinterest. Such significations as words have, then, are wholly discontinuous from the subjectivity of the speaker, but that they exist at all assures us of his existence as well. The language of *The Marble Faun* carries, as it were, at once but separately, the interpreter and his interpretation. When the words signify transcendentalism, they do not, however, *embody* the speaker, even if we know him to be a transcendentalist. We may call such speech "discourse." Discourse does not tell itself. It is not independent, self-validating. It implies a speaker, but one outside the language, disinterested in what he speaks. Discourse signifies a good deal, but what it signifies is wholly impotent. It may affect our opinions, but it can never affect us. In such a situation, language cannot result in possession by virtue of what it communicates. The message discourse may present us with is itself of no interest to us, and insofar as we are interested in the person who presents it, no matter what he speaks—so long as he does speak—we will in any case be possessed.

There is nothing, I suppose, necessarily wrong with a language of this sort. Indeed, the limitations inherent in it may even be a check to Romantic excess. Proper use of discourse, however, requires a consciousness difficult to maintain. Messages spoken, but never assented to, may be a vehicle of play, a sheer demonstration of exuberance as yet uncommitted. The speaker remains open to a variety of opinions he tests out, but to no one of which he is yet ready to subordinate himself.[14] He tries on forms, as it were pre-formed, but that are in no danger of forming *him*. Hilda, for example, on the banks of the Tiber, discusses the seven-branched candlestick of the Jews. It is an allegory completed, "an admirable idea for a mystic story, or parable, or seven-branched allegory, full of poetry, art, philosophy, and religion" (p. 371). Or Miriam elaborates on the Etruscan bracelet of seven gems from seven tombs. It is "the connecting bond of a series of seven wondrous tales, all of which, as they were dug out of seven sepulchres, were characterized by a sevenfold sepulchral gloom" (p. 462). We are back to the style of *Seven Tales of My Native Land*. The teller reports a story that already exists. Indeed, Miriam and Hilda engage themselves even less than that, telling not the stories themselves, but the structure of their telling. Hawthorne's earlier practice of grouping a number of anecdotes around a central focus has so firmly established a formal procedure that the execution is complete in the naming. The speaker is in no danger of beginning something that will ever envelop him, that will, in its course of development, define him against his will. He is from the start, which is the end as well, in absolute control.

[14] Cf. Jacques Derrida, "Structure, Sign, and Play in the Discourse of the Human Sciences," in *The Languages of Criticism and the Sciences of Man: The Structuralist Controversy*, ed. Richard Macksey and Eugenio Donato (Baltimore: Johns Hopkins Univ. Press, 1970), pp. 247–72.

Hilda, as we might expect, chooses a tale fully formed of transcendence, Miriam of gloom. The characters use what otherwise might threaten to use them.

In much the same way Kenyon construes the story of Donatello as a fortunate Fall. Arguing from Hawthorne's earlier practice is somewhat more difficult here. Perhaps the story of Hester Prynne has established the fortunate Fall as a pattern sufficiently mechanical to pose no threat. At any rate, it is clear that Kenyon cuts himself off from the story by categorizing it so summarily. He refuses to be moved. He will not engage action except in such a way that it is powerless to affect him. He classifies it in order to dispose of it, closes the fiction off before it can enclose him. Significantly, Kenyon has no great commitment to his interpretation, no especial stake in it. When Hilda objects he quickly recants. Adroitly he turns his error into a plea for her constant guidance. A hermeneutical basis, indeed, is given for marriage: " '. . . the mind wanders wild and wide; and, so lonely as I live and work, I have neither pole-star above, nor light of cottage-windows here below, to bring me home. Were you my guide, my counsellor, my inmost friend, with that white wisdom which clothes you as with a celestial garment, all would go well. Oh, Hilda, guide me home!' " (pp. 460–61).

The interpretation turns in on itself, for the moment abandoning its object. Interpreting alone remains, an action that never yields results. Hilda, of course, has no "wisdom," has no version of Donatello's story to substitute for the one she rejects. "Oh, hush!" she responds. "You have shocked me beyond words!" Kenyon, abandoning message, however, will not abandon words. If the criticism has ceased, the act of criticizing has not. The message recedes, but the community that considers it remains. Critical dialectic has become a language of love. Again, Kenyon remarks, discussing St. Peter's:

" 'But, what a delicious life it would be, if a colony of people with delicate lungs (or merely with delicate fancies) could take up their abode in this ever-mild and tranquil air! These architectural tombs of the Popes might serve for dwellings, and each brazen sepulchral door-way would become a domestic threshold. Then, the lover, if he dared, might say to his mistress, "Will you share my tomb with me?" and, winning her soft consent, he would lead her to the altar, and thence to yonder sepulchre of Pope Gregory, which should be their nuptial home. What a life would be theirs, Hilda, in their marble Eden!' " (p. 369).

The passage's death imagery, like that of the opening description of the room of the Dying Gladiator, is consistent with the images of a dying Rome that appear throughout the book. Ostensibly, Kenyon offers a critique of the "Old" World. But the critique is beside the point. To it, too, Hilda objects, and once again Kenyon can recant. He uses it only as a simple and most available medium of exchange.

More generally, however, discourse of this sort degenerates. The form tried on begins to surround. The writer loses self-consciousness, and messages originally spoken innocently are, where they should not be, "meant." A sort of basic dishonesty creeps into *The Marble Faun*, what we have called in an earlier chapter bad faith[15] and which we may now explore more fully. Opinions provisionally maintained, ideas "copied" but not possessed, the author now holds are his own. Forms the writer has offered as free of his presence, he now comes to believe present him. The author, trying on various attitudes, comes to accept them as fact. What he asserts, he unthinkingly believes.

Consider a discussion of St. Peter's comparable to Kenyon's, Hawthorne's own description of its effect on Hilda. The cathedral "marvellously adapts itself to every human need" (p. 344). It is "The World's Cathedral" (p. 354). It has "room for all nations," and in the

[15] See above, p. 42.

various confessionals set specifically aside for the purpose, "there was an ear for what the overburthened heart might have to murmur, speak in what native tongue it would" (p. 356). Hilda, therefore, bearing the burden of her terrible knowledge, enters it and is comforted. The importance of cathedrals to Hawthorne is unassailable. His flirtations with Catholicism, the conversion of his daughter, all point to a deep, abiding concern that cannot be doubted. And yet he makes the mistake of assuming that his interests outside the novel can be of interest within. Ideas however firmly held, however much of the self outside the book they involve, become, once inside *The Marble Faun*, opinions disconnected from the self. We may care about them, we may enjoy discussing them, but we do so in a disinterested way. Unlike Kenyon, then, Hawthorne commits himself to an idea in a context that makes commitment ridiculous. He attributes to St. Peter's a power it simply never earns. For all that he claims its universality in affecting humanity, St. Peter's would seem to possess Hilda but by virtue of a spurious analogy with the spaces of Hawthorne's earlier fiction. The growing hold of the cathedral repeats the progress of Hawthorne's writing. It appears at first, to Hilda, much smaller than she had imagined it, "a great prettiness; a gay piece of cabinet-work on a Titanic scale; a jewel-casket, marvellously magnified," "all inlaid, in the inside, with precious stones" (p. 349). The cathedral is Hawthorne's art, the little "jewel box" "inlaid with a fanciful tracery of pearl" that housed the beautiful butterfly. As he extended the ground of his art, so, "after looking many times, with long intervals between, you discover that the Cathedral has gradually extended itself over the whole compass of your idea . . ." (p. 350). We have here no Province-House whose force Hawthorne has worked hard to establish, no House of the Seven Gables, the result of an arduous career. Here, instead, is a pathetic imitation, the assertion of a power to engage which is never established, a projection of the development of power on a work which is, however, powerless.

Consider a more complex example. Donatello describes the banquet hall of Monte Beni: "It was meant for mirth, as you see; and when I brought my own cheerfulness into the saloon, these frescoes looked cheerful too. But methinks they have all faded, since I saw them last" (p. 226). Here is the presentation of a mood, an enforcement, as with Hilda's doves or the other "transformations," by repetition. It is a substitution of iteration for interest. It is an affirmation of a gloom that Hawthorne need not have thus tried to corroborate could he have validated it on his own. It is one more example of how little he is invested in his work, how little he possesses it. More importantly, however, Hawthorne seems unaware of how far away he really is. The description of the hall is no story playfully assumed. Beginning, perhaps, but as a fiction, a myth Donatello consciously proposes to express his changed mood, the change in the frescoes becomes a reality of its own. The fading is more than apparent. It is not simply a distortion of Donatello's morbidity. Hawthorne seems to think his morbidity has indeed effected the change. Kenyon, examining a figure in the frescoes, demonstrates how confused the situation has become:

"It [the figure] formed the principal link of an allegory, by which (as is often the case, in such pictorial designs) the whole series of frescoes were bound together, but which it would be impossible, or, at least, very wearisome, to unravel. The sculptor's eyes . . . soon began to trace through the vicissitudes—once gay, now sombre—in which the old artist had involved it, the same individual figure. He fancied a resemblance in it to Donatello himself; and it put him in mind of one of the purposes with which he had come to Monte Beni.

" 'My dear Count,' said he, 'I have a proposal to make.

You must let me employ a little of my leisure in model-ling your bust' " (p. 227).

Kenyon cannot "unravel" the "allegory." Evidently the action portrayed involves "vicissitudes," but of what sort it appears impossible to say. And yet Kenyon re-fuses to be hampered by ignorance. Taking Donatello's fiction seriously, he uses it as the ground for interpret-ing what he does not understand. Evidently, he reads the fading of the frescoes as a whole back on the progress within the frescoes, the movement of the figure from vicissitude to vicissitude. He takes the degenera-tion of the figure in all the pictures from gay to som-bre to be a development—though he acknowledges he cannot unravel it—of the figure from one picture to the next. This is why there seems to be a "resemblance" of the figure to Donatello: their two stories are similar. Donatello suggests a reading of the figure; the figure suggests Donatello. And now, as a final, circular step, Kenyon would turn the Donatello thus suggested back into, if not the fresco figure, yet a work of art like it, a bust. Here is a circle of confusion validating itself, of ignorance taken for knowledge, body for spirit, art for life, fiction for reality. It is a circle Hawthorne never does quite escape. It is the dominant tone of the book.

For years *The Marble Faun* served as a tour-book for Americans abroad. It is a tour-book such as Americans have come to use increasingly, a guide that, as Roland Barthes has so incisively analyzed,[16] stands in for what it claims to describe. Hawthorne paints the landscape. Here is the picturesque masquerading as observation, a description neither of nature nor culture, but of a hu-manized geography on the one hand, a naturalized civilization on the other:

"Emerging from the courtyard of the edifice, they looked upward and saw the sky full of light, which

[16] "The *Blue Guide*," in *Mythologies*, pp. 74–77. I have used Barthes throughout the following discussion.

seemed to have a delicate purple or crimson lustre, or, at least, some richer tinge than the cold, white moonshine of other skies. It gleamed over the front of the opposite palace, showing the architectural ornaments of its cornice and pillared portal, as well as the iron-barred basement-windows, that gave such a prison-like aspect to the structure, and the shabbiness and squalor that lay along its base. A cobler was just shutting up his little shop, in the basement of the palace; a cigar-vender's lantern flared in the blast that came through the archway; a French sentinel paced to-and-fro before the portal; a homeless dog, that haunted thereabouts, barked as obstreperously at the party as if he were the domestic guardian of the precincts" (p. 142).

What elsewhere is, admittedly, a "cold, white" moonlight is here a "delicate purple." Hawthorne backs down from scenery, refuses to confront it on its own austere terms. On the other hand, what would seem to be men, the cobbler and the cigar-vender, are just two more pieces of scenery. Hawthorne backs down from humanity, too, refuses to engage the men except as they add to the pretty spot. In other terms, the picturesque, as one eighteenth-century theoretician has remarked, "corrects the languor of beauty or the tension of sublimity."[17] Items are arranged to soften the high with the low, correct the low by juxtaposition with the high: the palace has a shabby, prison-like basement; the French sentinel is matched by a guardian dog; the natural light of the sky is reflected in "architectural ornaments" and a "pillared portal." Opposites, here, are never in any serious way resolved. No placing purpose relates one to the other. The point between them is vacant. But Hawthorne, once again through iteration, pretends it is full. By positioning the opposites side by

[17] Uvedale Price, *Essay on the Picturesque* (1794), quoted in Martin Price, *To the Palace of Wisdom: Studies in Order and Energy from Dryden to Blake* (1964; rpt. New York: Anchor, 1965), p. 382. Price offers a fine analysis of the picturesque.

side and then repeating the position a number of times, he makes opposition itself come to stand in for relation. The picturesque is a labor-saving device, as Barthes has called it,[18] a short-cut to interanimation. It is the sign of a union that has, however, never been achieved, a sign that substitutes for the union itself.

Hawthorne's landscape, accordingly, is fundamentally factitious. It passes over precisely what it claims to be. There is no significant history in Italy, no people with no story he cares to investigate. Golden Age fauns are translated to modern times. There is a "great chasm between our own days and the Empire" (p. 110). There is a simple layering of present on past without causal relation: "If we consider the present city as at all connected with the famous one of old, it is only because we find it built over its grave" (p. 110). History, indeed, is rather an atmosphere "with which our narrative is not otherwise concerned, than that the very dust of Rome is historic, and inevitably settles on our page, and mingles with our ink . . ." (p. 101). Superficially, this resembles the historic atmosphere of the Province-House, the legendary dust in its rafters. But the similarity is precisely a measure of the difference. The space of *The Marble Faun* is a copy in bad faith of the space of the Province-House. Little knowledge, little cultural presence, informs it. Hawthorne, as we have seen, frankly admits his ignorance of Italian ways. The audience does not associate itself with Italy as it does with America. Here is a space empty of meaning but pretending to meaning, a sign, as we have said, that substitutes for its signified.

Ultimately, then, the story *The Marble Faun* has to tell is a pseudo-story. Sequence, causality, action are replaced by a travelogue that serves in their stead. The Cook's tour through places of interest in Rome in successive chapters in the first half of *The Marble Faun* and places in Tuscany in the second gives the book its

---

[18] *Mythologies*, p. 74.

most consistent structure. As Hawthorne puts it: "Thither [to Monte Beni] we must now accompany him [Kenyon], and endeavour to make our story flow onward, like a streamlet, past a gray tower that rises on the hill-side, overlooking a spacious valley, which is set in the grand frame-work of the Apennines" (p. 213). Or again: ". . . we now follow the course of our story back through the Flaminian Gate, and threading our way to the Via Portoghese, climb the staircase to the upper chamber of the tower, where we last saw Hilda" (p. 326).

In place of story we have touring. In place of the more usual narrative connectives, the temporal "meanwhiles," "durings," and "afterwards," it is geography that leads us from scene to scene. Here is the novel reduced to space and space emptied of all meaning, reduced to a structural device. Perhaps the story of the nymph sums it up best. In a little dell in the countryside around Monte Beni, "hollowed in among the hills" like the "Hollow" of Hawthorne's earliest work, before a reforming art was ever attempted, geography takes over narrative completely (p. 243). In the "least artfully" told manner possible, in a manner, that is, presumably free of even the playful use of conventional forms, Donatello relates the story of a water maiden and her knight. But it is a story worse than conventional, yielding convention itself. Reversing the procedure that we found in relation to the seven-branched candlestick and the Etruscan bracelet, the practice of decorating a work of art with a tale, it begins as a tale only to end in a work. Donatello recalls: A knight, accustomed to bathe his sorrows in the fountain of a water nymph, loses her forever when he attempts to wash away a blood-stain on his hands. Mourning her the rest of his life, he employs a sculptor to carve the figure that the story thus explains. Here is a recapitulation of the grand theme of the book, the struggle, like Donatello's own, of innocence with guilt. But it is a struggle arrested now in a statue and a fountain. It is a "sweet old story connected with this spot" (p. 244), a story "transformed," eliding time, eliding any genuine relation of man to landscape, replacing it with a metamorphosis. "Descriptions of various Italian objects, antique . . . and statuesque," as Hawthorne says, have, indeed, come to dominate his book. It is no wonder Hawthorne will divide the rest of his career between travelogue and a timeless tale of eternity.[19] There is nothing else left.

[19] Most notable are *Our Old Home* and the two fragments, *Septimius Felton* and *The Dolliver Romance.*

Conclusion

HAWTHORNE'S "career" has come to an end. Of course, he continues to write. But the fragments and the travel essays he produces are a mere wreckage, an extension of a career outliving its function. This study cannot begin to deal with them. They are outside the particular purpose of Hawthorne's writing as we have defined it, the action the other works discussed perform. They are, despite any thematic connections they might exhibit with the fiction—despite possible similarities of concern or consistent psychic patterns they might manifest— unvalidated by that place in his development that establishes their "meaning." They are beyond the reach, that is to say, of our method, the limitations of which, as well as what I take to be the achievements, it is now time to sum up.

The progress of this book was a journey through our native habits of thinking. Two main currents dominate modern American criticism, the historical and the New Critical, neither of which could explain my reaction to Hawthorne as I first read through his works one by one—a reaction not untypical and since confirmed by students and colleagues. Dissatisfaction with individual stories yields, inevitably, to a sympathy at once too limited and too general for either methodology to explain. Hawthorne's historical achievement, his reconstruction of Puritan and transcendental thought—the special expression of American thinking that his works presumably constitute—has little or nothing to do with the matter. For history unappreciated in one story is not likely to appear to improve by repetition. Moreover, American culture, as I have attempted to demonstrate, has always seemed to me to be rather the condition of Hawthorne's writing than its subject, an opinion shared by a notably American writer himself, Henry James. Hawthorne was concerned, as James saw it, *in* his heritage, but hardly *with* it. For example, the Puritan sense of sin has, as a subject, an "almost exclusively *imported* character":

"He had ample cognizance of the Puritan conscience; it was his natural heritage; it was reproduced in him; looking into his soul, he found it there. But his relation to it was only, as one may say, intellectual; it was not moral and theological. He played with it and used it as a pigment; he treated it, as the metaphysicians say, objectively. He was not discomposed, disturbed, haunted by it, in the manner of its usual and regular victims, who had not the little postern door of fancy to slip through, to the other side of the wall."[1]

Hawthorne's fancy, it seemed to me, was precisely what historical analysis left out. A thorough immersion in his intellectual background, so far from enhancing appreciation of his American concerns, might subvert them. It would neglect my sense that they were, for Hawthorne, not very momentous, that they were important neither as positive nor negative issues on which he took an impassioned stand, but his literary horizon, what James called a "black patch" that, at mid-century, was inescapable. Here was a peculiar circumstance that needed to be explored. There was, in Hawthorne's work, a too easy atmosphere, a lack of intensity that served to cut it off from the continent it might otherwise appear to represent. It was an atmosphere whose very strength was its feebleness, whose value lay in the fact that what was a subject of passion and discord outside it became simply necessary within. A challenge presented itself to ordinary modes of criticism. We must give up further efforts at historical imagination, must cease to inquire after Hawthorne in his era, thereby obscuring what he has accomplished. The answer to his attraction, the path through the postern door, lay not, it seemed clear,

[1] *Hawthorne*, p. 471.

in historical research, but in close, sensitive reading of the text as it provided its own context, in a thorough investigation of the work.

Interestingly enough, that criticism most closely concerned with the context the work itself creates, the New Criticism, provided very little help. As I mentioned in the first chapter, New Criticism is a verticalization of literary history, an application of the results of historical research to the work at a series of interpretive levels. And it makes mistakes similar to literary history's. It considers each story of such potential importance—as important as the historians consider Puritanism or transcendentalism—that, on the one hand, the story becomes greater than it is or, on the other, is written out of the canon as unworthy, as too slight for analysis. Formalism places far too much weight on works too small to bear it. It would serve, perhaps, for *The Scarlet Letter* and a few others. But what of "Little Annie's Ramble" or "Buds and Bird Voices," sketches that evaporate upon close observation and yet that seem too characteristic to dismiss simply as minor. Was not even *The Scarlet Letter* minor if one thought, with Henry James, that Puritanism, the question of sin and salvation, was a cultural accident, a circumstance never elevated to substance. Formalism's tack was wrong from the start. Analysis geared to individual stories, like analysis that places the individual in a far too general context, could hardly explain that unique experience of *developing* interest that I sought to understand. All the close reading in the world would not help. One might sharpen one's analytic tools, might learn, say, the set of paradoxes particular to Hawthorne's fiction, might come to read his code more rapidly, see more quickly his peculiar figure. But intimacy with Hawthorne grew not as clarifying the experience of each work—indeed, not even as deepening it—rather almost as eliding it, as if the work were a vehicle for something happening through it but not in it.

Hawthorne invites us into his study—quite literally, in at least one story, "The Old Manse," figuratively in virtually all the others—and gives us his manuscripts to read. Like or dislike the particular works, we love the room and respond to the gesture. We grow comfortable in the study and find it unpleasant to leave. After a while, is one reading the text at all or responding purely to Hawthorne's sociability? One had to do the one to get to the other. Hawthorne invited one in on no other terms. But was not one's sense of the text defined by what loomed beyond? I determined to build an aesthetic on this response, determined that no "work" even existed except in the context of a growing intimacy that was far more real than the printed page. Let the meaning of Hawthorne's writings be his attitude towards them, the purpose they served in the writing. Let the messages the works communicated be seen as the means of an action larger than message. Here was a partial solution of the initial problem, a non-historical, non-formalistic explanation of a response to reading.

How to validate such an aesthetic, however, remained a problem. On what basis besides my own intuition could I claim to regard the clear communication of a work as secondary? Where, in other words, was this central purpose to be located, how known? I had rejected already the authority of the printed work. Nor could I, surely, appeal to history—to Hawthorne's biography or intellectual situation—without beginning all over again the problem of historical research, without risking a loss of that Hawthorne who invites us, after all, to intimacy only by reading.

William Charvat, for example, has written a fine study of the situation of the American writer in the nineteenth century in relation to publishers and the public.[2] The writers presented here, however, are pro-

[2] *The Profession of Authorship in America, 1800–1870: The Papers of William Charvat*, ed. Matthew J. Bruccoli (Columbus, Ohio: Ohio State Univ. Press, 1968).

fessionals, men of commerce engaged in the business of selling their wares. Hawthorne is such a man, too, but it is a different Hawthorne from the one whose study we enter. The tables Charvat provides, the figures of costs, income, and sales, may even help us, by establishing the constraints of the printing and publishing processes on authors, determine certain formal characteristics of what we read—the size of the work, its structure, scope, and the like. But they can never explain for us why we are being asked to read such forms in the first place. They can never prove that the invitation we sense has in fact really been offered. There was a danger, in responding as I did, of a real lack of rigor. To give up tables and charts was to run the risk of extreme subjectivity, of distortion at every turn. And, perhaps worse, even if such distortion were somehow avoided, if my sense of Hawthorne was, in fact, correct, would not any articulation of it yet lapse immediately into impressionism? With formalism and historicism put aside, even the sharpest perceptions would be obscured for lack of rigid analytical tools. The problem was a serious one, for it threatened to dissipate every insight. Evasion would not do. Nor was compromise possible, for too long a distance had already been traveled.

Surprisingly, the answer lay in the question itself. The solution to the problem was a restatement of it as no problem but the very condition of what I would say. If Hawthorne's purpose could not be corroborated directly, if no existing definitions of literature seemed to provide a ground for it, yet it might be entertained as a working hypothesis, corroborating itself after the fact, so to speak, in the various aspects of the writing it would explain. Purpose, it must be admitted, could not be proved. But as the center of a system revolving around it, it could most emphatically be demonstrated. The apparatus of historical and formalistic analysis might now be reclaimed. Although what I took to be Hawthorne's meaning could not finally be validated by

traditional methods, yet by turning the tables, by employing such methods in the service of his meaning, an
argument might be presented as objectively as could be
desired. A founding arbitrariness but redefined objectivity as strictly relational. The "history" of Hawthorne's
career was no biography or intellectual development,
but the progress of his work toward intimacy; his
"works" were not formal elaborations of ideas or messages, but units significant as elements aiding or frus-
trating this intimate history. The analysis that was to
follow is the book that has preceded. It must make its
own case, and I can do little more, here, to help it. But
certain ideas not strictly necessary to the argument that
has been made about Hawthorne, certain implications
that may be drawn from it, might briefly be sketched
out.

The time has long passed, as noted in the first chapter, when "burrowing" would bring to light new facts
about American literature. The "discoveries" of the last
decades have yielded, we may safely assume, a reason-
ably stable canon, and further attempts at "uncovering"
have but multiplied, at a variety of allegorical levels,
what is already known. The situation of the contemporary critic is radically different from that of the critic
in the Twenties or Thirties. He faces no uncharted territory, but a literature whose boundaries, at least, have
been fully delimited, a literature academicized, firmly
enshrined in the critical institution. The danger of
sterility is great. The very enthusiasm of previous readers, who, pursuing their interest, have mapped out the
literary landscape, stands in the way of our own enthusiasm. Accordingly, the path open to us, as I have
been maintaining, is not in a repetition of the burrowing method. A slavish imitation of conventional procedures denies, in the very attempt to recapitulate them,
the achievements such procedures have accomplished.

What is needed is a radical reorganization of material we must finally admit has been uncovered fully

enough so that it is beyond our capacity to uncover very much more. There are no longer any large dark areas in the literary landscape, nor any very great mysteries about the messages the classic American works convey. There is no new territory to explore, or, at any rate, if there is, the old canon still retains its fascination. Rather, there are new maps to draw of the old landscape, new lines to define, relations to establish among material now fully visible. New works, in our terms, are those made up of bits and pieces reorganized from the old; new writers, new purposes at the center of such reorganized works; new literary histories, new progresses of the new centers. The guiding principle, here, must be interest, rather than definitiveness. We must give over the security of generally agreed upon criteria of verifiability. We must strive for self-consistency, rather than some eternal validity. Let us allow, even, for a degree of subjectivity. The "objectivity" of historical and New Critics, after all, was but a subjectivity of another age. It was a necessity of the first stage of American criticism, a product of a particular time, need, purpose that demanded the as yet obscure facts. But recognition of our own very different purposes is the only objectivity our own age now permits. This is not license to say whatever one wants, to be unhistorical and faddish; it is a recognition, instead, that there are fads in history, too. It is to demand the rights of the earlier generation of critics, to criticize as an act of cultural affirmation, to commit oneself to a literature of one's choosing, which is to say a history of one's making. To do this properly, of course, is no easy matter. Impressionism, as has been said, must be avoided by the use of carefully honed tools. Rigor requires that one's commitment be systematized, mechanized, even, so that analysis does not degenerate.

This leads to a second point, the work that needs at this juncture to be done beyond what I have been able to say about Hawthorne. I have suggested, especially in the chapter on *The Blithedale Romance*, a way in which certain modalities might be redefined. Romance, naturalism, realism, are attitudinal terms. They express a relation between a writer and a reader, an appeal by the author to us or against us or, finally, his refusal to make any appeal at all. More needs to be written about these matters. To interpret the message a work communicates without first investigating the particular appeals sorts of communication make is to undermine the validity of interpretation by taking it for granted. It is to interpret in despite of a question all the more insistent because unacknowledged. No convincing hermeneutic is possible that fails to consider the demands on the reader that the place of the text in relation to its culture—the place the author puts it in—makes. Thus critics have divided literature into certain formal categories, genres described structurally or thematically, but with no reference to affectivity. They miss about a work precisely what engages them in it. Worse, they fail to see "works" that are all around in the interstices of those they have defined. Beyond the boundaries of simple modality or genre for which the conventional definitions alternative to my own might seem to serve, in the delineation of areas for which we have names, but, as yet, no adequate explanation—history, fiction, essay, journalism—are not such considerations as I have been suggesting a potentially productive line of investigation? The commitment of the writer calls for a corresponding commitment of the reader, and we are in danger, if a literature transcends mere communication, of substituting form for value, description for involvement. The "burden" of the prophet is not the teachings he proclaims, but prophecy itself, vision as an attitude toward the world, which, when we understand it, makes prophets of us all.

It is in relation to such larger questions, then, that a final point should be made. It is ironic that Americans, especially, have turned for so long from the methodological inquiries that on the Continent, for example, have become a general matter of interest. It is odd that students of American literature, of all people, have concerned themselves so little with the question that tormented American writers from the first—the status of literature, the meaning of fiction-making as an enterprise, the justification of authorship itself. As I mentioned in the first chapter, a certain lingering insecurity, perhaps, has made us defensive. The apparent unskillfulness of so much of early American fiction, the quantity of writing that is poor by the standards of a long-established British tradition, has caused us to protest too much that our fiction, though young, does, however, have terribly important things to say. We deny, because we are too busy rationalizing, what classic American literature is most concerned with—its own being, function, effect. The American novel is from the beginning an experimental novel. It is literature that, as writer after writer tells us, is unsure of its own usefulness, afraid to trouble the reader with reading it, ashamed to present itself as something significant. It is fiction that knows it is only fiction. But because it knows this as a birthright, as it were, as a condition of writing in a country that doubts the validity of writing, it goes far beyond the need of the contemporary novel to debunk itself. It is a novel debunked from the start, concerned not so much with its inability to be real, as with the uses to which its acknowledged unreality may be put. It is a self-conscious fiction, not a sterile one. It is only in self-conscious reading that we can avoid sterility ourselves.

Index

Abel, Darrel, 12
Adams, Henry, 173
Adams, Robert M., 63n
"Alice Doane's Appeal," 44,
    52n, 159
allegory, 13-16, 17, 50, 95,
    100, 127, 128, 130, 133,
    167, 180, 196, 204, 210;
    in *The Scarlet Letter*,
    107-110, 113ff, 118, 126;
    and symbolism, 19-21, 90n.
    See also criticism:
    allegorical
The American Notebooks,
    42, 43, 83
The Ancestral Footstep, 195
Arthos, John, 100
"The Artist of the Beautiful,"
    56, 81-86, 87, 89, 119,
    123-24, 169, 183, 213
Arvin, Newton, 43n, 56n,
    141n
Austen, Jane, 167
Austin, J. L., 11

Bachelard, Gaston, 65, 67
bad faith, 42, 44, 113, 212,
    217
Barthes, Roland, 21, 42n, 182,
    215, 217
Basket, Sam, 36, 37, 38, 40
Baym, Nina, 13
Bell, Michael Davitt, 104n
Bell, Millicent, 49n, 56n
Blackmur, R. P., 114
The Blithedale Romance, 35,
    123, 148, 149-92, 193, 194,
    195, 196, 208, 209, 228
Bloomfield, Morton, 11n
Booth, Wayne C., 10n
Borges, Jorge Luis, 40-41, 42,
    43
Bridge, Horatio, 116
Brodhead, Richard H., 9n

Brooks, Cleanth, 26
Brooks, Van Wyck, 4-5
Brown, Charles Brockden, 88,
    89n
Brown, Norman O., 73n, 75
"Buds and Bird Voices," 223
Bunyan, 14, 108
Burke, Kenneth, 95, 98

career, 24-25, 34, 37-38, 45,
    47-48, 50, 53, 64, 149,
    221, 226
"The Celestial Railroad," 14
Chandler, Elizabeth Lathrop,
    51n
Charvat, William, 100, 102,
    224
Chase, Richard, 100-101,
    171n
Clemens, Samuel L.
    (*Huckleberry Finn*), 171
Coleridge (*The Rime of the
    Ancient Mariner*), 157
Cooper, 56, 87, 112n
Cowley, Malcolm, 96
Crane, R. S., 21
Crane, Stephen, 184-85, 197
Crews, Frederick, 13, 24, 28,
    30, 82n, 84, 155n, 169
criticism: allegorical, 11-13,
    16, 25, 26, 29-30, 67-68,
    107, 131, 182, 185, 189,
    226; historical, 67-70ff;
    psychological, 13, 24, 28,
    67-70ff, 176. *See also*
    formalism, historicism,
    interpretation, New
    criticism
Cunliffe, Marcus, 148n
"The Custom-House," 36-40,
    45, 48, 57, 91-95, 105, 106,
    115, 116, 119, 121, 122,
    123, 128, 144, 145, 193,
    194, 198

231

Howe, Irving, 172
Howells, William Dean, 125
"Howe's Masquerade," 68, 69,
70-72, 74, 78, 79

"interest"/disinterest, 150,
152, 166, 169, 193, 194,
202, 208, 209, 213
interpretation, 25, 28, 29, 36,
37, 68, 189, 191, 202ff, 205,
211, 215, 223, 228; defined,
11; in "discourse," 209;
and the reader, 50, 51, 121,
196, 204, 206; and realism,
156, 165; of romance,
176; and symbol, 185,
188, 200. See also criticism
Irving, Washington, 93, 105

James, Henry, vii, 4, 60,
114, 115, 156, 157, 167,
172, 196, 222, 223
Jones, Buford, 14n
Jones, Howard Mumford, 3n

Kellogg, Robert, 51n, 52
Kermode, Frank, 98, 125n,
147n
Kern, Edith, 158

Lacan, Jacques, 74n
"Lady Eleanore's Mantle,"
14, 69, 75-78
Lawrence, D. H., 3
Legends of the Province-
House, 14, 48, 65-81, 87,
96, 103, 125, 144, 213, 217
Lesser, Simon O., 59n, 135n
Levin, Harry, 7
Lewis, R. W. B., 83n, 95n
The Literary History of the
United States, 7
"Little Annie's Ramble," 223
Love Letters of Nathaniel
Hawthorne, 124, 173n
Lowell, Robert, 199, 200
Lubbock, Percy, vii
Lundblad, Jane, 88n

MacShane, Frank, 36, 38

"Main Street," 90
Male, Roy, 12, 25-27, 30
The Marble Faun, 15, 42, 113,
115, 150, 183, 192,
193-219
Marks, Alfred H., 135n
Minter, David L., 155n
Matthiessen, F. O., 6n, 15n
"The May-Pole of Merry
Mount," 52n, 53
Melville, Herman, 3, 15, 18,
19-21, 90, 90n, 114, 131,
157, 171, 182, 183
Milton, John, 114
"The Minister's Black Veil,"
109
"Mr. Higginbotham's
Catastrophe," 52n
modality, 35, 46, 174-79, 228
Morris, Wesley, 8n
Murrin, Michael, 14, 15
"My Kinsman, Major
Molineux," 52n, 53, 67

naturalism, 173, 184, 228;
defined, 177-78
New Criticism, 6-7, 12, 16-17,
26, 36, 221, 223, 227.
See also formalism
"Night Sketches," 14
Normand, Jean, 24
Norris, Frank, 184-85, 197

Ohmann, Richard, 11n
"Old Esther Dudley," 72,
78-81, 124n, 129, 130
"The Old Manse," 65, 224
"An Old Woman's Tale," 52n
Orians, G. Harrison, 100, 102
Our Old Home, 195n, 219n

paradox, 23, 26, 27n, 99
Parrington, Vernon Louis, 3
"Passages from a
Relinquished Work," 23,
43, 52n, 53, 158-59
Pattee, Fred Lewis, 6n
Peabody, Sophia, 142, 182
Pearce, Roy Harvey, 8n, 11,
112n, 204

LIBRARY OF CONGRESS CATALOGING IN PUBLICATION DATA

Dauber, Kenneth, 1945-
  Rediscovering Hawthorne.

  Originally presented as the author's thesis, Princeton,
1973.
  Includes index.
  1. Hawthorne, Nathaniel, 1804-1864–Criticism and
interpretation.   2. Fiction.   I. Title.
PS1888.D3   1977   813'.3   76-45893
ISBN 0-691-06323-0